Spreading the Dhamma

Southeast Asia

POLITICS, MEANING, AND MEMORY

David Chandler and Rita Smith Kipp

SERIES EDITORS

OTHER VOLUMES IN THE SERIES

HARD BARGAINING IN SUMATRA:
Western Travelers and Toba Bataks in the Marketplace of Souvenirs
Andrew Causey

PRINT AND POWER:
Confucianism, Communism, and Buddhism in the Making of Modern Vietnam
Shawn Frederick McHale

INVESTING IN MIRACLES:
El Shaddai and the Transformation of Popular Catholicism in the Philippines
Katherine L. Wiegele

TOMS AND DEES:
Transgender Identity and Female Same-Sex Relationships in Thailand
Megan J. Sinnott

IN THE NAME OF CIVIL SOCIETY:
From Free Election Movements to People Power in the Philippines
Eva-Lotta E. Hedman

CAMBODGE:
The Cultivation of a Nation, 1860–1945
Penny Edwards

THE TÂY SƠN UPRISING:
Society and Rebellion in Eighteenth-Century Vietnam
George Dutton

ART AS POLITICS:
Re-Crafting Identities, Tourism, and Power in Tana Toraja, Indonesia
Kathleen M. Adams

Spreading the Dhamma

Writing, Orality, and Textual Transmission in Buddhist Northern Thailand

DANIEL M. VEIDLINGER

UNIVERSITY OF HAWAIʻI PRESS *Honolulu*

Printed in the United States of America
11 10 09 08 07 06 6 5 4 3 2 1

Library of Congress Cataloging-in-Publication Data

Veidlinger, Daniel M.

Spreading the Dhamma : writing, orality, and textual transmission in Buddhist Northern Thailand / Daniel M. Veidlinger.

p. cm.—(Southeast Asia—politics, meaning, memory)

Based on the author's dissertation (University of Chicago).

Includes bibliographical references and index.

ISBN-13: 978-0-8248-3024-3 (hardcover : alk. paper)

ISBN-10: 0-8248-3024-5 (hardcover : alk. paper)

1. Buddhism—Thailand, Northern—History. 2. Communication—Religious aspects—Buddhism. 3. Pali literature—Thailand, Northern—History and criticism. I. Title. II. Series.

BQ568.N675V45 2006

294.309593—dc22

2006008330

University of Hawai'i Press books are printed on acid-free paper and meet the guidelines for permanence and durability of the Council on Library Resources.

Series design by Richard Hendel

Printed by The Maple-Vail Book Manufacturing Group

CONTENTS

Acknowledgments *vii*

Note on Transliteration and Translation *ix*

Abbreviations *xi*

Introduction *1*

1. Monks and Memory: The Oral World *21*
2. Early Thai Encounters with Orality and Literacy *42*
3. Golden Age, Golden Images, and Golden Leaves *63*
4. The Text in the World: Scribes, Sponsors, and Manuscript Culture *103*
5. Turning Over a New Leaf: The Advance of Writing *133*
6. Overlooked or Looked Over? The Meaning and Uses of Written Pali Texts *164*

Conclusion *204*

Notes *213*

Bibliography *233*

Index *249*

NOTE ON TRANSLITERATION AND TRANSLATION

All isolated names of people, places, and things that are derived from Pali or Sanskrit are written according to their Indic pronunciations, which generally accords with their Thai spellings, but not pronunciation. This should allow those familiar with both the Thai spellings and the Indic languages to recognize the word immediately. Thus Haripuñjaya instead of Hariphunchai, Sukhodaya instead of Sukhothai, *vihāra* instead of *wihan*. However, except where this would cause undue confusion, place names that incorporate *both* Thai and Indo-Aryan words are transliterated following their Thai pronunciation—for example, Wat Phra That instead of Wat Phra Dhātu.

Thai words are transliterated following pronunciation according to the Royal Institute general system of transliteration, with minor concessions to typesetting constraints that should present no problems for the reader. The system is described in detail in the *Journal of the Siam Society* 33. Also, note that text from manuscripts, inscriptions, and other primary written materials has often been transcribed exactly as found in its original state. This has resulted in the doubling of some letters and the omission of others and in misspellings, grammatical errors, and other realities that the paleographer is doomed to wrestle with. I have not attempted to gloss over or otherwise occlude the various mistakes that occur in actual texts as found in the world—doing so would defeat the purpose of my analysis, which, after all, is an attempt to harvest information about writing itself from just this kind of predicament.

Translations are my own unless otherwise indicated.

ACKNOWLEDGMENTS

This book developed around my dissertation, which was prepared for the Department of South Asian Languages and Civilizations at the University of Chicago, where I had the good fortune to have Steven Collins as my adviser. He saw the project through from a nebulous complex of ideas years ago to the dissertation and beyond. Without his interest, encouragement, and discerning criticism, this book never could have been completed. My sincerest thanks are also extended to the other members of my dissertation committee, Frank Reynolds and Matthew Kapstein, whose insightful comments and clear direction always kept me on track.

Much of the information in this book was collected while I was a research associate at the Social Research Institute at Chiang Mai University in 1999. There were many people in Thailand who offered their time and wisdom to aid me in my research. In particular I would like to thank Justus Neuser, to whom I owe my deepest gratitude. One of the few people with the language skills required for a project of this nature, he happily offered to assist me in any way he could. He helped me struggle through many of my first Thai colophons and inscriptions. Endowed with a true thirst for knowledge, the more I requested of him, the more satisfied he was. Bali Buddharaksa, who was curator of the manuscript project at the SRI, encouraged me to look at as many manuscripts as possible, and, what is more, helped me to do so. Samli Mulkæo taught me how to read the Lan Na script and was very patient during the many occasions when I was confronted with letters that seemed to me, though thankfully not to him, to be indecipherable. The rest of the faculty and staff at the SRI made the research and my time in Chiang Mai pleasant and fruitful.

I have had the pleasure of meeting or otherwise being in contact with numerous people in the field to whom thanks are due for answering my often obscure questions. Louis Gabaude, Oskar von Hinüber, Michael Rhum, Donald Swearer, and Hans Penth deserve particular mention in this regard. Peter Skilling was not only an endless fount of information, but also a gracious host, and I thank him for welcoming me to Thailand.

I also owe many thanks to series editor David Chandler and an anonymous reader as well as Justin McDaniel, who graciously read the entire manuscript with a fine-toothed comb and responded with amazingly detailed and helpful comments. Copy editor Margaret Black's suggestions and corrections were always spot on, and any mistakes that I have managed to sneak past these able scholars are thanks only to my own deviousness. Pamela Kelley at University of Hawai'i Press patiently answered my many queries and ensured that the whole process ran smoothly.

Financial support for the research was generously provided by the Committee on Southern Asian Studies at the University of Chicago, whose organized and friendly staff made the task of supporting this endeavor much easier than it might have been. The transformation of the dissertation into this book was supported by the Research Foundation at California State University, Chico, through two Summer Scholars grants.

My father, Otto Veidlinger, and brother, Jeffrey Veidlinger, read much of the manuscript and greatly helped improve my writing. My beloved Saman provided enormous emotional support and believed in me even when I did not. And finally, I happily acknowledge my colleagues at the Department of Religious Studies CSU, Chico, for creating the perfect environment in which to work each day.

ABBREVIATIONS

AN	*Aṅguttara Nikāya*
BEFEO	*Bulletin De L'École Française D'Extrême Orient*
CDV	*Cāmadevīvaṃsa*
CDVe	*Cāmadevīvaṃsa: The Legend of Queen Cāma.*
CLNI	*Corpus of Lan Na Inscriptions*
CNPT	*Charük Nai Prathet Thai*
DN	*Dīgha Nikāya*
EHS	*Epigraphic and Historical Studies*
Epochs	*Jinakālamālī: The Sheaf of Garlands of the Epochs of the Conqueror*
EZ	*Epigraphia Zeylanica*
HH	Manuscript Number in Harald Hundius (1990)
IHP	*Inscriptional History of Phayao*
JIABS	*Journal of the International Association of Buddhist Studies*
JKM	*Jinakālamālī*
JKMI	*Jinakālamālī Index*
JKMp	*Jinakālamālīpakaraṇaṃ*
JPTS	*Journal of the Pali Text Society*
JSS	*Journal of the Siam Society*
LNI	*Lan Na Inscriptions.* Part I.
MF	SRI Manuscript Microfilm Number
MS	*Mūlasāsanā Samnuan Lan Na.*
MV	*Mahāvaṃsa*
Nan	*The Nan Chronicle*
Otani	*Catalogue of Palm Leaf Manuscripts kept in the Otani University Library*
PSC	*Prachum Sila Charük*
PTS	*Pali Text Society*
PTSD	*Pali Text Society Pali-English Dictionary*
ROB	*Royal Orders of Burma*
SN	*Saṃyutta Nikāya*
SRI	Social Research Institute, Chiang Mai University
SRIcat	*Warnakon Pali Nai Lan Na*
SS	Siam Society Manuscript Number in von Hinüber (1987)
SV	*Sāsanavaṃsa*

TCM	*The Chiang Mai Chronicle*
TPD	*The Pa Dæng Chronicle*
Vin	*Vinaya*
VRI	Vipassana Research Institute
VRI-Dev	Chaṭṭha Saṅgāyana Devanāgarī Script Edition of Pali Tipiṭaka

Spreading the Dhamma

Source: Thongchai (1994)

Introduction

In its 1967 entry on Marshall McLuhan, *Current Biography* notes the criticism that has been directed toward the father of media theory for often taking his ideas too far; it cites as an example his notion that the outcome of the 1960 presidential election was influenced by the simple fact that most people accessed the Kennedy-Nixon debates through the new medium of television rather than radio. In time, this, like many other of McLuhan's pronouncements, became conventional wisdom, and the insight at the core of his thought—that human culture and technology arise in tandem and are bound by an intimate and mutually affective relationship—has animated many recent studies in a variety of disciplines. Central to these studies has been the idea that we can improve our understanding of a culture by being sensitive to the distinctive ways that it has adopted and adapted to the various technologies with which it has had contact. While McLuhan and his school have many detractors, key themes that they promoted have made their way onto the general scholarly palette. For example, most scholars, McLuhanite or not, would find it curious if an exploration of the rise of values such as democracy and individualism in Asia did not at least touch on the contributions of such things as electricity, automobiles, radio, and telephones to this process.

As modern life is greatly impacted by ever-changing technologies, so the lives of Theravāda Buddhist monks in premodern northern Thailand were affected by the technologies of their day. The key decisions they took regarding technology—how and when to use it, who could use it, what status to assign it—brought a variety of forces into play that shaped the experience and practice of Buddhism, as well as the success of their orders and the very identity of the region. Historically, for monastic groups in Thailand, communications technology has been essential, for the religion could not have flourished without the successful transmission through diverse media of the canonical texts known in the Pali language as the Tipiṭaka, as well as commentaries, translations, and ancillary literature. When I speak here of "technology," I refer to the application of human knowledge to fashion a system that solves a particular problem. It need not require advanced scientific knowledge, so both writing and mnemonic systems are no less technologies than is the Internet.

Most scholars currently believe that the texts of the Pali Tipiṭaka were transmitted orally for about four hundred years,[1] from the time of their genesis until the first century BCE,[2] when Buddhist chronicles tell us they were written down.[3] The oral transmission of the Pali texts was aided by mnemonic features such as repetition, formulae, meter, and numbered lists, and was entrusted to specially trained monks called *bhāṇaka*s (reciters). The *bhāṇaka*s were divided into several groups, each of which was responsible for the retention of a different part of the canon. Like the scholarly *paṇḍita* tradition in India,[4] there was a division of labor among the various branches of *bhāṇaka*s, and again as in the case of the *paṇḍita*s, the oral tradition continued to be an important force even once the texts were committed to writing. Although no version of the Tipiṭaka was printed until 1893 CE, when the project was executed under the sponsorship of the Thai king Chulalongkorn, in recent years monks, scholars, and patrons have busied themselves making up for lost time with numerous dissemination projects that have led to the mass availability of Tipiṭaka texts for free on CD-ROM and through the Internet.[5] This book focuses on one part of the story of the transmission of the Tipiṭaka and related Pali texts, namely, the development of writing and its complex relationship to the oral tradition in the kingdom of Lan Na in northern Thailand.

BRIEF HISTORY OF LAN NA

The inhabitants of historical Lan Na consisted largely of people descended from the early Mon of the region, from aboriginal Austronesian tribes, and from Tai[6] people speaking a language known as Yuan. The Tai Yuan, who soon became the culturally and linguistically dominant group, had spread from their ancestral homeland in southeastern China, probably in the area of the Red River delta, towards the end of the first millennium. Their language was and is very similar to that of the Tai in the central region of Sukhodaya, as well as the Tai Yai and the Tai Khün. It is not far, in fact, from what is the standard Thai of modern Thailand. The main differences are phonological, with only moderate lexical variations. There are fewer words of Khmer origin in Yuan than in standard Thai, and Sanskrit-derived words have generally been replaced by Pali terms, reflecting the strong Theravāda influence that permeated Lan Na.

In the mid-thirteenth century, the Tai ruler Mangrai began to bring various warring areas of northern Thailand under his control, and in 1292 CE he established a major political and religious center in the newly built city of Chiang Mai. At this point the kingdom of Lan Na, meaning "a million rice paddies," began to assume the form that it would more or less retain for several centuries. In the late 1360s the Lan Na king Kü Na invited the monk Sumana from the central Thai capital of Sukhodaya to bring a Sinhalese forest-dwelling monastic lineage to Lan Na. Sumana did arrive shortly thereafter, and this event laid the seeds for the flourishing of the Mahāvihāra interpretation of Theravāda Buddhism in the kingdom. This order soon became known as the flower-garden order (*pupphārāmavāsī*), because their chief monastery was the Flower Garden Monastery (Wat Suan Døk) just outside of Chiang Mai. The Sinhalese form of Buddhism was strengthened during the reign of Sam Fang Kæn (1401–1441 CE), when a group of twenty-five monks from Lan Na went to Sri Lanka to be reordained and brought yet another forest-dwelling lineage (*araññavāsī*) back to Thailand. This lineage became based at the Red Forest Monastery (Wat Pa Dæng), another monastery somewhat farther from the city of Chiang Mai than Wat Suan Døk.

Lan Na experienced a Golden Age in the fifteenth and beginning of the sixteenth centuries,[7] during which political power expanded and solidified, and Buddhist cultural production reached its apex. The Golden Age, presided over by Sam Fang Kæn, Tilaka (1441–1487), Yot Chang Rai (1487–1495), and Muang Kæo (1495–1526), witnessed the composition of dozens of original Pali works, including pseudocanonical, cosmological, and commentarial works,[8] but the fortunes of Chiang Mai and Lan Na waned quickly. After the assassination of Ket Chettharat in 1545 CE, there was no clear heir to the throne, and a prince from the Lao center of Luang Prabang came to power on the basis that his mother was related to the royal line of Chiang Mai. After his short reign, a Shan ruler was installed, but he was unable to ward off the Burmese, who conquered Chiang Mai in 1558 CE. The rest of Lan Na gradually came under Burmese control over the next few decades.

The following years did witness some rebellions and brief periods of Burmese retreat, but the Burmese never failed to reassert their suzerainty until the late 1770s, when much of Lan Na was freed from their yoke by Kawila, a warrior who had the backing of the central Thai (Siamese) powers. By 1804 CE, Kawila had taken Chiang Mai, Chiang Sæn, and other northern cities and began to repopulate them—a necessary project since the people had been decimated from decades of war and conscription by the Burmese. He initiated a massive reconstruction and ruled as a vassal of the Chakri king in Bangkok, as did his successors until 1933, when Lan Na was divided into a number of provinces of Siam.

The dissemination of Pali texts played a large role in the cultural development of Lan Na both before and after the Burmese conquest. The monks and the rulers wished to accompany the expansion of their influence with the extension of Buddhist institutions and practices, and these were supported by canonical and commentarial texts. While the texts were at first primarily transmitted orally, residing in the heads of monks who had gone to outlying areas, they were later transmitted in manuscript form. In time, the characteristic Lan Na Dhamma script became so strongly identified with the region itself that we can now virtually delineate the borders of Lan Na based on where manuscripts employing this script have been found.

MEDIA THEORY AND ITS APPLICATIONS IN THE BUDDHIST CONTEXT

While the past few decades have seen growing interest in the ways that different communications technologies affect both the texts that are transmitted and the way they are received, very little scholarly attention has been paid to the forms taken by Buddhist texts in premodern Asia, let alone Lan Na. We know that the texts were initially spread orally and then in written form, but even when texts were written, it must be emphasized that the people of Lan Na, like all premodern Buddhists, did not engage them in anything remotely resembling the critically edited, printed books now available. This book will look at the forms in which they actually encountered these texts and will ask how these experiences might have affected the way they construed and practiced their religion. This will entail an examination of the role that Pali texts in oral and written form played in different communities in Lan Na—the social life of texts, as Justin McDaniel has called it in his work on Thai and Laotian manuscripts (McDaniel 2003, 88). Another objective will be to assess the attitudes that different sectors of society held regarding orality and writing during the periods under study. These attitudes were determined by social, political, and psychological factors, as well as practical considerations pertaining to the physical features of different media. Often a particular medium was central to one's social position, such as orality in the case of the *bhāṇaka*s. The attitudes of these monks towards writing would certainly have been affected by the degree to which they saw writing as a threat to their position. Likewise, monks belonging to traditions more amenable to the written word would have naturally had other opinions. Rulers also had different perspectives on orality and writing that depended at least in part on their view of the utility of these technologies for stabilizing their rule. As in the adoption of any technology, opaque personal preferences doubtless played an important role as well. Regardless of their etiology, such attitudes tell us a lot about the ways that particular groups may have approached and interpreted the texts.

When looking at the "roles" that manuscripts in particular have played, it is essential to realize that manuscripts can fit into the lived practice of religious communities in a variety of ways beyond their obvious function as supports for the words of texts. It is important not to obscure the unintended consequences that arise once the key functional advantage of writing—the materialization and hence preservation of ephemeral sounds—has been addressed. For example, when the word enters the physical world, it becomes something that can be bought, sold, and owned, and thereby feeds the fires of possessiveness while at the same time opening up unwanted possibilities such as defilement, which would happen if an animal left droppings on the pages or a human used the leaves to make a mattress.

In order to focus my account of the world of writing, I would like to highlight two main categories of manuscript usage—*cultic* and *discursive*—that frame much of what I will say. Cultic usage of a manuscript may be divided into two modalities, seen and unseen, in which the manuscript itself occupies a substantially different place. An example of seen cultic usage is the offering of flowers to a manuscript in the context of *pūjā* or the procession of a manuscript through the kingdom on the back of an elephant. In both of these situations, an actual manuscript, preferably one that has aesthetic value, is required. However, there are also cases where an unseen manuscript is honored, most notably in the event of its being installed within a *stūpa*. As in the case of the Buddha's relics, which are often similarly treated, the manuscript—since it will never be seen—may not actually possess the characteristics that are attributed to it; in fact, it may not even exist.

Under the rubric of what I call discursive usage there are also a number of possible modalities. The main feature that distinguishes the discursive from the cultic category is that in the discursive, the words of the text are actually read, whereas in the cultic, the manuscript as a whole is treated iconically, generally as a physical embodiment of the teachings of the Buddha.

Following Paul Griffiths (1999), I divide discursive usage into three modes: composition, display, and storage. The first mode indicates the way in which written or, more properly, writeable surfaces may be used for composing a work. Generally one will write one's ideas down, and then rewrite them, alter them, and rethink them in the turbulent process of composition. This is generally, although not always, a private or at least narrowcast usage of writing that awaits completion before being displayed. In the use of writing to display a work—to make it accessible to those wishing to gain knowledge of its linguistic contents—two distinct modes can be distinguished: the work may be read silently or read out loud. Note that when a text is read aloud, those present will, strictly speaking, be accessing the text through the oral medium. This is a secondary orality, and must not be confounded, as has often been done, especially by modern graphocentric scholars, with a more general literacy. Even if most of the texts are *stored* in writing, if only a few literate people read these to the vast majority who are illiterate, then one should not assume that the texts, although actually written, enter into society and are engaged as written texts. A second aspect of the discursive display of texts pertinent here is whether they are read in a bounded ritual/liturgical context, or whether they are studied, discussed, and commented upon in a scholastic environment. The role of a manuscript at a Paritta ceremony, where it is used as a support for the recitation of protective verses, is quite different from that of the well-worn palm leaves of a copy of a doctrinal compendium, such as the *Visuddhimagga*, that generations of scholarly monks have studied and debated.

The final mode mentioned by Griffiths is storage, which of course is what gives a work that has been composed and displayed the ability to be redisplayed and thus transmitted over time. In Lan Na, those responsible for the production of manuscripts were quite conscious of their importance for storing texts. As we will see, many of the manuscripts possess colophons stating explicitly that they were made in order to preserve the teachings of the Buddha for 5,000 years.

There are important reasons for wanting to establish just which roles were being fulfilled by the media available in Lan Na. An intimate symbiotic relationship exists between the word and the medium through which it is communicated, for the one cannot exist without the other. This is certainly the case with Pali texts. The English word "text" in its most basic meaning, like the Pali words *sutta* and *gantha*, refers to a series of items strung together, but it has come to be used primarily to denote a series of words put together to form a linguistic work. The word "text" may be used to refer not only to the discursive or semantic contents of a work, but also to its physical receptacle—what we might call the "book." Scholarship about South and Southeast Asian textuality, however, has focused largely on only one aspect, semantic content. The nature of the vessel has been largely ignored. This is unfortunate, because the medium is deeply involved with how the text is assimilated. A textual encounter that is mediated through the written word has qualities that differ from the encounter that occurs through speech; the physical presence of an unchanging written document has an effect on the interpretive strategies available to the reader that is qualitatively unlike the effect engendered through hearing a text.

Many scholars have argued that there are strong theoretical reasons, beyond the quest for mere historical particularities, for wanting to know precisely what methods of communication have been used in various instances. McLuhan has argued that the medium greatly affects—in fact, *is*—the message of a text. There can be little doubt today, even among those who are not media savvy, that certain media are more appropriate for certain forms of communication. Hence the joke behind the 1971 record album *The Best of Marcel Marceau*: each side of this recording of the great French mime consists of twenty minutes of silence followed by a minute of thunderous applause. But many scholars have made far-reaching claims about the effects of various media that go beyond any such casual observations. Walter Ong holds that writing actually restructures consciousness in fundamental ways, and Jack Goody[9] believes that written texts funnel thought into a more linear mode, nourishing logical processes and individualism along the way, whereas hearing allows for more open, participatory patterns of thought.[10] They are joined by a host of other scholars from disparate fields, such as classics (Havelock 1963), medieval studies (Stock 1983), international relations (Deibert 1997), and psychology (Olson 1994), to name just a few, who all adhere broadly to the belief that

> the transformation of basic information into knowledge is not a disembodied process. It is powerfully influenced by the manner of its material expression. In other words, the medium is never neutral. How we organize and transmit our perceptions and knowledge about the world strongly affects the nature of those perceptions and the way we come to know the world. (Paul Heyer, quoted in Deibert 1997, 3)

The main difficulty with this theory is that, like all materialist theories, it often rears its head in a strong version that leads inevitably to technological determinism. Such theoretical zealotry sees all social and historical transformations as products of changes in the modes of communication only. On this view the Renaissance would be understood as a necessary, linear result of the invention of the printing press, and globalization as the child of television and the Internet. In response to this, I would argue that communication technology is but one in a complicated nexus of factors that shape a society at any given time, but one that is, however, particularly important in the context of religious communities that arrive at many of their beliefs and practices through the guidance of texts. Of course, it was not approaches to writing or the oral tradition alone that differentiated one monastic group from another and that preoccupied the minds of kings. I am only using communication technology as one of many possible lenses through which to view the Buddhist world of northern Thailand.

Besides totalizing tendencies, another problem that has hounded media theory is that it has often been deployed deductively to make predictions about the facts regardless of their fit. For instance, it has been surmised, based on his particular use of scientific and analytic principles, that the fifth-century BCE systematic grammarian Pāṇini *must* have used writing to produce his comprehensive Sanskrit grammar, the *Aṣṭādhyāyī*—despite hardly a shred of empirical evidence to support the claim (Goody 1980, 12). Regardless of whether certain theories concerning communication are tenable, one cannot even begin to address them in a Buddhist context until the forms in which the texts were communicated are known. What is called for at this juncture in the study of the communication and transmission of Buddhist texts in Thailand, and Southeast Asia generally, is to get the historical record straight. Our understanding of the contents of these texts should be supplemented with more thorough knowledge of the actual forms in which the contents were delivered. My aim, then, is to help cultivate this knowledge with particular attention to the use of writing and manuscripts and how they related to the oral tradition.

My second objective is to supplement our understanding of the *role* of manuscripts in the region under study by looking at the *attitudes* that were held towards this new technology. While it may be difficult in today's dizzying digital landscape to think of dusty old manuscripts as new technology, it nevertheless remains the case that in fifteenth-century northern Thailand the writing of religious texts was a new enterprise that was welcomed by some but viewed with apprehension by others. In this, at least, it is no different from what is seen today. It will become clear that the introduction of writing to transmit Pali texts was not a seamless process, but was an arena of contestation, elaboration, and consolidation.

Evidence for *attitudes* towards writing is of a somewhat different nature than evidence for the actual *existence* of writing and its permeation into various arenas. Evidence for the attitudes must be abstracted from such things as the tone in which writing is described, the frequency and centrality of references to it, and the veneration accorded written items. This task must often be fixed within a comparative framework, where attitudes towards other entities vying for similar positions are also evident. For example, that relics possess wondrous powers is a common feature in both Pali and vernacular chronicles. However, I have never come across any such powers being attributed in Lan Na to a manuscript or book of any sort. This, then, I read as evidence that writing was not exalted as relics were, even though both could be interpreted as representations of the Dhamma of the Buddha. Many such examples will be presented in this book.

PREVIOUS SCHOLARSHIP

Little research has been done regarding communication and the transfer of information in premodern South or Southeast Asia.[11] As Richard Gombrich states regarding the oral tradition, "somehow scholars have not given much thought to the mechanics of how [monks] would have remembered what to preach" (1990, 25). The actual techniques of memorization and oral transmission of the Pali tradition have been little studied, and there are few occasions where we are told exactly how the *bhāṇaka*s went about their trade.[12] Nevertheless, Steven Collins[13] has managed to bring to our attention a commentarial work that discusses how to memorize the text of a meditation subject. This apparently includes the recitation of parts of the body in forward and backward order. Because oral traditions leave no direct records, evidence attesting to methods of oral transmission of the early texts can best be gleaned from the traces left behind in the style and format of the texts after they were written down.[14] I would add that scholars have also not given much thought to the chirographic production of written texts, to their storage, or to the accompanying reading practices.

It is important to keep in mind that the existence of written copies of the canon since the first century BCE does not necessarily mean that the texts were thereafter always engaged as written documents. Indeed, individual reading of the texts was the exception rather than the rule for many centuries for a variety of reasons. It may have been difficult, for example, to gain access to manuscripts in some regions, or the culture itself may have respected a long-standing tradition to focus more on memorized texts than on written documents.[15] Seemingly unrelated things such as diet may have affected literate culture by causing poor ocular health; even today, about one quarter of all adults over forty worldwide cannot read without glasses, a technology that was unavailable to the societies in question.

Ruth Finnegan discusses the problems involved in the definition of "oral" and "written" literatures in a way that illuminates the often spurious distinction between the two. She adeptly demonstrates how the categories flow into each other, especially through the three modes of composition, transmission, and performance. She provides examples of orally composed texts subsequently being transmitted in writing, written texts being performed orally, and other similar cases that blur the definition of what "oral" and "written" mean (1977, 16–24). The realm of Theravāda Buddhism provides examples of these points. Subsequent to the writing down of the Tipiṭaka in the first century BCE, there is little mention of written scriptures in the historiographical literature from Sri Lanka, where the writing of the scriptures took place, until the reign of the seventh-century Sri Lankan king Kassapa II (MV 1925, 45.3). The one notable exception is the interesting account of Buddhaghosa's writing of the commentaries (MV 1925, 37.215ff), which will be discussed in Chapter One. Indeed, the oral tradition, although not institutionalized as it once was, is today still alive in the Buddhist world. *The Guinness Book of World Records* has the following entry:

> **Human memory**: Bhandanta Vicitsara recited 16,000 pages of Buddhist canonical texts in Rangoon, Burma in May 1974. Rare instances of eidetic memory, the ability to project and hence recall material, are known to science. (McWhirter 1986, 22)

William Graham (1987) has written about the loss of a consciousness of the oral aspects of sacred texts that has permeated much scholarship about religious "scripture." He argues that the most useful conception of scripture must include its oral and aural aspects. Even the meaning of the text must embody not only a raw knowledge of its discursive contents, but also the way it is used in oral frameworks, how it enters into language itself, and how it sounds when chanted or read. These aspects he calls the sensual or aesthetic meaning. This must be kept in mind when trying to understand the popularity of the oral tradition—it captures some aspect of the text which cannot be conveyed in writing. It calls the listener into its world more thoroughly than can written texts. As I will demonstrate, the hearing and memorization of texts was a prominent feature of Theravādin historiographical literature even into the eighteenth and nineteenth centuries.

THE SOURCES

The Theravāda monks were the most energetic and prolific historiographers in all of South and Southeast Asia. Beginning with the *Dīpavaṃsa* and *Mahāvaṃsa* (MV) they chronicled the religious, political, and textual history of Buddhism. These chronicles are ordinarily centered around one of three themes: the history of Buddhism in general, the history of specific Buddha images, and the history of religious sites such as monasteries and reliquaries. While the chronicles are often based solely and uncritically on earlier records, and may thus be secondary or even tertiary sources, they nevertheless constitute the best literary sources available for learning about the region's past, as I will discuss below. Pali texts such as the *Sāsanavaṃsa* (SV), *Saddhammasaṅgaha* (Law 1963), *Gandhavaṃsa* (Kumar 1992), *Cāmadevīvaṃsa* (CDV), and the *Jinakālamālīpakaraṇaṃ* (JKM) purport to relate the transmission of the teachings of the Buddha to Burma, Thailand, and other countries. These last two texts were produced in Lan Na during the Golden Age and will be used extensively in this book.

The CDV and the JKM were composed by monks from different orders in Lan Na who lived about one hundred years and forty kilometers apart. The CDV was composed at Haripuñjaya in the first part of the fifteenth century, probably around 1410 CE (CDVe, xxvi), by Bodhiraṃsi Mahāthera, who was also the author of a Pali chronicle about one of the most important Buddha images in Thailand, the Sīha Buddha (otherwise known as Phra Buddha Singh).[16] The JKM, on the other hand, is the work of the *araññavāsī* Ratanapañña Mahāthera, who composed it at Wat Pa Dæng in Chiang Mai between 1516 and 1528 CE. The JKM is based on various sources, some from Sri Lanka and others from Thailand, most likely including the MV, CDV, and the *Tamnan Mūlasāsanā* from Wat Suan Døk (MS).[17]

In addition to the Pali chronicles mentioned above, information garnered from vernacular Thai chronicles known as *tamnan* and *phongsawadan* adds color to the picture of the textual world of Lan Na. The *tamnan*s commence with an account of the Buddha himself and seek to connect him to the place or object that is the main subject of the text; the *phongsawadan*s, while similar, tend to focus on dynastic history. The works of this type I have considered include the MS, the *Chiang Mai Chronicle* (TCM), the *Nan Chronicle*

(Nan), the *Wat Pā Dæng Chronicle* (TPD), *The Crystal Sands: The Chronicles of Nagara Śrī Dharmarrāja* (Wyatt 1975), and the *Phongsawadan Yonok* (Notton 1926). There are numerous *tamnan* that narrate the history of an individual image or relic,[18] but there are no known works of this genre that deal with the history of a specific important or magically powerful manuscript.

One cannot simply open traditional chronicles and read them as history. Some people have considered it inappropriate to use them as anything but the most rudimentary of guides to the main events that constitute the history in question. Beginning with Alberuni and continuing through Hegel and Weber to the modern period of western scholarship, there has been a tendency to divide the world into a historically conscious West and an East blissfully unaware of the very passing of time, let alone historical development.[19] This position can still be heard even in the face of countless inscriptions throughout the region that date and mark for posterity specific historical events and an entire genre of literature, called *itihāsa*, which claims to tell of the past. In the Buddhist countries of Southeast Asia, as I have said, there is a particularly strong historiographical tradition. However, these texts, in contradistinction to western ones, have often been seen as "uncritical" and ideologically driven, whereas "proper" history, executed by western scholars, is thought to provide a clearer picture of the past. This viewpoint predisposes one to focus on the mythical aspects of many of these texts and to claim on the strength of these that the texts are not to be valued as history (Wyatt 1994b, 3).[20]

In the realm with which I am presently concerned—the media through which Buddhist texts were transmitted—the serious chronicles provide a general sense of development from a strictly oral framework of transmission in the distant past, to one which is increasingly more literate as time progresses. People from different eras are depicted using the communications technologies appropriate to their times. Thus we never hear of kings sponsoring the copying of Dhamma texts until well after the fourth council, when all the chronicles agree they were first written down. This is significant, given that an understanding of the diachronic progression of technological innovation is often not evident even in early modern artistic works of European provenance. For example, in Raphael's 1506 *Holy Family*, depicting Jesus in Jerusalem, gothic churches with crosses can clearly be seen in the background; in Rembrandt's *Holy Family with Angels*, from 1645, contemporary tools hang from the walls of Joseph's carpentry shop, and the Holy Mother is reading a book even though the codex format was unknown until at least two centuries after Christ. To this list could be added the famously anachronistic clock strike in Shakespeare's *Julius Caesar* (2.1.190), as well as countless other examples culled from the western canon. One might therefore expect to encounter anachronisms in Pali chronicles that betray historical accuracy in the service of certain ideological goals. It would surely be no great surprise to come across a passage in which the paradigmatic third-century BCE king Asoka sponsors a royal copy of the Tipiṭaka. Such a story could serve to demonstrate that a ruler, in sponsoring a canonical copying project, is emulating the glorious, model deeds of Asoka. This kind of strategy is commonly deployed in other contexts in the Theravādin world, as Kevin Trainor (1997) highlights in his study of the relic cults. In the MV, for example, the Sri Lankan king Duṭṭagāmaṇī enshrines relics of the Buddha in the Mahāthūpa at Anurādhapura in a process similar to what was done earlier in the chronicle by the first Lankan Buddhist king Devānampiyatissa as well as by Asoka even earlier.

> The early chronicles' depiction of these exemplary kings provided models for later rulers whose own actions on behalf of the *sāsana* could be seen as congruent with the ideals of Buddhist kingship. In this respect, the king's enshrinement of relics in *stūpas*, his maintenance and restoration of those *stūpas*, and his celebration of great festivals to honor the relics of the Buddha all served to demonstrate his fidelity to the Theravāda ideal of righteous rule. . . . By acting in conformity with this model, Sri Lankan kings no doubt reinforced their standing both in the eyes of the saṅgha members and among the populace at large. (Trainor 1997, 100)

In the realm of manuscript production, it would have been easier to inspire the scribes themselves to undertake the laborious, painstaking, and time-consuming process of making a manuscript if they could have been made to feel that they were thereby following the example of great and revered figures. Nevertheless, Pali or Thai historical narratives of important early Buddhist figures copying canonical texts are never found in the scholarly chronicles and are rare indeed in the more fanciful tales, even though their actions would have had an almost injunctive force which could easily have been translated into great support for such an endeavor.

I must also distinguish between two types of historical claim that I am making, which call upon different aspects of my sources. As I have stated already, I wish to create as accurate a chronology as possible of the development and expansion of written religious culture in the region, but I also hope to paint a picture of what that culture entailed. In pursuit of this, the sociocultural aspects of the chronicles may be separated from their description of specific events. The overall sense of the textual forms and media that were being used when these chronicles were written can be distilled irrespective of the accuracy of certain dates. For example, if a text claims that a letter was sent from one ruler to another at some time in the past, one can safely say that, regardless of whether that particular instance of communication was actually effected through writing, written missives were used for interregnal communication at least by the time the account was written, otherwise the author would not have thought of it.

Whenever a chronicle focuses on the gilding of Buddha images rather than on the making of palm-leaf manuscripts, or on the building of *vihāra*s but not on libraries, this can be interpreted in both event-historical and cultural or social-historical terms. In terms of the first, there are claims being made about how many of these items were actually produced, by whom, and when, which may or may not conform to reality.[21] The veracity of the statement can be evaluated in light of other evidence in many cases, helping gradually to clear the haze surrounding the world under examination. However, even in the absence of any other evidence, we can still harvest valuable information from such accounts about the attitudes the author of the text held towards books, libraries, or images. And we can use this to help answer some crucial questions about a culture: What are the symbols around which its members coalesce? What practices does it marginalize, and why? How are social relations mediated through the institutions and practices that form around key technologies? Far from hindering my investigation, the ideological viewpoints of the authors are instead rich mines for information about the views that various social groups held about what position the growing technology of writing ought to have.

Northern Thai manuscripts, and especially their scribal colophons, constitute another major source for the study of textual transmission in the Lan Na kingdom. I have chosen to focus on palm-leaf manuscripts from Lan Na because they are among the oldest Pali documents available; a few date from the fifteenth century and scores from as early as the first half of the sixteenth century. Outside of these, the bulk of traditional chirographic Pali texts in the Theravādin world exist in nineteenth-century manuscripts. The oldest Pali manuscript yet found dates back to the sixth century and is from Śrī Kṣetra, once a major Pyu center in Burma; it consists of a selection of passages written on gold plates fashioned to look like palm leaves. Some stone wheels from seventh- or eighth-century Dvāravatī with brief extracts from Pali texts[22] and a few isolated, short inscriptions have also been found in

Southeast Asia (Skilling 1997b). The earliest extant manuscript from Sri Lanka is of the *Saṃyuttanikāya* from 1411 CE, and the oldest Pali manuscript from Lan Na is part of a Jātaka from 1471 CE (von Hinüber 1985, 1).

Thousands of manuscripts from northern Thailand, of which some ten to fifteen percent are in Pali, have been microfilmed and cataloged by the Social Research Institute (SRI) at Chiang Mai University. The SRI has published its own catalog with the colophons of eighty-nine manuscripts (SRIcat), and several German scholars have also published useful information about these manuscripts. The Siam Society in Bangkok maintains a library of several dozen northern Thai manuscripts, as do the Royal Danish Library and the Otani University Library in Japan.[23] These manuscripts and their colophons can provide valuable information, not just about the provenance of the work, but also about the circumstances under which it was made, how it was intended to be used, and how it was valued. The fact that the colophons are in the vernacular in itself opens up a range of questions about the knowledge of the scribes, the intended users of texts, and the interplay between Pali and other languages. I will address some of these issues in what follows.

I will supplement the literary-historiographical sources and the manuscripts with epigraphical and archaeological evidence. There are numerous inscriptions which provide information about such things as royal sponsorship of libraries and manuscripts, lay donations of lecterns for books, learned monks who know the Tipiṭaka by heart, and other matters pertaining to the transmission of Pali texts.

With few exceptions, Lan Na inscriptions from the earliest times until well into the twentieth century are to be found in one of two scripts, the Fak Kham or the Tham script. The Fak Kham script (named after its similarity to the shape of tamarind pods) was used from at least 1411 CE in official inscriptions, important letters, and other documents (Penth 1992, 52). It looks similar to the classical Sukhodaya script and, like it, probably developed out of a proto-Thai script that was based upon the scripts of the Mon as well as Tamil and Andhra *grantha* scripts. The Tham or Dhamma script, also known as Tua Müang (local letters), is far more rounded and, as its name suggests, was used mainly for religious texts in Pali, but was also adapted for the vernacular. Almost all palm-leaf manuscripts from the region employ this script, as well as many inscribed Buddha images and about 10 percent of lithic inscriptions. The Tua Müang script also developed out of the proto-Thai script but was apparently more heavily influenced by the Mon in use more recently at Haripuñjaya.[24]

While consideration may be given to historical information found in these inscriptions, it is important to avoid the temptation to see them as providing a clear window onto the past that trumps the chronicles or other literary sources. Their agreement or disagreement with other texts should be taken neither as confirmation nor repudiation of the points under examination. The inscriptions may be based on the same source material as the more ephemeral historiographies, on hearsay, on the imagination of the author, or on the ruler's desire to make history as he wishes it to have been.

One of the most difficult questions to answer in connection with inscriptions is that of their purpose. Should they be approached in the same way as any other textual form? Is their main function to convey some body of knowledge to a reader through a discursive engagement with the text, or are they more properly to be considered as physical representations of their text, perhaps embodying some numinous power, regardless of whether it is read or not? Petrucci, grappling with this issue in the context of Lombard inscriptions, emphasizes the "special solemnity of lapidary writing" (1995, 50) that comes through because of its monumental nature. He asserts that epigraphy, while conveying a verbal message to those who can read it, also imparts a figural message to the illiterate or semiliterate populations, who have only the slightest notion of what the text is about or who put it there. In a similar vein, Bierman (1998) in her study of what she terms the Fatimid public text, focuses on the context, placement, and appearance of Arabic text in both public and private spheres in Fatimid Egypt, arguing that these can offer up information about both the authors and the intended recipients. The historian should bear in mind that "meaning as understood here is not completely contained in the writing itself but, rather, grows in the web of contextual relationships woven between the official writing, the patrons, the range of beholders, and the established contexts in which that writing was placed (Bierman 1998, 15).

Does the efficacy of inscriptions lie mostly in the act of inscribing and installing the inscriptions themselves, what, following Bierman, we might term their territorial aspect, as opposed to their ability to be read many years in the future—their referential dimension? The idea of actually reading an old inscription to garner information from the text that it bears seems to be rather a modern phenomenon. Perhaps the utility of monumental writing differs according to the nature of the text; the intended uses of a commemorative epigraph marking the establishment of a new monastery might differ from those of an inscription of the Four Noble Truths. There are some instances where the inscription is clearly not intended for discursive engagement, because it has been sealed inside a reliquary or positioned high atop a pillar or in a hard-to-reach cave. And, most importantly for the purposes of this study, what does all this say about the position of writing in the society that is home to such inscriptions?

KEY TERMS AND THEIR IMPORTANCE

Since much of the evidence that I present from literary and epigraphical sources is terminological, certain key words must be carefully considered. When dealing with Pali sources, I have looked for such words as *likhita* (written), *potthaka* (book), *pāṭhā* (reading), *vāceti* (literally: to cause to speak—and thus by extension to read aloud), as well as words connected with the oral tradition, such as *āha* (said), *vuttaṃ* (said), and *uggaheta* (grasped/taken up [in the mind]). I am fully aware, however, that one should be careful about what some words mean. The word *vuttaṃ*, for instance, does not necessarily mean only "said," but can be taken to mean "written" as well. For example, one finds the following: "*Rājavaṃse pañcahi bhikkhusatehi āgamāsī ti vuttam. Silālekhane pana vīsatisahassamattehi bhikkhūhī ti vuttam*" (SV, 37). This quote states that in one text, the *Rājavaṃsa*, it is said (*vuttaṃ*) that the Buddha traveled with 500 hundred monks, but in an inscription it is said (*vuttaṃ*) that it was 20,000 monks. An inscription is by definition written, so the term *vuttaṃ* must have a semantic field extending to a number of possible forms of communication. Because the tropes that are used in this literature derive from the primarily oral milieu of ancient India, the meanings of the words connected to orality extend into the realm of writing, and not vice versa. Thus the term "to say" in Pali texts may refer to writing as well, because oral discourse is taken to be primary, whereas the term "to write" (*likh*) would not refer to a spoken text, as it can in English (for example, "Paul McCartney wrote 'Blackbird' on his favorite guitar").

Key Thai terms that have guided my research, such as *nang süa* (letter/book), *an* (read), and *khian* (write), are somewhat less ambiguous than their Pali counterparts and help to clarify the question of what communications media were used in a number of instances. In the case of both Pali and Thai terms, context must always play a highly important role in determining the best meaning. This basic hermeneutic principle has not been deployed as often as might be desired in many Buddhological works, which is why I have mentioned it here. For example, a Pali or Thai statement that one might find in a chronicle to the effect that an individual "brought the Tipiṭaka" with him or "came with the Tipiṭaka" no more insists that a corpus of physical books was delivered than does the English statement "he brought the Gospel into his house." Only a full consideration of the particular environment in which such transmissions would have occurred can complete the picture of what transpired.

The picture of textual transmission that emerges using the methodology I have outlined is one painted in small strokes that are suggestive, rather than sharply defining. But when one stands back and looks at that picture, a clear image does take shape, like an impressionist painting. In the case of Lan Na, I will show that the general canvas is one of an oral society, on which the literate aspects stand out like dashes of color.

Before turning to that society, I would like to discuss one more term salient to this study: Tipiṭaka. Literally, it means "three baskets," which refers to the three main divisions of Pali scriptures: the Vinaya (the monastic code); the Sutta (the discourses of and stories about the Buddha and his disciples); and the Abhidhamma (the psychophilosophical analyses of Buddhist doctrine and ontology). The word Tipiṭaka is often translated as "the Pali Canon," and since within the ocean of Thai literature I am really looking at how this Pali Canon reached various shores, it is fitting that I explore just what it is that is the subject of this transmission.

The problems start with the name itself. If these texts were maintained orally for centuries, why would they have been associated with the word for "basket"? As Steven Collins has noted, "it is intriguing to speculate on what could be the metaphor underlying its use to mean 'tradition' given that one cannot literally put oral 'texts' in baskets" (1990, 92).

It has been suggested that the metaphor may be that the tradition is passed on in baskets just as earth or water is so passed by laborers in a chain, or perhaps the idea is simply that baskets contain things and knowledge can metaphorically be one of those things.[25] The question for us, however, is what exactly were the contents of these three baskets and how do they map on to the notion of a "canon." Perhaps I should go even further back and discuss the term "Pali" in the expression "Pali Canon." The term *pāli*, like the term Tipiṭaka, is not found in the core canonical texts themselves but rather becomes current around the first century CE in commentarial and ancillary literature,[26] where it is used to refer to text upon which the commentaries (*aṭṭhakathā*) offer their insights. When the term *pāli-bhāsa* is found in the commentarial literature, therefore, it means "the language of the root text," as opposed to what is found in the other layers of commentary. The word Pāli, then, strictly speaking refers to the core collection of canonical texts around which the commentarial tradition developed, and it is in this sense

synonymous with the term Tipiṭaka. However, the word Pāli also has come to refer to the language in which these and other texts are written.

The word "canon" denotes a list of texts regarded as having particular authority within a tradition, but that list may be "open" or "closed." Mahāyāna Buddhism has an open canon, to which texts have been added through the ages using various strategies, all of which claim for such texts agreement with the message of the Buddha. Theravāda Buddhism, on the other hand, developed a closed canon like Judaism and Islam, to which texts cannot normally be added. New ideas and stories can be introduced through the commentarial literature and receive wide dissemination and traditional authority in that manner, but strictly speaking they cannot become a formal part of the Tipiṭaka. This closed canon, though, was *developed*; it did not appear as a complete corpus all at once, like a bird bursting forth from its shell, but was collected and edited in the centuries following the death of the Buddha. It is impossible to say precisely which texts were recited at the councils held periodically after the death of the Buddha, but the Tipiṭaka surely includes significant portions that are very similar to many of the texts there recited, even though it should not be entirely identified with the body of literature produced through these councils as the tradition would have us believe. Collins has pointed out that Theravāda Buddhism did not arise around the Tipiṭaka but rather produced it (1990, 89). But once this process was complete, at the latest by the time the commentaries were set in the fifth century,[27] acceptance of this particular canon became a defining feature of the Theravāda school. Defining though it may have been, the actual contents of this body of literature were not known by most Buddhists, or even by most monks. Certain parts would, for practical no less than philosophical reasons, have been studied and preached more commonly than others, and conversely, noncanonical texts such as the *Paññāsa Jātaka* (Jaini 1983) and *Māleyyadevatheravatthu* (Collins 1993), which will be discussed in later chapters, were and are both widely known and highly influential.

Again I turn to Collins, who observes that "the evidence suggests that both in so-called 'popular' practice and in the monastic world, even among virtuosos, only parts of the Canonical collection have ever been in wide currency, and that other texts have been known and used, sometimes very much more widely" (1990, 103).

Collins suggests that we can refer to a "ritual canon" that is the collection of texts from the Tipiṭaka as well as other sources deemed to be authoritative for any particular community of Buddhists that are actually in use in the cultic and scholastic life of the faithful. This kind of corpus is so common that when the historical and other texts that have been used as the sources for the present study speak of the transmission of the Tipiṭaka, we must assume that this term is being used to stand for the canon, but does not necessarily mean that in each instance the entire body of literature so defined was actually transmitted. Indeed, it is extremely rare to find a complete copy of the Tipiṭaka in monasteries today in any medium, and its existence in palm-leaf manuscript form in any of the older collections in monastic libraries in Thailand is, in fact, unknown. When the texts that will be examined in this book speak of the transmission of the Tipiṭaka, we might best take this to connote that all three parts of the canon (as opposed to, say, only the Vinaya texts) were well represented, but not necessarily that they were complete. We can see evidence for this contention in a text called *Pitok Tang Sam*, which purports to be a summary of the three sections of the canon (*tang sam* means "all three") but actually focuses only on a few portions (Coedès 1966, 70). When tracing the transmission of the Tipiṭaka, one should keep in mind François Bizot's statement that the Tipiṭaka is an ideological concept rather than a specific collection of texts (1976, 21).

There is no doubt that Louis Renou's assertions about the Vedas can be applied at least in part to the Tipiṭaka as it appears in the chronicles and inscriptions that will form the fabric of this study. In Laurie Patton's words, "Renou asserts that over time the Vedic canon became a kind of empty icon, signifying various kinds of prestige and power, but little else. According to Renou, in the classical and modern religious traditions of India, only the 'outside' of the Veda has survived" (Patton 1994, 1).

As found in the sources used for this study, the "outside" of the Tipiṭaka is far more important than its contents. It achieves iconic status and symbolizes for those who have the resources to produce it the power and authority of the Buddha, depending on the context within which it is produced. It has syntactic value within the constellation of objects, ideas, and practices that constitute the world of Buddhism, but little semantic value that can be adduced from the sources I have used. Perhaps nothing could endorse this notion better than the fact that throughout Southeast Asia, copies of canonical texts are repeatedly found with their leaves gilded together.

I Monks and Memory

The Oral World

It is difficult perhaps for most people in the modern western world, tied as it is to the written word, to understand just how much textual knowledge was maintained in the memories of monks in the ancient world. Indeed, as the *Guinness Book of World Records* suggests (McWhirter 1986, 22), great amounts of text are still maintained in people's heads in the Buddhist world today. In Thailand, as in other Buddhist countries in Asia, one often hears Pali chanting emerging from the mouths of monks who are gazing straight ahead rather than down at books. One of the impediments to a serious, sustained study of orality in premodern societies is simply that orality, by its very nature, does not leave records, and therefore the true state of this medium in historical periods has been difficult to discern. However, a sensitive reading of the written records left from the earliest stages of writing in Lan Na reveals a lot about the state of the oral tradition and its relationship to the written tradition.

This chapter will examine how Pali textual history from the earliest period in India until the establishment of the Lan Na kingdom is presented in traditional Buddhist sources. While it is difficult to map the events related in chronicles to the actual state of the world during the time being narrated, one is on surer footing when trying to discern the attitudes of those producing these chronicles towards certain subjects, in this case writing and its interface with oral media. In the absence of contradictory evidence, the narrative may also serve as a rough guide to the development of literate culture in the Theravādin world.

The present chapter is based upon two important Pali chronicles of northern Thai provenance, called the *Cāmadevīvaṃsa* (CDV) and the *Jinakālamālīpakaraṇaṃ* (JKM), as well as a vernacular chronicle called the *Tamnan Mūlasāsanā* (MS). Each text was composed by monks from one of the three different orders widespread in Lan Na during the Golden Age—an old Mon-derived order, a new Sinhalese forest-dwelling order, and an older Sinhalese forest-dwelling order, respectively.

Of the two Pali chronicles, the CDV is written in a more informal and less scholarly style. Composed by the monk Bodhiraṃsi in the second decade of the fifteenth century, it is less influenced than the JKM by reforms that were introduced in the late fourteenth and early fifteenth centuries by two forest-dwelling (*araññavāsī*) Sinhalese schools of Buddhism. One of these schools—or more properly ordination lineages—was brought to Lan Na by Sumana Mahāthera from Sukhodaya a few decades prior to the compilation of the CDV, and the second by a group of Thai monks who studied in Sri Lanka about a decade after the CDV was completed.[1] The JKM was written, as will be discussed in more detail in Chapter Three, by Ratanapañña, a monk who belonged to the lineage established by this second group. Bodhiraṃsi, when he composed the CDV, was most likely a member of the city-dwelling order (*nagaravāsī*), which was based on the Mon tradition that was adopted by the Tai at an early stage.[2] Bodhiraṃsi's greater tolerance for popular beliefs and practices is quite evident from a reading of the CDV, which contains far more numerous references than does the JKM to such things as the transfer of merit and the apotropaic benefits acquired through reverence of the Three Jewels and various divinities (*devatā*s).[3] In fact the JKM, which was completed about a century after the CDV, frowns upon such practices, noting disapprovingly, for example, that King Tissa worshipped wooded groves, trees, and rocks with offerings (Epochs, 128).

The CDV synthesizes narratives about the coming of Queen Cāmadevī to Haripuñjaya and the establishment of the city and its religious edifices with stories of a more parochial nature, such as the exploits of local tree and mountain spirits. Sommai Premchit and Donald Swearer suggest that among the reasons that Bodhiraṃsi may have had for compiling the CDV were the desire to assert the effectiveness of popular devotional piety and the importance of Wat Phra That Haripuñjaya in the face of the growing prestige of religious centers in Chiang Mai (CDVe, 22).

The MS was written at a Chiang Mai monastery called Wat Suan Døk, which had been the headquarters of the sect of forest dwellers ever since it was established by Sumana Mahāthera in 1371 CE. The name of this monastery translates as The Flower Garden Monastery in English (Pali: Pupphārāma) and therefore the sect based there came to be known as the "flower-garden sect" (Pali: *pupphārāmavāsī*). The MS was composed in two sections. The first and main section of the text originated in the 1420s and was the work of Buddhañāṇa, the fourth abbot of Wat Suan Døk; the second section was added about eighty years later by Buddhabukāma, the twelfth abbot of the monastery (EHS, 324). Thus the first part is contemporaneous with the CDV and the second with the JKM. The MS tells of the life of the Buddha, of the first three councils, and of the coming of the teachings and religion (Sāsanā) of the Buddha to Thailand, especially to Haripuñjaya and Chiang Mai.

All three texts are in general agreement about the early history of Buddhism, and in particular about the oral nature of the early transmission of the texts, although each one has a different focus that emerges from the distinct backgrounds and inclinations of the authors.

THE EARLY ORAL TRADITION

Pali canonical texts were not written down until the fourth council, which was held circa 70 BCE in Sri Lanka under King Vaṭṭagāmiṇī, roughly four centuries after the Buddha's death. Until that time the oral *bhāṇaka*s were the sole vehicles for transmission of the copious body of Pali texts. Thus the teachings were handed down orally even in the days of Asoka, the great third-century BCE Buddhist king who helped to spread the religion through much of South and possibly parts of Southeast Asia.

The oral nature of the transmission of the Buddha's teachings emerges in the early history of the religion as narrated in the MS through the use of phrases such as *tæ muk thuan* (Pali: *mukhadvārā*; English: "from the oral portal") and the attention given to the unbroken chain of people who bore the teachings through the ages:

> The religion which was established in our land of Thailand ought to be understood in the hearts of wise, learned people as follows: Mahā Upāli learned the *Vinaya* from the very mouth of the Buddha and thus it is said that Upāli was the first [in the line of transmission]. Then came Dasako, who was the second . . . then came Ariṭṭha, who was the eighth, and then all the noble people such as Tissadatta, Kālasumana and Dīghasumana, who passed it down far and wide from one generation to the next and without end from the monastery of Ariṭṭha, all the way to Kassapa [who spread it] in yonder island of Laṅkā. (MS, 175)

Harry Falk (1993) and Oskar von Hinüber (1989) have executed comprehensive studies of textual transmission in India during this period, both of which conclude that writing, if known at all prior to Asoka, was seldom used and certainly not for transmitting lengthy religious texts. Writing utensils are not included among the eight requisites for a monk, nor are they ever mentioned in the Vinaya as being part of the monastic wares. As Rhys Davids and Oldenberg point out in their introduction to the Vinaya:

> Every moveable thing, down to the smallest and least important domestic utensils, is in some way or other referred to, and its use is pointed out. . . . But nowhere do we find the least trace of any reference to manuscripts; much less of inks, or pens, or styles or leaves or other writing materials.
>
> And we do find, on the contrary, passages which show the difficulties which arose every time that the memorial tradition by word of mouth of any of the sacred texts was interrupted, or threatened to be interrupted. (Vin 1881, xxxiii–xxxiv)

There is, then, little reason to doubt the veracity of the MS account. The historical imagination of the author of the MS is remarkably sensitive to the varied realities of textual transmission in this early stage; the MS acknowledges that writing was known at the time of Asoka, for when Asoka decides to propagate the 84,000 divisions of the teachings, he sends a minister with a letter (*nang süa*) announcing his intentions (MS, 73). Falk, von Hinüber, and other scholars of South Asian textual history agree that the earliest uses of writing in the region were for state purposes such as royal decrees and other short communications, and not for the recording of religious texts, except insofar as a king might wish to include a quote. The degree to which the MS author was aware of this situation is difficult to say, but it is imperative to keep in mind that the realization among western historians that Asoka utilized writing at all emerged only when his inscriptions were deciphered by James Princep in 1837. When the MS was composed, Asokan writing was unknown and the Buddhist tradition held (as it still does) that the Tipiṭaka was written down at the fourth council, about two centuries after Asoka. It is therefore all the more astonishing that the author seems to have gotten it just right, namely, that the proclamation to spread the teachings could have been rendered in writing, while the teachings themselves would have remained oral.

This latter point brings up two important questions: if writing was known several hundred years before the fourth council, why was it not used to record the teachings of the Buddha? And secondly, why was it finally used when it was? In South Asia generally, writing was not viewed with the esteem accorded it in the neighboring civilizations of the Middle East and China. The Brahmanical culture placed great emphasis on memory and oral transmission of the Vedas and other sacred texts, but writing was viewed as a cause of impurity. Scribes were assigned very low caste status, and Brah-

mans engaged in writing were forbidden from studying the Vedas afterwards.[4] As a heterodox sect attempting to exist independently of the established Vedic cult, early Buddhism would no doubt have wanted to exercise every means for legitimacy at its disposal, and the maintenance of its core texts through an unbroken oral tradition would have been an important part of this project. Relying on written texts for the maintenance of religious literature would have lessened the value of Buddhism in the eyes of society at large and thus of potential converts. Presumably by the first century BCE, the religion was stable enough to be able to forge its own traditions without having to copy those of Brahmanical society.

Collins (1990, 98) suggests that one of the catalysts for the writing down of the canon may have been the growing rivalry between the Mahāvihāra and Abhayagiri monasteries. The fixing of the canon in writing by the Mahāvihāra, perhaps inspired by farseeing monks, would have helped to establish their hegemony and would have guarded it against the vicissitudes of political and hence religious instability. However, regardless of the actual reasons that the canon was written at that particular historical moment, I am concerned here with what is said in the traditional Buddhist sources about the reasons for writing down the texts. The JKM holds that while the monks handed down the texts and their commentaries orally at first, they eventually had them written in order to preserve them (*ciraṭṭhitatthaṃ dhammassa potthakesu likhāpayuṃ*). If the oral tradition was more prestigious, what accounts for the suggestion here that oral memory was at one point no longer sufficient to ensure the preservation of the texts? For insight into this question, I turn to the *Sāsanavaṃsa* (SV), a Pali chronicle from Burma that took its final form in the nineteenth century but which was based on much older sources. The SV includes a particularly involved section about the fourth council in Sri Lanka at which the Tipiṭaka was first written down. This section helps us to understand better what traditionally educated Buddhist monks may have perceived to be some of the benefits and handicaps associated with the oral medium (although it cannot be said to be identical to what Thai Buddhists may have thought).

> *Yathāvuttatheraparamparā pana bhagavato dharamānakālato paṭṭhāya yāva potthakārūḷhā mukhapāṭhen'eva piṭakattayaṃ dhāresuṃ. Paripuṇṇam pana katvā potthake likhitvā na ṭhapenti* (SV, 21).

The succession of monks mentioned already bore the *Tipiṭaka* orally from the time the Buddha was living until it was written down in books. But when this was complete and it was written in books, they did not establish it.

Here there is no indication that the written is more prestigious than the oral tradition and in fact the final cadence laments that the understanding, interpretation, and instantiation of the Dhamma—indeed its very life—is better served by the oral tradition. When inscribed on leaves, the canonical texts lie only on the surface of the written page, whereas when borne on the waves of sound, they tunnel deep into the recesses of the mind and become steadfast inhabitants of the cognitive world.

Mary Carruthers (1990) has written about the medieval European equation of textual knowledge with memorization. In the middle ages it was felt that one did not truly know a text if it was not (to use a Pali idiom) "established" in one's mind such that one could recite and quote from it liberally. The question of what the benefits are of memorizing a text has, of course, always been a central pedagogical problem. The current trend, especially in America, away from rote memorization in school may allow for more critical thought, but the educated person certainly has a very different relationship to the classic texts than someone reared even a generation ago. In the premodern Southeast Asian Buddhist world, attitudes towards knowledge were much more similar to those discussed by Carruthers than to what might be found today in all but the most traditional societies. Southeast Asian Buddhists, like the medieval European thinkers, "reserved *their* awe for memory. Their greatest geniuses they describe as people of superior memories, they boast unashamedly of their prowess in that faculty, and they regard it as a mark of superior moral character as well as intellect" (Carruthers 1990, 1).

The SV makes it clear that the great merits of the oral tradition do not appear with ease but rather arise only when the felicitous environment required for the proper memorization of texts exists. Just before the commitment of the canon to writing, there is a drought in the island of Lanka, so Sakka tells the chief monks to go to Jambudīpa in order to properly maintain their studies. The monks end up staying on the island, however, and with great difficulty (because conditions are so poor), they manage to keep the knowledge of the texts alive long enough for them to be recorded. This is but one instance of many in the chronicle that speak of the challenges facing those attempting to keep the memorization of the texts alive. All these stories end with a trope that emphasizes the difficulty of such a task: "Thus it should be understood that in bearing the Tipiṭaka orally the monks carried out a difficult task. And that they bore the teachings without missing even a single word is indeed a very difficult task" (SV, 22).

The community of monks is portrayed as being well aware of the demands of this arduous project of maintaining an unbroken, orally transmitted, textual lineage; when they finally gather to commit the canon to writing, they think to themselves: "In the future, beings who are deficient in mindfulness, wisdom, and concentration will not be able to bear it orally" (SV, 23). Great respect is offered to those who carry the torch of the oral tradition. It is implied that this form of transmission will no longer be appropriate for the humble denizens of future times (including the authors of the SV account), who are fated to exist during the course of the religion's 5,000-year decline. This rhetoric has something of the character of an excuse for the reliance upon written texts that came to dominate the Buddhist textual tradition in Burma with the passage of time. While on one hand it praises the oral tradition, on the other it appeals to the harsh realities of the world in order to legitimize the written one. It is likely that the Thai authors with whom I am primarily concerned would have shared similar views, endorsing the prestige of the oral tradition while acknowledging the necessity of the written one.

The JKM uses the causative form of the verb *likh* (to write) in its account of the commission of the canon to writing. In Pali, the causative generally connotes that the agent causes someone else to perform the action denoted by the word. It is highly possible, then, that even at the time of the fourth council, monks did not write and that they directed others to record the Tipiṭaka. In contrast to this, according to the colophons of manuscripts from Thailand centuries later, the vast majority of texts were written by monks or novices (*sāmaṇera*). Clearly, at some point, scribal duties became an important part of monastic life in northern Thailand, if indeed they were not in early Sri Lanka.

Even after the canonical texts were committed to writing, examples of the transmission of Pali texts, as narrated in Thai chronicles, remain by and large in the oral register (with the single exception of Buddhaghosa, as will be discussed below). For example, the succession of kings of Lanka reported in the JKM includes the first account in any of the northern Thai chronicles of a specific text being communicated from one region to another (JKMp, 64). About BE 780 (237 CE) two students are sent from Pagan in Burma[5] to Lanka to learn the *Vinayagaṇṭhipada*. The students are then brought back to Pagan, presumably to teach what they have learned. The JKM does not say that they brought written copies of this text back with them, but the stronger evidence that the text was transmitted orally stems from a consideration of the nature of the text they were studying. The *Gaṇṭhipada* genre consists of lexical texts that serve as a type of commentary insofar as they provide glosses for difficult words (von Hinüber 1996b, 100). In the absence of indexes, the facility of a text of this nature is expressed only if it is learned by heart. Only then can the definitions of difficult terms be accessed with any degree of efficiency when they are confronted in the root text. Lexical and grammatical texts such as these come under the rubric of *śabdavidyā*, or the "linguistic sciences," and are still learnt by heart in many places in India; the seventh-century Chinese pilgrim Yijing remarks that texts of this type were commonly memorized when he was studying in India (2000, 149).

Again, the mere existence of writing is not sufficient to displace orality as the prime mode in which texts are engaged. In fact, as Carruthers has shown (1990, 8), writing was often seen in the premodern world as just another mnemonic technique—a particularly good medium through which to learn a text by heart. We should therefore not be at all surprised that the colophon of a Paritta manuscript written in 1677 CE in northern Thailand suggests that it be used to learn the text by heart (*khün cai*) (von Hinüber 1996a, 53). Before print, what books there were would have been expensive and largely inaccessible. To be of any use, the limited exposure that one might have had to written works would have best been employed by fixing the contents of the works in the mind by means of memorization.

BUDDHAGHOSA AND EARLY REFERENCES TO WRITING

Most early accounts of textual composition and transmission in the JKM make no mention of books of any kind and eschew the use of the verbal root *likh*; however, writing and books do play a significant role in the story of Buddhaghosa. It is the only section in the JKM dealing with the period before the Golden Age that touches unambiguously upon literate culture.

> *Dīpañ ca pana patvā so yaṃ Mahindattherena Sīhalabhāsāya abhisaṅkharitvā kathitaṃ Buddhavacanaṃ yañ ca khīṇāsavehi potthakesu likhāpitaṃ, taṃ Sīhalabhāsāto parivattetvā Māgadhabhāsāya likhāpesī ti idaṃ paramparāgate Buddhaghosācariyanidāne pākaṭaṃ* (JKMp, 71).

> And having arrived at the island [of Sri Lanka] he [Buddhaghosa], having prepared the teachings of the Buddha which were recited in the Sinhalese language by Mahinda and which were caused to be written in books by enlightened ones, having translated them from the Sinhalese language, he had them written in the Māgadhī [Pali] language. This is well known through the legend of Buddhaghosa's deeds.[6]

As in the account of the fourth council, we find the causative form of the verb *likh*, possibly indicating that he was not the scribe. Perhaps the chronicle wishes us to believe that he dictated the texts in question. Regardless, this story of Buddhaghosa is one of the few times that the actual process of writing makes an appearance in the chronicles from northern Thailand. Since it features so prominently in all the stories of Buddhaghosa, both of Thai and non-Thai provenance, such an emphasis must be based on the highly literate and productive quality of the historical figure himself. Buddhaghosa, even if he was only the leader of a school of exegetes, and not the sole author of the commentaries bearing his name, must have produced a large volume of texts and was surely known in his day as the most prolific writer in Sri Lanka. This reputation would have carried through to all the historical traditions and expressed itself through the common references to literate cultural production on his part. But having mentioned writing in their accounts of Buddhaghosa, most Southeast Asian chroniclers wasted no time in concentrating once again on the subjects that they and their audience cared most about—images and relics, powerful kings, and knowledgeable monks.

There was one author, however, whose work on Buddhaghosa appears to have emerged from an environment in which literacy played a substantial role. Mahāmaṅgala wrote the *Buddhaghosuppatti* (Gray 1892), a somewhat romantic account of the life and deeds of Buddhaghosa, in the fifteenth century in Burma. Half of the chapters concern themselves with details bearing on the process and importance of writing, reflecting its growing prominence in the Burmese culture where this text arose. As we shall see, Burmese culture of the fifteenth and sixteenth centuries and beyond has been one in which the written word played a more prominent role than in Lan Na.

In the *Buddhaghosuppatti*, while Buddhaghosa is on his way to Sri Lanka, he meets another well-known scholastic, Buddhadatta, in the middle of the ocean. The latter urges the great commentator to continue his work in translating the commentaries and subcommentaries into Pali and gives him a writing stylus and a balsamic ointment called myrobalan, which he says will ease any back pain that might arise from the task (Gray 1892, 50).

Another telling detail found in the *Buddhaghosuppatti* is that while on his alms rounds, Buddhaghosa picks up palm leaves that have fallen and uses these when writing his books. Such behavior is never attributed to important religious figures in Thai chronicles and again presumably is included in the account because it is something that the audience would have been interested in.

In another scene Buddhaghosa witnesses an altercation between two women, which he promptly records in writing for use in clearing up the matter, figuring that he will be asked about it in the near future: "Thinking 'when I am asked, I will display this' Buddhaghosa established the matter by writing down the belligerent words of the two women in his own book" (Gray 1892, 52). Since this incident is not related in other, earlier versions of the story, it strongly suggests that at the time of the composition of this text in Burma, writing was felt to be a better recorder and truer arbiter of the truth than oral communication.

The account of Buddhaghosa's translation of the commentaries is also laden with chirographic references. In the story, Buddhaghosa is listening to a disquisition by the Saṅgharājā, who soon runs into a difficult textual problem that he cannot understand. When the Saṅgharājā retires to think about the problem, Buddhaghosa writes the meaning of the difficult phrase on a slate. When the Saṅgharājā sees the answer, he has Buddhaghosa brought to him and tests his mettle by giving him some stanzas to contemplate. That night, Buddhaghosa writes the *Visuddhimagga* with great ease (*Visuddhimaggapakaraṇaṃ atilahukena likhi* [Gray 1892, 56]) only to have it snatched by the god Sakka twice. After each incident he rewrites the text, leaving him with three identical copies the next day. The Saṅgharājā is greatly pleased and bids him complete his task of translating the whole canon and the commentaries.

The preceding examples of various uses of writing serve as good models for the type of accounts we might expect to find in Thai narratives of important figures in the history of Buddhist textual production. However, this kind of detailed concern for and discussion of writing features in neither the JKM nor the other Thai historical accounts of textual composition and transmission that I examined. For example, in the course of narrating the production of Pali literature in Sri Lanka, the JKM employs a number of different terms to denote the composition of a text. Buddhadatta is said to have "bound" (*ganthe bandhitvā*) the *Jinālaṅkāra*, *Dantadhātuvaṃsa*, and the *Bodhivaṃsa* and to have made (*akāsi*) the *Vinayavinicchaya* and other works. The use of the verb *bandh*, especially in conjunction with the word *gantha*, is interesting. *Gantha* is very similar to the English word "text" and denotes a series of items woven together. The verb *ganth* can refer, for example, to putting beads on a string. The root *bandh* has a semantic field similar to the English word "bind." So the use of the term here may refer to a process much like redaction—the joining together of several elements into one text, but should not be taken to indicate that he was physically binding leaves together. Most importantly, the use of the verb *likh* (to write) is assiduously avoided in this section, a fact that should not be regarded as insignificant.

While these features alone would not be sufficient to allow us to make claims about the degree of literacy that was likely to have been found in Lan Na, the lack of attention to writing coupled with a pronounced tendency to focus on oral aspects of the textual world does begin to paint a picture of a society in which writing was still overshadowed by orality.

TIPIṬAKADHARAS AND THE COMING OF THE SĀSANĀ TO HARIPUÑJAYA

It is not at all clear how Buddhism reached the Mon city of Haripuñjaya, now known as Lamphun, and spread from there to the rest of northern Thailand. However, the chronicles are fairly consistent in their identification of the Mon-Lavo queen Cāmadevī as the catalyst for the introduction of the texts and institutions of Theravāda Buddhism to this region. The main story, as it is found in the JKM, not only sets the stage for the development of Buddhism in the north of Thailand—what later will become known as Lan Na—but also provides a very clear picture of the way in which the texts central to the religion were transmitted to this remote area. In the JKM, when Cāmadevī comes by ship to Haripuñjaya in the seventh century, the text specifically says that she is joined by a retinue of monks well versed in the Tipiṭaka (*tipiṭakadhara*). The term *tipiṭakadhara*, which translates literally as "bearer of the Tipiṭaka," occurs numerous times in the chronicles and is a key to understanding the organizational and institutional composition of the oral tradition. In traditional Pali sources, both from within and outside Thailand, this term is always used in descriptions of the first three Buddhist councils. For example, the JKM tells about the second council in the following manner:

> *Evaṃ te therā tipiṭakadhare pattapaṭisambhide sattasate bhikkhū uccinitvā Vesāliyaṃ Vālikārāme sannipatitvā sabbaṃ pi sāsanamalaṃ sodhetvā Kālāsokena upatthambhiyamānā dhammasaṅgahaṃ kariṃsu* (JKMp, 42).
>
> Those Elders, having chosen 700 analytical monks who were *tipiṭakadharas*, assembled at the Vālikārāma in Vesālī, cleansed the teachings of all blemishes and, with the support of King Kālāsoka, compiled the Dhamma.

In this case, since the JKM acknowledges that the Dhamma was not yet written down, the use of the term *tipiṭakadhare* must denote people who know the texts of the Tipiṭaka by heart. Further evidence of such a technical meaning of the term is provided by the account of the monk Mahinda, who was the first to preach the Dhamma in Sri Lanka. It is said that he became a *tipiṭakadhara* when his father, King Asoka, had been consecrated for nine years (*Mahindatthero pana piturajino navavassabhisekakāle . . . tipiṭakadharo ahosi* [JKMp, 46]). Such a specific time designation indicates that the label *tipiṭakadharo* was not merely a loose description of someone who was familiar with the Dhamma or the canonical texts, but rather was conceived as a title which was conferred when certain requirements were met. These requirements were a mastery[7] of all three different collections of texts, the Vinaya, Sutta, and Abhidhamma, including the memorized knowledge of a significant part, if not all, of the Tipiṭaka. Later in this section of the JKM, we are told that Mahinda preached the *Lesser Simile of the Elephant's Footprint* (*Cūlahatthipādopamasuttaṃ kathesi*) and the *Samacittasutta*. This further suggests that according to the JKM, Mahinda knew several *sutta*s by heart and was able to recite them from memory when necessary.

Because it is such an important term, I would like to explore further what learned Pali scholars such as the authors of the chronicles under study might have meant by the term *tipiṭakadhara*. Certain illuminating passages appear in the commentarial literature produced in fifth-century Sri Lanka and commonly found in the collections of early Pali manuscripts from Lan Na. They would have been a major resource to which the authors of the chronicles would have turned for answers to doctrinal and terminological queries. As such, we can infer that the authors would have attempted, in their drive to share in the legitimacy conferred upon those whose interpretation of the texts is in accord with those of the classic commentarial corpus, to use key terms in a manner that is in accord with their usage in these texts. In the commentary to the Vinaya, we find the following episode:

> "Why are you coming?" "To take up the Buddha's words, sir." The elder monk, having said "Take them up now, novice," from that day on taught the Buddha's words. Tissa, having become a novice, and having studied the teachings, took up [by heart] the entire Vinaya along with its commentary. At the time of his higher ordination, though he had not even been in the robes for a year, he was a *tipiṭakadhara*. His teacher and preceptor, having firmly placed the entire words of the Buddha in the hand of Moggaliputtatissa, when their life ended, went to *nibbāna*. Moggaliputtatissa in the future, having developed his meditation practice and being an enlightened one, recited the Dhamma and Vinaya to many people.[8]

Here, the image of placing the entire teachings in the hand of the monk as well as the emphasis on his taking up the entire Vinaya (*vinayapiṭakaṃ sabbaṃ*) strongly suggests that the memorization of large amounts of text, if not the entire Piṭaka, is the subject of this narrative.

The next passage deals with a group of monks who are *tipiṭakadhara*s and who come to the Buddha to complain that they recited some verses but were not praised by the gods afterwards.

> The teacher, having said "I do not, O monks, call one who has taken up much [by heart] or who says a lot, a *dhammadhara*. Rather, he who only knows one verse by heart but pierces the [four noble] truths, he is called a *dhammadhara*," teaching the Dhamma he spoke these words: "One is not a *dhammadhara* insofar as one speaks a lot [of Dhamma texts]. Rather, one who, though having heard little, sees the Dhamma with his body, one who is diligent towards the Dhamma, he is surely a *dhammadhara*."[9]

The Buddha, in saying that one does not measure a *dhammadhara* by the quantity of texts that he knows, is of course acknowledging that such a measure is precisely what is generally used to determine who is a *dhammadhara*, a term synonymous with *tipiṭakadhara*.

Turning now to the JKM passage describing the actual voyage of Cāmadevī, we see that there is no indication of any physical texts being involved in the mission to bring the religion to the north. Instead, it is clear that this is supposed to be an instance of oral transmission.

> *Sā ca sabbapañcasatikena mahāparivārena pañcasatehi ca tipiṭakadhara-mahātherehi nāvam abhiruhitvā sattahi māsehi Biṅganadiyā 'nusārena idha anuppattā* (JKMp, 73).[10]
>
> And she [Cāmadevī] boarded the boat with a great retinue of five hundred people of all kinds and five hundred elder monks who were *tipiṭakadharas* and following the river Biṅga for seven months she arrived here.

The picture that one gets from this passage is of an entourage surrounding the queen, headed by the monks who are the guardians of the oral tradition. Note that they are differentiated from all the other groups in the queen's retinue. This conveys a sense of the great prestige that accrued to these monks, who were viewed as noble players in an honorable tradition of textual preservation and transmission.

This episode is substantially the same in the MS, in which there is no mention of books. On the contrary, the phrase *song pitok tang 3* in apposition to the monks suggests that they knew all three sections of the canon by heart. In the last line of the passage describing the coming of the teachings to Haripuñjaya, the copula *khüa* is used to relate the 500 monks to the teachings, suggesting a translation that in English should read: "Cāmadevī brought the teachings, *in the form of 500 monks*, to prosperity in Haripuñjaya." The identification of the teachings, and thereby the texts, with the monks themselves is a common feature of oral transmission. The monks embody the teachings both figuratively through their actions and literally through their maintenance of them in their memory.

It is important not to build an image of a seminal event based on one or two words, however. While it seems clear that the term *tipiṭakadhara* refers to monks who had memorized all or most of the canonical texts, it is of course possible that they also brought written copies with them to further ensure that the transmission would be a success. The absence of any record of written texts does not in itself tell us that they were not part of this momentous occasion; the chronicles may have simply overlooked the bringing of manuscript copies of canonical texts to Haripuñjaya. Perhaps books were simply beyond the purview of the author of the chronicle, rendering their absence in the account of Haripuñjaya of little historical significance?

This question must be answered in the negative because the JKM does, when appropriate, bring the transmission of physical texts into the picture. In the story of the transportation of Pali texts from Sri Lanka to Burma by Anuruddha, the JKM does provide information about the books that were brought back and about how they were delivered, in this case by boat. If such particulars about *Burmese* textual history are included in the JKM, it is inconceivable that they would not be included when relevant for Thai history as well.

The account of King Anuruddha of Pagan (Epochs, 142–144) is highly pertinent to the topic of textual transmission in Thailand because it is the first time in the JKM that we are told specifically about the transfer of written versions of the Tipiṭaka. As such, it serves to show that the JKM author was not *totally* unconcerned with the transfer of physical texts and provides reason to wonder why so little attention is directed towards this subject in his accounts of Lan Na itself. I commence with a full presentation of the episode:[11]

> This king who had gained faith in the Dispensation, being desirous of having the Tipiṭaka written down (*piṭakattayaṃ likhāpetukāmo*) asked the learned men, "Is the Tipiṭaka found in our land free from errors or not (*Kiṃ*

> *ambhākaṃ dese piṭakattayaṃ viruddhaṃ udāhu viruddhan ti*)?" On hearing the reply given by them that it contained errors and that what is found in the island of Laṅkā was free from error, he went to the island of Laṅkā travelling through the sky mounted on his thoroughbred horse, thinking of obtaining the Tipiṭaka from there (*tato piṭakattayaṃ gaṇhissāmī ti*). And his followers went by ship. And when he had gone there, he told the King, the Sovereign of Laṅka, "We wish to obtain the Tipiṭaka." The King, the Sovereign of Laṅkā, said, "If that be so we will write it for you (*tena hi mayaṃ likhissāmā ti*)." But Anuruddha replied, "Your writing of it does not meet with my approval (*tumhākaṃ lekhākiriyaṃ mayhaṃ amanāpaṃ*); I myself will write it down (*sayam eva likhisāmā ti*)," and he transcribed the Tipiṭaka and the Piṭaka of Exegeses (*piṭakattayañ ca niruttipiṭakañ ca likhitvā*),[12] and placing two Piṭakas in one ship and two Piṭakas and the Jewel Image in another he returned. (Epochs, 142–143)

In this account, which speaks in a clear manner about the mechanics of writing and transporting the Tipiṭaka, we do not find the causative form of the verb *likh* that is so common when someone of high status is involved in a writing project. On the contrary, the word *sayam* is used to emphasize that it is the king himself who copies out the text and not scribes working according to his orders. The king also seems to have fancied himself something of an aesthete, for he has very strong views about how writing should look and rejects the Sinhalese offer to copy it for him. This, and the fact that in this story he is himself able to read and write, indicate that the author of the JKM believes that writing already played a major role in Pagan, which accords well with the rich inscriptional record from Pagan.[13] It is clear from this passage, then, that the author of the JKM recognized the possibility that the written word could centuries earlier have been used to record and transmit the canon but that this did not enter into his picture of the voyage of Cāmadevī.

The CDV creates the same picture of an oral world during the time of Cāmadevī as do the other chronicles I have been looking at. In fact there is only one instance in which written texts appear in the CDV, but this occurs during an episode that lays the foundations for the journey of Cāmadevī. The sage Vāsudeva wishes to inform his friend Sukkadanta, who resides in Lavo, about his desire to found the city of Haripuñjaya. He therefore writes a letter and gives it to a tree deity to deliver (CDVe, 49). Sukkadanta, in turn, sends his emissary Gavaya with a letter to the Lavo king telling about the project and requesting that his daughter Cāmadevī come to rule the city.

The letter itself is not a particularly important detail in this story, and in fact in the JKM's account of this episode, the emissary Gavaya is not sent with a letter, but rather is said to relate the story of the sages and their city orally (*katham kathesi*). It is thus quite possible that the letter was an element that would have been embellished in an oral context over the core story.[14] It is easy to picture Bodhiraṃsi or someone from whom he heard the story adding this detail for color, especially at a time when the large majority of the population could not write. Such things would have been considered quite technologically advanced and thus rather interesting by most of the people, akin perhaps to our fascination today with movies where the heroes use the latest high-tech communications devices. It is notable that in another chronicle by Bodhiraṃsi, the one reference to writing is in a very similar context. In the *Sihiṅgabuddharūpanidāna*, an account of the Phra Buddha Singh image, there is an episode in which a king sends a letter to another king. Recall that in the account of the propagation by Asoka of Buddhism found in the MS, a text written in part during the same period as the CDV, the king uses a letter to announce his intentions, but the texts themselves are transmitted orally. We can therefore be sure that, regardless of the specific case of Gavaya, letters were sometimes used for communication between rulers during Bodhiraṃsi's time but writing was probably not commonly used to record religious texts.

Other than this one incident, there is a conspicuous absence in the CDV of any reference to writing, libraries, manuscripts, or other accoutrements of Buddhist literate culture, even when other aspects of religious culture are discussed. At one point Cāmadevī builds a number of religious edifices

> complete with a *vihāra* and a Buddha image. Afterward she [gives the following to the *saṅgha*]: a residence for the community of monks headed by the *saṅghathera*; the Māluvārāma Monastery, including a *vihāra*, at the northern corner of the city to accommodate the monks from the four directions; . . . the Mahāvanārāma Monastery to the west of the city along with a *vihāra* and a monk's residence (*kuṭī*) as well as a Buddha image and food and drink for the resident monks. (CDVe, 79–80)

Library buildings or canonical texts do not feature in any such donative lists in the CDV. Following this passage, however, we are told that the Buddhist religion prospered through the efforts of the queen and her family, who were supported by 5,000 learned monks well versed in chanting (*bhāṇakā-*

dipaññāya) and 500 *tipiṭakadharas*. This indicates that the *bhāṇakas*, the oral purveyors of the canon, were at least perceived by the CDV author to have been prospering at this time. It also clearly differentiates between *bhāṇakas* and *tipiṭakadharas*, suggesting that the ability to recite some portions of the canon is not in itself sufficient to give one the latter title. Rather, as mentioned already, a *tipiṭakadhara* was most likely someone who was able to recite a very large portion of the canon. E. W. Adikaram, in his classic study of Sri Lankan history, says that while we can surmise that the *bhāṇakas* were actively practicing their charge at least until the time of Buddhaghosa, little is known for certain about their history after the sixth century (1946, 22–34). He may not have been aware of the CDV and other texts of Thai provenance, which as we can see suggest that they were still operating in Thailand into the seventh and eighth centuries and beyond.

The inattention to anything related to literate culture in the CDV is also evident in the speech given by Cāmadevī's son, Mahantayasa, at her funeral. He tells mourners to perform meritorious deeds—to give *dāna*, observe the precepts, to build *cetiyas* and images, and to dedicate the merit to their families, but mentions nothing about making or reading manuscripts (CDVe, 96).

MON INSCRIPTIONS IN RELATION TO THE LITERARY EVIDENCE

At this point, it is important to look at evidence that pertains more directly to the Mon in order to see if it creates a divergent picture of the role of writing in their civilization. Mon hegemony was strongly felt in the Buddhist civilization called Dvāravatī[15] that flourished from about the sixth to the ninth centuries in the central plains of what is now Thailand. The Mon also had major centers in lower Burma and played an important role in the culture of Pagan. Mon political influence was felt as far north as Haripuñjaya well into the thirteenth century, and their language and religion has left a heavy mark on both Thai and Burmese writing, religion, and culture.

Published Mon inscriptions from east of the Salween River are scarce,[16] and experts in this field scarcer still. However, the few inscriptions that I will present here are enough to give the impression that the Mon in fact had considerable respect for written Buddhist texts. The few, short, old-Mon inscriptions available boast about as many references to written texts as are found in hundreds of Thai inscriptions. They also contain many more canonical passages than do Thai inscriptions and suggest that the Mon had a considerable knowledge of Pali Buddhist texts. It is not without relevance that one of the teachers of Lüthai, the Sukhodaya ruler who composed the first vernacular Thai Buddhist work, called the *Traibhūmikathā*, was from Haripuñjaya[17] and thus probably of Mon descent.

As for the inscriptions, Robert Brown has published a detailed study of forty-two Dvāravatī *dhammacakka* wheels in which he discusses the recently deciphered epigraphy found upon them (1996, 96–120). It is difficult to date these inscriptions, but they probably belong to the seventh century. Some of the wheels have inscriptions on the spokes or felloe that appear to have been taken from the *Dhammacakkappavattanasutta*, while other inscriptions on stone *dhammacakka*s seem to come from such texts as the *Dhammapada*, *Vinayamahāvagga*, and the *Visuddhimagga* (Skilling 1997b, 133–157). Peter Skilling (1997b, 123–133) has written about some Dvāravatī inscriptions on a stone bar from Nakhøn Pathom inscribed with two lines on each of the four thirty-centimeter sides. They consist of the essence of the Buddha's teachings in highly terse form, but cannot be related directly to any one text. The first side includes key words from the Four Noble Truths as well as the twelve links of the chain of conditioned origination (*paṭiccasamuppāda*); the next side lists the thirty-seven factors conducive to enlightenment; the next side bears a canonical verse about enlightenment; and the last side also includes some common verses about the path to enlightenment as well as about the Buddha that are found in numerous places in the Pali canonical texts.

Lest one believe that these inscriptions were intended for the edification and education of the people of the region, it must be said that many of the wheels from Dvāravatī were elevated on pillars, rendering the inscribed texts unreadable for the earthbound observer. This leaves one wondering about the motivation behind the production of these monuments. Were the words themselves deemed to have had some apotropaic or other power, effected through their being carved in stone? Were these inscriptions used to accentuate the power of local rulers who sponsored their construction? Were they intended to be taken down and read at some distant time in the future when knowledge of the texts was declining? Regardless of the exact reasoning behind the making of these texts, they prove that the Mon did indeed have knowledge from early on of written forms of Pali Buddhist canonical and possibly commentarial texts. This lends credence to the SV account of the Pagan king Anuruddha, which differs from the account in the JKM in asserting that he sacked the Mon city of Sudhammanagara and wrested from there (and not from Sri Lanka) several copies of the Tipiṭaka.

An inscription now kept at Wat Phra That in Haripuñjaya (Coedès 1925, 189–192), marks the establishment of a monastery called Jetavana by King Sabbādhisiddhi, a member of the Mon royal lineage established by Cāmadevī who later became a monk. The date mentioned in the inscription in connection with the founding of the monastery corresponds to 1213 CE. The stele itself is in fairly good condition, with only the first seven lines, which are in Pali, having any lacunae. The remainder of the two faces are in Mon. After saying that he built the monastery and populated it with monks who follow the precepts, the text says that the king made many golden Tipiṭakas and hopes that beings are released from pain and pleasure through faith in the Three Jewels.

In the MS there is also a reference to this king that echoes the information given in the inscription: "When the king reached seven years, he gave the city to his mother and went forth to become a novice monk. . . . When he returned he had twelve sacred books made and after ten years he made a great forest retreat and *cetiya*" (MS, 134).

The term *nang süa* used here can refer only to written books, unlike *khamphi*, which may denote any form of text. In the next MS passage, we are given further information: "To put in the library he had a set of all three Piṭakas made in which all the texts were complete." This project is included in a list of other meritorious and costly deeds done or gifts made by Sabbasiddhi, such as a golden flower covered in jewels, and a *cetiya* covered in gold leaf.

Another inscription, this one from Wat Sen Khao Ho, which once stood near the center of Haripuñjaya (Coedès 1925, 194–195), tells us about the literary concerns of yet another Mon king. The inscription is not dated, and unfortunately the king to whom it is attributed, Tjum, is unknown from other sources. In it, the king has a large cave built as an offering, into which is put an image of the Buddha. However, in this cave are also placed some apotropaic Paritta texts as well as another book whose title is not provided, but which is obviously Buddhist in content. Here the physical book itself is apparently viewed as being an item which adds merit to an offering just like an image would.

What evidence there is of old Mon civilization in the Menam basin, then, suggests that the Mon had a closer relationship to writing than did the early Tai, even though the latter adopted many of the customs, beliefs, and linguistic habits of the Mon. Strengthening the impression given by the inscriptional record is a statement by Emmanuel Guillon in his comprehensive study of the Mon:

> Writing is the obligatory means whereby great messages are to be introduced. In one of the versions of the Mon cosmology *Mūla Mūli*, towards the end of the organization of the world and the moral order the Buddha hesitates before transmitting his message of salvation to mankind and decides to teach humans writing and grammar first. (1999, 29)

If it is indeed the case that writing occupied an elevated position in classical Mon civilization, then what accounts for its decline within the fifteenth-century Mon-derived monastic order that produced Bodhiraṃsi, author of the CDV? There are four points that I wish to bring forward in order to help explain this phenomenon, although with the paucity of evidence available, these must remain conjectures. First, while Mon culture from Haripuñjaya was one of the main sources for many aspects of Lan Na religion and culture in general, the exact relationship of this culture to the earlier Mon culture from the time of Cāmadevī and classical Dvāravatī is unclear. Guillon has recently hypothesized that one can distinguish between a first and second Haripuñjaya (1999, 140–141). He argues, based on archaeological, inscriptional, and historiographical evidence, that the city was largely abandoned for about a century from 1050 to 1150 CE, perhaps due in part to an epidemic mentioned in the chronicles. Whatever the reason, he says that the architecture and statuary, among other things, leave no doubt that a new period began in the middle of the twelfth century. It is therefore possible that the affinity for writing dwindled during that century of upheaval and neglect, such that when the city was reinvigorated the concern for writing was eclipsed by the more immediate task of resettling the city. The dearth of later Mon inscriptions from the region is itself a testament to the possibility that the Mon themselves began to move away from a heavier reliance upon written texts after their conquest by the Khmer and Tai. If writing was intimately connected to the Mon/Dvāravatī state and cultural apparatus, then, as it waned, writing may have waned with it, as happened, for example, with the decline of the western Roman Empire. Second, we can look at the way in which Mon words entered the Tai languages to get an idea of the manner in which cultural attitudes, including those directed towards writing, may have been transferred. Guillon says that

> Thai has retained without change both the meaning and the phonetics of the Khmer terms that it came to reuse . . . in contrast, when the Thais took over terms or expressions from Mon . . . they often distorted the meaning

> or the phonetics . . . [scholars have] postulated "an imperfect bilingualism with a certain lack of comprehension in the exchanges." (1999, 144)

This imperfect adoption of Mon words leads us to expect Mon customs, and in particular ones related to language and communication such as writing, to have been altered considerably through their confluence with Tai practices. Third, it is important to realize that Mon culture, like all cultures, was not monolithic, and thus those parts that were assimilated by the Tai need not have reflected all aspects of the culture. Even within the realm of Mon Buddhism at Martaban, there were at least seven different schools that followed quite different practices (Guillon 1999, 154–155). Some of these schools had close connections to Sri Lanka and the Mahāvihāra, and others did not. Dhida Saraya even brings to our attention some recently discovered Sanskrit inscriptions from Dvāravatī that may be associated with Sarvāstivādin or even Mahāyāna influence, which is also evident in some of the architecture and iconography of Haripuñjaya.[18] One can only assume that, like the various orders in Lan Na, they also had different approaches to writing, and there is no way of ascertaining with our current state of knowledge just what role writing might have played in the particular order or orders that developed into the *nagaravāsī* order of Lan Na. Finally, perhaps the literary simply did not resonate with the Tai people who were initiated into these orders, for ultimately an order is defined by a specific ordination practice. Cultural or other features of monks from one order may or may not be transmitted to another ethnic group along with the ordination lineage itself, depending on such things as the amount of actual intercourse among the two groups of monks, their educational framework, and the original degree of difference between the two groups.

The conflicting images of Mon literacy that emerge from the Thai literary and Mon epigraphical sources may complicate our understanding of early Mon civilization, but when we turn to literacy and orality in early northern Thai civilization, as will be done in the next chapter, we will see that our sources build a clearer picture of the methods of textual transmission that were then current.

2 Early Thai Encounters with Orality and Literacy

In the thirteenth century the city of Chiang Sæn grew steadily in size and power. Located strategically at a bend in the Mekhong, it was populated primarily by Tai-speaking people who had probably come in the not-too-distant past from the far southeastern regions of China. In 1259 CE, the Tai warrior-king Mangrai took the throne and easily conquered the neighboring warring principalities. To consolidate his power as he moved south, he built a new capital, which he called Chiang Rai. According to the chronicles, hearing of the beauty and riches of Haripuñjaya, he desired to add this city to his rapidly growing empire. Therefore he sent an agent to the coveted city who was able to turn the people against the ruling Mon king, allowing Mangrai to take the city without meeting much resistance. Mangrai was able to establish a strong ring of Tai, Mon, and Shan allies, mainly to ward off the Mongol tribes. This circle of allies established a precedent for ties that continued off and on for several centuries with Sukhodaya and Mon and Shan regions. Mangrai eventually established his most important capital in the newly built city of Chiang Mai in 1292 CE, and this city, still one of the largest in Thailand, has remained the center of the north to this day. Mangrai was a strong supporter of Buddhism, perhaps as much out of the desire to offer something to unify the diverse constituents of his empire as out of piety. He built *stūpa*s to enshrine relics and encouraged the growth of Buddhist practice and scholarship in the region. Unfortunately, Lan Na suffered both politically and culturally under Mangrai's successors, who were unable to regain the stability of the founding ruler because of both internal squabbling and external strife.

In 1355 CE a king well versed in Indian cultural and political traditions, named Kü Na, ascended the throne and was able to consolidate the kingdom once again and sponsor religious and other cultural advancements. One of his most significant acts was to invite a monk named Sumana from Sukhodaya to bring the stricter Sinhalese forest-dwelling ordination lineage to Lan Na, thereby planting the seeds for the flourishing of the Mahāvihāra interpretation of Theravāda Buddhism that was soon to culminate in a Golden Age of Buddhist culture in Lan Na.

It is fair to say, then, that the decline of Mon power and the conquest of Haripuñjaya by the Tai king Mangrai ushered in a new era in the history of northern Thailand; but how was the transmission of texts affected? We have seen that the Tai-authored literary sources from Lan Na portray the world of Mon Buddhism as an oral one and that the Mon epigraphical record apparently contradicts this. It is therefore likely that the Tai-speaking Buddhists who gained ascendancy in Lan Na inhabited a cultural world in which the written word played a less prominent role, and that this accounts for their portrayal of the Mon world as such. The appropriate place to search for more positive evidence for this contention is in portrayals of the introduction of the new Buddhist monastic lineage by Sumana, for this is the most influential event of the early Tai period that would have involved the transfer of Pali texts and other information salient to the Buddhist religion. The native historical sources generally identify the movement of the religion itself—the Sāsanā—with the establishment of the ordination lineage in various areas, a fact that testifies to the central importance of this procedure and the likelihood that communication of texts would occur concomitantly.

INTRODUCTION OF THE FIRST SINHALESE FOREST-DWELLING ORDER

The story of Sumana and the Sinhalese order features prominently in the JKM, where in CS 701 (1339 CE) Sumana Mahāthera goes from his native Sukhodaya to Ayudhyā to study the Dhamma with teachers there (*garūnaṃ santike dhammaṃ uggahetvā* [JKMp, 84]). Sumana then goes, around 1355 CE, to study with a monk named Udumbara who had come to Rāmaññadesa, generally understood to be Martaban in lower Burma,[1] from Sri Lanka at the behest of the king, who wished to strengthen and purify the religion there. Udumbara belonged to the Udumbaragiri (Sinhalese: Dimbulāgala) fraternity, an *araññavāsī* or forest-dwelling, sect from Sri Lanka well-known for its learned and erudite monks (Epochs, 117, n. 4; JKMp, xiii).[2]

To understand who these *araññavāsī*s were, it is necessary to look briefly at some key aspects of the history of Buddhism in Sri Lanka. During the classical Anurādhapura period, which lasted from the beginnings of Buddhism in the island until the eleventh century CE, the Mahāvihāra monastery was vying for influence and royal patronage with the Abhayagiri and Jetavana monasteries. Besides disagreements on certain points of monastic discipline, there were also doxological differences among these monasteries, with the latter two being somewhat more sympathetic to the ideas found in the Sanskrit *sūtras* of what is called the Vetullavāda in the MV and would today be referred to as the Mahāyāna. The Mahāvihāra regarded itself as the most orthodox of these orders, being less willing to accept these doctrines and demanding of its monks stricter adherence to the traditional Vinaya rules. Towards the middle of the twelfth century, rivalry between these monasteries became so turbulent that King Parakkamabāhu I intervened and imposed royal authority upon the Saṅgha that privileged the tradition of the Mahāvihāra. Part of this program of what he termed "purification" led to the reordination of monks from the other sects according to the Mahāvihāra protocols. From that juncture, then, the monks in Sri Lanka were no longer divided by points of discipline and ordination; however, divisions based on lifestyle later emerged. The monks soon became divided into town-dwelling (*gāmavāsī*) and forest-dwelling (*araññavāsī*) fraternities. The main Mahāvihāra monastery complex itself was located inside the capital of Anurādhapura, with monasteries in its lineage prevalent in towns and villages throughout the kingdom. A group led by Mahā Kassapa Thera, who was a trusted advisor to the king and an important figure in the purification of the Saṅgha, founded the Udumbaragiri forest monastery which became the center of the forest-dwelling fraternity for a time. It was at this monastery that Udumbara Mahāsāmī, the teacher and preceptor (*upajjhāya*) of Sumana, was most likely trained. Forest-dwelling was one of the thirteen *dhutaṅgas*, or ascetic practices, open to monks and as such was an option for those monks who sought a life removed from the hustle and bustle of city life that would provide a framework more amenable to discipline and quiet contemplation. It must be stressed, however, that the forest-dwelling monks, although traditionally expected to focus on meditation (*vipassanādhura*), did not in practice do this to the exclusion of the study and preservation of the texts (*ganthadhura*). Many forest monks were renowned as scholars and commentators. The most important Sinhalese text of its period, the fifteenth-century *Saddharmaratnākaraya*, an involved commentary on the *Dhammapada,* was composed by Vimalakīrti, a forest-dwelling monk who came from a long line of scholars at the Palābatagala forest monastery (Ilangasinha 1992, 58). Even the founder of the forest fraternities,[3] Udumbaragiri Kassapa, himself authored an important work called the *Bālāvabodhana,* a scholarly Sanskrit grammar.

In the JKM, Sumana is ordained anew into this Sinhalese lineage by

Udumbara, and then he studies the Dhamma with him *(Udumbara-mahāsāmino santike puna pabbajitvā dhammaṃ ugganhi* [JKMp, 84]).[4] The Pali phrase *dhammaṃ ugganhi* used in the JKM here literally means "he took up the Dhamma" and connotes a very thorough assimilation of the Dhamma into his cognitive world—the kind of integration that can only occur through memorization. Words derived from this verb "*ut* + *gah*" can be used to refer to the learning of nonverbal skills, similar to saying in English that one has "taken up" a hobby (Collins 1992, n. 22). Any doubts as to the nature of the information transfer occurring in this passage should be assuaged by the explanation of the term in the commentarial literature, where the verb *ut* + *gah* is often glossed as *tuṇhībhūto suṇanto* (listening in silence).[5] Thus it would seem that Sumana learned the Dhamma from Udumbara in this case through an oral interchange of ideas and texts. It is important to realize that a very large amount of information can be transmitted orally, especially when one has trained in various mnemonic techniques for many years. As the seventh-century Chinese Buddhist pilgrim Yijing says in his account of learning in India, through acquiring the various techniques for memorization, "one can understand whatever one has heard once without resorting to a second discussion. As I have seen such men with my own eyes, it is certainly not a falsehood" (2000, 153).

Although such intensive styles of learning are not common in the modern West, musicians still regularly and effortlessly learn long pieces by heart. Many professional instrumentalists are able to play a complicated piece after hearing it just a couple of times, and there is little reason to think that a monk well-versed in mnemonic techniques would not be able to perform a similar feat in his own medium. The JKM, then, leads us to believe that Sumana returned to Sukhodaya carrying with him the new ordination, but not new manuscripts.

An inscription at Wat Phra Yün in Haripuñjaya commemorating the building of a pavilion there in 1371 CE continues to elaborate the story of the career of Sumana and suggests as well that he carried great knowledge not in his arms but in his head. Alexander Griswold, the doyen of Thai paleography, translates a line from this inscription describing Sumana as "skillful in expounding all the texts" (*ru chalat nai wohan artha tham tang lai* [EHS, 614, Face 1: ln. 17]). One possible meaning for the Pali-derived term *wohan* is simply "words" or "language." Thus this line could be saying that the monk had expertise (*ru chalat*) regarding wording (*wohan*), meaning (*artha*), and Dhamma. In this case the emphasis on his personal knowledge of the very words of the Dhamma texts connotes that he knew many texts by heart.

Based on this inscription and other sources, it can be surmised that

Sumana was invited to go from Sukhodaya to Haripuñjaya by King Kü Na (Pali: Kilanā) in 1369 CE (EHS, 614). After two years he continued on to Chiang Mai, where he established Wat Suan Døk, which was to be a center for the new forest-dwelling order of Sinhalese provenance that Sumana had brought with him. According to the inscription at Wat Phra Yün, the king greeted the monk with banners and flags, grilled rice and flowers, torches and candles, xylophones, stringed instruments, gongs, drums, clarinets, cattle-horn trumpets, small double-headed drums, curved trumpets, and conchs; however, there is no indication that Sumana returned the king's greeting with a gift of manuscripts. The next few lines indicate that Sumana's first act was to initiate restoration of damaged Buddha images and that he had the king build a pavilion in which to place four standing Buddha images (hence the name Wat Phra Yün—Monastery of the Standing Buddhas). When the pavilion was complete, a relic of the Buddha that Sumana also brought with him was placed in a tabernacle of exquisite beauty and stored presumably in the center of the pavilion. If Sumana had had more accurate versions of seminal texts with him, surely the arrangements for their preservation would have also been a prime concern and would have been mentioned in this detailed account of the proceedings.

While such arrangements are not mentioned in other sources, both the MS and the TPD, chronicles which we will examine in more detail in the next chapter, say that Sumana brought with him the relic *and* the Tipiṭaka (TPD, 17).[6] Perhaps these chronicles mean to say that the *thera* brought the knowledge of these texts, rather than the manuscripts themselves. It is possible that some texts were brought from Sukhodaya, but the fact that this is mentioned neither in the JKM nor in any inscriptions, coupled with the lack of archaeological evidence for a library for what would have been a very important artifact, force us to question the assertion.

There is other evidence that as a resident of Sukhodaya Sumana would have come from a predominantly oral world. Amid the copious archaeological evidence from the Sukhodaya period lurks no clear evidence of any libraries or other buildings that might specifically have been dedicated to the maintenance of literate culture.[7] Needless to say there are no extant manuscripts from this period, and I am not aware of any inscriptions bearing more than a few words taken from the Pali canon.

The third face of the Rama Khamhæng inscription of 1292 CE (EHS, 259–264)[8] lists important assets of local monasteries, such as image houses, *kuṭīs*, and massive images (EHS, 262, Face 3: ln.1–5). However, it does not mention copies of the Tipiṭaka or libraries. The king is very proud that the inhabitants of the area are diligent in observing the precepts, and are faithful Buddhists, but there is mention neither of the texts themselves nor their study. By the mid-fourteenth century, just prior to Sumana's mission to Lan Na, we do find inscriptions (EHS, 496, Face 2: ln.46; EHS, 513, Face 3: ln. 40) in which the Tipiṭaka is said to be kept in the royal palace: "Salute and pay respects to the golden Buddha image and the Tipiṭaka which are kept in the royal palace."

There are some rather detailed accounts of the donation of items to monasteries in the area, as well as lists of monastic buildings,[9] none of which mention books or libraries. It is possible, then, that the only existing copies of texts from the Tipiṭaka were kept ceremonially in the palace, and the monks, such as Sumana, in the course of everyday study and liturgy had to engage the texts orally. In fact, in some Sukhodaya inscriptions contemporary monks are described as *phu song trai pitok*, "people who maintain the Tipiṭaka" (PSC, 7: item 14, Face 1: ln. 26)—a standard translation of the Pali term *tipiṭakadhara,* which as we saw was used to refer to monks who knew large portions of the texts by heart.

The *Traibhūmikathā* is considered to be the first Thai vernacular text, and as it was composed around the period in question probably by Lüthai, also known as King Mahādharmarāja I, it is necessary to say a few words about what it does and does not tell us about the state of literacy and textual history at Sukhodaya during Sumana's time. The *Traibhūmikathā* is a Buddhist cosmological text that describes the three main worlds, the *kāmāvacara, rūpāvacara*, and *arūpāvacara*—the planes of gross, sensuous beings; of subtle beings of pure form; and finally of formless or immaterial beings. These are the various worlds through which beings may progress on their journey through *saṃsāra*, a journey that beings hope will end in the blissful, eternal state of *nibbāna*. As one would expect, the author tells us that the text ought to be heard, not read:

> Whoever wishes to reach the celestial treasure, which is the deliverance of Nibbāna, let him listen to this *Sermon on the Three Worlds* with care and interest, with faith in his heart, and without being heedless in any way. He will then be able to meet the Lord Sri Ariya when he is born in the future, to pay his respects to him, and to listen to the Dhamma that he will preach. (Reynolds and Reynolds 1982, 350)

The problematic issue to be considered here is that both the prologue and the epilogue present a detailed list of almost three dozen canonical, commentarial, and extracanonical texts that Lüthai supposedly used to compose the treatise. This extensive list of texts that includes some obscure titles has led scholars such as Likhitanonta to exclaim that there was a large collection of Pali texts in and around Sukhodaya at this time (1987, 169). However, in light of the textual history of the region a closer look at the situation suggests that the framing prologue and epilogue are probably later additions. It has already been pointed out by Vickery (1974) that the present form of the *Traibhūmikathā* is probably not the original one. Although the core text may well have been composed by a committee headed by Lüthai, it may have been a very much shorter and simpler version than the present one, which might have been expanded some generations later. The basic text relates standard Buddhist cosmology and soteriology, which could have been compiled by learned monks from memory and from basic canonical texts, along with some additions of their own, and does not require the many texts cited in the epilogue.

The date found in the epilogue states that the text was written in the year of the cock, in the fourth month of the twenty-third year of the era, but Vickery (1974) convincingly argues that it was assigned to the reign of King Lüthai through a copyist's error in the Ayudhyā period, when the knowledge of Sukhodaya's chronology had been lost. He believes that even based on the epilogue alone, the author was not Lüthai but Sai Lidai, also known as Mahādharmarāja III, who was the grandson of Lüthai. In a later article (1991) Vickery goes on to analyze the text as a whole and suggests that based on philological, stylistic, and comparative grounds, the text as we have it now is probably not from the reign of Lüthai. His claims rest on such things as the presence of royal titles that are unknown in Sukhodaya inscriptions (1991, 28) and the muddled, unsystematic understanding of Buddhist cosmology found in inscriptions such as Inscription 45 that are dated after the supposed composition of the *Traibhūmikathā* (1974, 25).

Regardless of whether Vickery's assertions about the body of the *Traibhūmikathā* are entirely correct, they should raise enough questions at least about the date of the prologue and epilogue to preclude their being taken as automatic proof of the presence of many lesser-known Pali texts at Sukhodaya in the early fourteenth century.

THE ORAL WORLD OF KING LAKKHAPURĀGAMA

Having taken a good look at the Sukodaya world out of which Sumana came, let us now move on to examine the kingdom of Lan Na into which

Sumana brought his new ordination. King Lakkhapurāgama, who reigned at Chiang Mai not long after Sumana had established the monastery of Wat Suan Døk but before Bodhiraṃsi composed the CDV, was known in northern Thailand as a very righteous and devout ruler. His acts of faith recorded in the JKM include the erecting of the large Chedi Luang, as well as covering the Mahathat Chedi in Haripuñjaya with 210,000 sheets of gold leaf. However, for all his faith, it is not recorded that he sponsored any manuscripts or erected any libraries. This suggests that manuscripts, if they existed at all in the region at the end of the fourteenth century, were regarded as very marginal to the practice and maintenance of Buddhism.

The passage in the JKM that describes the king's attitude to the teachings of the Buddha is as follows:

> King Lakkhapurāgama, who is devoted to the Three Jewels, is well educated, a bearer of the Dhamma, one who learns and questions and always has the Dhamma spoken to many groups. He even provides the four requisites to all those who study only grammar beginning with euphonic combinations and substantives. (JKMp, 91–92)

We can see in this some standard epithets that are used to delineate a person in an oral context who is familiar with the Buddha's teachings. The phrase translated as "well educated" is literally "one who has heard much" (*bahussuto*), and the king is also described as "a bearer of the Dhamma" (*dhammadharo*). The next phrase includes the causative form of the verb *vac* (to speak) and means literally that he "causes the Dhamma to be spoken." This term, while indicating at least that the Dhamma is presented orally, sometimes implies that it is being read aloud from a written text. In this sense the text is metaphorically being "caused to speak" by the person reciting it. However, this is not necessarily the case, for in the *Sela Sutta* we find the passage "*brāhmano . . . mante vāceti*" (VRI-Dev, *Majjhimanikāya*, 2: 356). Because Brahmans never read mantras from books, in this case "the priest . . . recited the prayers from memory" is the only possible interpretation. The other terms used in this passage such as *bahussuto* are less ambiguous, at least in their literal meaning, and do seem to refer specifically to orally transmitted learning. This is in keeping with the internal logic of the JKM, in which no transfer of written copies of the Dhamma to the region ruled over by this king has yet been mentioned.

The second part of the passage is slightly different in emphasis. In it the king provides the four requisites to those people who have taken up the grammatical texts treating such subjects as *sandhi* (euphonic combinations) and nouns. The list starts with *sandhi*, which is a feature of the language that is specifically an oral one, emerging as a consequence of pronunciation. Again, the word for study here is *uggahanti* (taking up). Would these grammatical texts have been learned orally or through written texts? Of all the texts that one ought to know by heart, grammar is the most important, because one must be able to recall all the rules at a moment's notice when one encounters them in a passage.[10] Searching through an unindexed manuscript copy of the *Saddanīti* grammar, for example, would be a decidedly impractical, if not impossible, way of accessing relevant grammatical rules. All of the above should serve to emphasize that the literary record of the period suggests that even educated Thai kings and monks operated largely within an oral milieu at the beginning of the fifteenth century.

WRITING AND ORALITY IN THE PRODUCTION OF THE *CĀMADEVĪVAṂSA*

We have now seen how the major events in Buddhist textual transmission until the time of Bodhiraṃsi at the beginning of the Golden Age are portrayed in Thai chronicles and epigraphical sources. A picture of a cultural world dominated by discourse in the oral mode emerges, with monks and learned kings bearing knowledge of the teachings of the Buddha in their minds and engaging and transmitting Pali Buddhist texts primarily in an oral form. Although the existence of writing and its use by rulers for official communication is admitted, the sources are concerned primarily with the oral tradition in the few passages where textual transmission is mentioned at all. It must be emphasized that textual transmission is greatly overshadowed in all the sources by a concern in the religious sphere for Buddha images and relics.

Having set the stage, I would now like to assess the role of writing and orality in the production of one of the earliest extant Pali works from Lan Na, the CDV. This chronicle emerged out of what can be characterized as the largely oral world of the early fifteenth century, but, as will be shown, it marks the start of a period in which the shift to a more literate society was beginning to occur. Because this text is a chronicle, the author tells us about the material circumstances of life in Lan Na as part of the narrative, but in assessing the modes of communication prevalent in the world inhabited by Bodhiraṃsi, we can rely as well on formal and structural features of the work that allow us to see beyond what the author intended.

The author of the CDV compiled the text from vernacular stories that were circulating during his time and that he edited and translated into Pali. Towards the beginning of the text he announces as his aim the elevation of the language of these tales (CDVe, 37) through the following lines:

> The language of those telling this story (*cārikaṃ bhāsamānānaṃ*), following the local language, is lesser and not suitable. I, a city dweller,[11] will turn it into a language whose syllables and consonants are those of Pali, which is strung into stanzas and verses, is pleasant to hear and delights the mind, and is a means to attainment for men and women whose aim is the generation of satisfaction. (my translation)

Besides establishing the preeminence of Pali in the linguistic hierarchy, this passage suggests that the vernacular stories utilized for the CDV were transmitted orally. The phrase *cārikaṃ bhāsamānānaṃ* means literally "of those speaking the story." It is difficult to conceive of the sources as written texts in light of the verbal root *bhās,* which was likely chosen out of the many possible words encompassing the various methods of communication because speaking was the method in question. The founding of Haripuñjaya was no doubt a favorite tale for inhabitants of the region, and it must have been told in many different versions by bards and elders in a process of oral communication well known to the field of folklore studies.

Unfortunately, Bodhiraṃsi did not succeed terribly well at his self-proclaimed mission of raising the level of the language of this text, for the language is often clumsy and grammatically irregular. Coedès, the first to publish the manuscript in Roman transliteration, points out that the many grammatical and other mistakes cannot be attributed to copyists' errors, because other texts from the region, such as the JKM and the *Maṅgalatthadīpanī*, which presumably descended through the same scribal lineage, are devoid of such errors and exhibit very well-formed language (1925, 14). Furthermore, Bodhiraṃsi's other work is characterized by the same poor language construction. Coedès also observes that many of the common grammatical problems met with in the CDV are morphological in nature and as such are indicative of an author whose native language—in this case Thai—is uninflected (1925, 15). It is also likely that there were not many people at that time in Haripuñjaya who had the erudition to point out the inaccuracy of Bodhiraṃsi's claim to have ameliorated the text.

Upon commencing an analysis of the CDV, one is immediately struck by the conformity of the form of the text to that often displayed by oral discourses,[12] and in particular those intended for a wide audience. As Swearer and Premchit, authors of the first English translation, remark:

> The *Cāmadevīvaṃsa* has much in common with the literary genre associated with preaching and other modes of popular instruction in the vernacular, e.g., *jātaka, nidāna*, and *tamnān*. (CDVe, 6)
> Even though Bodhiraṃsi wrote the text in Pali, it does not appear that the CDV was intended as a book for scholarly study or monastic edification as was the case with Sirimaṅgalācariya's commentary on the *Maṅgala Sutta*. It is more reasonable to assume that it was written to be preached. (CDVe, 9)

The translators' opinion is endorsed by the number of popular myths and legends woven into the story, which resembles the way that they are still today incorporated into sermons delivered to the faithful.

Furthermore, many of these accounts are in verse form, generally conforming to the *anuṭṭhubha* meter but occasionally employing other meters as well. Thus although the bulk of the text is in prose, Bodhiraṃsi includes numerous sections—at least one in almost every chapter—that are in verse, and most of these are attributed to his sources. It is well known that, as Olson says in his survey of the field, "mnemonic devices, coupled with figures of speech and metrical, poetized speech, permit the storage and retrieval of the verbal form of culturally significant information" (1994, 101). Moreover, in the CDV these sections often comprise the most important details of the story. For example, after having related in prose how Cāmadevī's son Anantayasa built and became king of Khelāṅga with the help of a seer (CDVe, 83), the tale of the founding of Khelāṅga is then repeated at length in the *tuṭṭhubha* meter.

A note by the translators helps to flesh out just what form Bodhiraṃsi's sources took, and how he engaged them:

> Throughout the narrative, [Bodhiraṃsi] quotes from "ancient sources." It is difficult to determine whether this pattern is a means by which Bodhiraṃsi is legitimating his story or if he is actually recalling specific quotations from various texts or consulting specific manuscripts. (CDVe, 150, n. 178)

The possibility that manuscripts were consulted, however, is highly doubtful. Before considering this, I will assess the possibility that the author was recalling quotations. This assessment, however, requires some understanding of oral communicative techniques that were likely to have been used in Bodhiraṃsi's day.

Some of the basic parameters that ought to be taken into consideration when considering oral texts can be found in the work of Milman Parry (1971) and Albert Lord (1960). Their theory of oral composition and transmission is based on the contention that for the oral poet, the moment of composition is the performance itself. The poet does not recite a poem which has been learned by heart, but rather composes it extemporaneously.[13] While the essential story of the text is the same, the way it is told, its length, and many of the details vary depending on the mood of the bard and the audience and what is required at the time.[14]

The CDV does not fit perfectly into this scheme because it combines long prose sections with short verses that are attributed to older sources. The verses themselves are short enough that they may not have been composed in the manner outlined by Parry and Lord, but rather may have been fixed and memorized by bards, with the prose sections embellished around them. In this respect the CDV is similar to many *suttas* from the Tipiṭaka, such as the *Mahāparinibbānasutta,* that can confidently be attributed to an oral milieu.[15] Richard Gombrich sums up the process that likely led to the current form of much of the Tipiṭaka and by extension the CDV:

> I think the earliest Pali texts may well be rather like the Rajastani folk epic studied and described by John Smith, in which the essential kernel is in fact preserved verbatim, but variously wrapped up in a package of conventional verbiage which can change with each performance. (1990, 22)

Throughout the CDV there are many such instances of a story being spun around a core almost like a piece of music that develops on a theme. Chapter three of the CDV revolves around the bringing of a conch shell by a bird to sages who use it to delineate the boundaries of Haripuñjaya magically. After this episode is told in prose, it is repeated in verse. In chapter fourteen, a prose section tells of the Lavo army marching towards Haripuñjaya, and then a verse section reiterates much of the same subject matter. Likewise in chapter fifteen a prose section tells of some crows coming to inform the king as to the whereabouts of a relic, and much of the conversation is recorded in verse. The story of Anantayasa, as noted earlier, follows a similar pattern, as do many other sections throughout the text.

Most of these embedded metrical anecdotes contain further evidence of their oral nature. Bodhiraṃsi places these passages in the mouths of previous compilers, in much the same way as he does the story of Anantayasa mentioned above:

> *Tena idaṃ vatthuṃ mahācārike dassento (saṅgāhiko) āha: Anantayaso . . .*
>
> The (previous compiler of several vernacular stories from which I am working) illustrating this tale in a major narrative, said: "The noble Anantayasa . . ." [metrical account continues here].

Although the word *āha* (said) is employed in this context, terms such as this do not automatically denote orality. Just as the English sentence "on page 26, Blackburn said that Buddhist devotion was influenced by *Bhakti*" does not refer to speaking, so in Pali, terms related to orality could connote literate communication. It is therefore crucial to investigate the nuances of each terminological application. Throughout the CDV there is a consistent use of the word *āha* when referring specifically to the earlier sources, without the deployment of other terms, such as those based on the root *likh* (to write), even for the sake of variety. If in these cases, the term *āha* was intended to include written as well as oral sources, one would expect that the dictates of prosody or aesthetics would lead at least once to the use of other terms relating more specifically to writing. But no such references occur in the CDV in relation to its sources.

The idea that the prose portions of the CDV represent earlier, orally transmitted kernels, while finding strong support in the form of the text, is nevertheless countered by some of Bodhiraṃsi's words. As mentioned already, he explicitly states that the earlier language was unsatisfactory and that he is translating the stories into Pali. If so, then the embedded verses, which are in Pali, would not have come from the older sources, but would have had to have been composed by Bodhiraṃsi. A possible way to reconcile these scenarios is to postulate a multilayered, multilingual textual field from which the particular CDV that has come down to us was compiled. The compiler (*saṅgāhiko*) referred to throughout the CDV may have composed the Pali verses some time before Bodhiraṃsi, who then used some of them as the basis around which to collect vernacular stories that he then translated into Pali. There are still many difficulties with the language of the text as we know it; accordingly, it is very likely that the sources that Bodhiraṃsi was using were even more grammatically problematic. There is a passage that does suggest that Bodhiraṃsi has clarified problematic words in the ancient records and also that he *wrote* the current text (CDVe, 99):

> People should listen well to her great story whose letters are well-written (*sulikkhitakkharaṃ*). The Pali stanzas employing meters such as *samāla-*

> *gandhi* and *vajira* have been prepared by me with regards to their etymology according to the meaning of the ancient tales. I clarify unclear meaning wherever it is found. Let good people reflect upon it in order to gain a share of merit. (my translation)

Perhaps the use of the term *sulikkhita* (well-written) serves to emphasize that Bodhiraṃsi, as opposed to those who came before him, has finally written it down. Even so, people are advised to listen (*suṇeyyuṃ*) to the story. Although it may have existed in written form, it was not by reading it that common people would have come into contact with it; it was written to be preached orally. The language of this passage does not indicate whether Bodhiraṃsi arranged the text into these particular meters himself or whether that is the form in which they were handed down to him. About the only thing that is clear from this is that the process leading to the actualization of the written manuscript upon which the 1920 Wachirayan Library edition of the CDV was based was a multifaceted one that ultimately involved numerous authors working in different languages.

THE SOURCES OF THE *CĀMADEVĪVAṂSA*

Most chapters of the CDV end with the following statement:

> *iti Haripuñjeyyaniddeso mahāporāṇacārikānusārena Bodhiraṃsinā nāma mahātherenālaṅkato*
>
> This is the description of Haripuñjaya embellished by the Mahāthera Bodhiraṃsi in accordance with important ancient stories.

This simple colophon actually presents a number of difficulties that were not overcome in the translations of either Coedès or Swearer and Premchit. They all translate the term *alaṅkata* as "composed" (French: *composée*), which, strictly speaking, is not a meaning attributable to the word. Rather, its semantic field, though wide, is limited to terms relating to embellishment or improvement. The term is primarily used to describe the process of beautifying a person or place. Here it should not be taken to mean "composed," but rather should convey the sense of "embellishing" an existing text. This is wholly in keeping with Bodhiraṃsi's intention to weave a series of popular vernacular tales into a piece of high literature in Pali. Swearer and Premchit translate *anusārena* as "from his recollection," which is probably a result of their confusing the word *anusārena*—from *anu* + *sṛ* meaning "to flow along with"—with *anussarena*—which does in fact come from *smṛ* meaning "to recall."

The translators argue (CDVe, 136, n. 32) that the texts Bodhiraṃsi was following were themselves likely to have been inscribed on palm leaves, but perhaps were not accessible at the actual time of composition. They believe that since the word *chan* is often used in northern Thai to refer to inscribing palm leaves (*bai lan*), the Pali word *cārika* probably denotes written manuscripts. They come to this conclusion based upon the observation that if the last syllable in the word *cārika* were dropped, as sometimes happens in Tai phonology,[16] it would be pronounced *chan.* This argument is not convincing for a number of reasons. First, *cārika* is not generally used to denote the physical text-bearing object itself in other contexts, but merely refers to any text, especially ones about the deeds of important figures. Second, and perhaps most important, there is not a single extant manuscript of a text in a northern Thai vernacular dialect from before Bodhiraṃsi's time.

The oldest manuscript among the more than 4,000 titles on catalog at the Social Research Institute at Chiang Mai University that seems to be a vernacular text is a legal treatise entitled *Avaharn* and dated CS 834 (1472 CE) (MF 80.046.03.052). Apart from this one text, however, the oldest texts that include vernacular passages are all Nissaya texts, starting with a *Nissaya Gāthā Dhammapāda* (SRI 07-02-019) from 1563 (CS 925). This is a copy of most of the *Dhammapada*, with explanations and discussions of the verses in the vernacular. The Thai Nissaya genre has just begun to be subjected to sustained scholarly examination,[17] which has suggested that the genre first appeared in the sixteenth century (McDaniel 2003, 1). The observation by John Okell (1963, 187) that Burmese Nissaya emerged just prior to the beginning of noninscriptional Burmese vernacular literature dovetails well with the idea that Pali manuscripts were in use prior to vernacular ones and that the production of purely vernacular manuscripts was likely heralded by the production of Nissayas.

External evidence also militates against the possibility of the existence of vernacular manuscripts from before Bodhiraṃsi's time. Although there are no known manuscripts of Thai provenance in either Pali or Thai that can be positively dated prior to the fragmentary Jātaka of 1471 CE, it goes without saying that it is possible that some were produced that simply have not survived. However, the dates, physical condition, and relative numbers of the manuscripts that have survived are not suggestive of a burgeoning manuscript-centered literate culture from much before this time. The state of many manuscripts from the oldest known strata is quite good, sometimes exceptional, and conversely many of the newer manuscripts, even from as recently as the late nineteenth century seem about to crumble in one's hands and are in very poor, almost unreadable condition. For example, the *Saddasāraṭṭhajālinī* (SRI 07–04–070), a grammatical treatise copied, according to the colophon, in CS 888 (1526 CE), is in excellent condition, and it was found at Wat Phra Singh in Chiang Mai without even the usual wooden boards sandwiching and protecting the leaves. Apart from a few holes along the edges that appear to be the work of hungry ants, the manuscript is undamaged, the leaves are still supple, and the writing is clear. There are numerous other old manuscripts in similarly good condition, which suggests that there is no physical reason for manuscripts of slightly greater age not to have survived if they ever existed in any great numbers. Furthermore, among the dozens of manuscripts that I examined first hand, there is no discernable pattern of decay that decreases as the manuscripts become newer. Some of the most damaged, brittle, and least readable ones are in fact from the nineteenth century, such as the *Dhammapāda Gāthā* from Wat Duang Di (SRI 19–04–039–00) copied in CS 1188 (1826 CE). It seems that the condition of a manuscript is more dependent upon the vagaries of chance, the individual quality of the leaves used, and of course the care taken to preserve it than on its sheer age.

In face of this evidence, it is difficult to argue that the only reason we do not have any manuscripts older than the middle of the fifteenth century is that they have all succumbed to the ravages of time. The best way to explain the sudden appearance of manuscripts in good condition from the latter part of the fifteenth century is simply to allow that they were not produced in any significant manner until just before that time. Von Hinüber presents further evidence to support this hypothesis. Based on his research, he has suggested that there are a total of eleven manuscripts remaining from the fifteenth century.[18] However he adds that there is

> a dramatic increase in the numbers of surviving manuscripts from the 16th century: nearly 80 dated and about 45 undated manuscripts of that century have come to light so far. After this peak of copying activities as mirrored in the extant material today, there is a marked decline with only about 25 manuscripts dated during the 17th century, and most of them, i.e. about 50% have been produced during the first three decades of that century. (von Hinüber 1990, 57)

The manuscripts from the two major repositories in Chiang Mai boasting older, accessible manuscripts—Wats Duang Di and Phra Singh—reflect this situation as well. Von Hinüber wonders how closely we can tie the beginnings of the Pali manuscript tradition in this area to the appearance of old manuscripts. He concludes that the oldest manuscripts that we have today probably coincide closely with the beginnings of the tradition itself.

The epigraphical record bears this out, with no evidence of writing being used by the Thai in any significant way in the area from before this period. The oldest firm epigraphic evidence in Lan Na of the Dhamma script is a statue of the Buddha from Wat Chiang Man dated CS 827 (1465 CE), and the oldest stone inscription is from Chiang Rai and dated 1488 CE (von Hinüber 1990, 58). Furthermore, von Hinüber demonstrates, based on research by Hans Penth, that "the number of dated inscriptions i.e., 1300–1400: 3; 1400–1500: 90; 1500–1600: 112; 1600–1700: 13 closely corresponds to the respective evidence of the manuscripts" (1990, 58).

This suggests that the tradition of writing Pali manuscripts in the Lan Na script started only in the fifteenth century. Perhaps it may somehow be connected with the delegation of monks that went to Sri Lanka in the 1420s and, according to the JKM, studied Pali and possibly even writing while there.[19]

In sum, based on evidence from outside the CDV, it is very probable that Bodhiraṃsi himself was working in an environment that was just beginning to taste the fruits of literate Pali culture, and it is most unlikely that, if his sources were indeed vernacular stories, he was working from written accounts. Nevertheless, it is said in the CDV itself that the final work was *written* by Bodhiraṃsi. It should come as no surprise, then, that the work exhibits features of both worlds.

THE FUTURE DISAPPEARANCE OF THE RELIGION

I would like to end this chapter by looking into the future from the perspective of those living in the fifteenth century. I have shown that the texts under study portray, both explicitly and implicitly, the Buddhist culture of the area that is now Thailand up to the beginning of the Golden Age as being largely an oral one, although one in which writing was known. Before looking in the next chapter at the situation during the Golden Age itself, I will jump ahead and look at the conception of the distant future in one of the texts, on the principle that notions of the future are strongly colored by the realities of the present. The section of the MS dealing with the gradual disappearance of the religion after 5,000 years will thus be used to shed further light on the world of the MS itself. The relevant text commences in this manner:

> Here the future will be told of: The teachings have three divisions, which are the study of the Dhamma (*pariyatti*), the practice of the teachings (*paṭipatti*), and insight into the teachings (*paṭivedha*). The first division includes study of all the Dhamma texts composed by the Buddha, with their commentaries and subcommentaries, on the part of good people. From studying, people can practice the teachings, which entails acting like good people. Then people can attain understanding of the teachings and reach the four stages of enlightenment starting with entering the stream, and they can thereby get the four fruits of these paths and thus master the nine supramundane attainments.[20] The teachings of our Lord Buddha rest upon good people who themselves study, hear, know, follow, and protect them. (MS, 176)

The section goes on to say that the teachings will only last 5,000 years, which is a common theme in Buddhism. In the future the religion will decay as people lose their insight into the meaning of the teachings, neglect their practice, and eventually lose the texts themselves. Thus the three divisions will fade from the world in the reverse order that they develop in people of faith, and Buddhism will be no more.

The use of the term *pariyatti* to denote the acquisition of the texts themselves is instructive for my purposes. Among the meanings listed in the PTSD is "study (learning by heart) of the holy texts" and "the Scriptures themselves as a body which is handed down through oral tradition." In the above passage, there is no word that means, or even implies, the act of reading, although hearing is featured.

The story of the decay of the religion details how the understanding and practice of the teachings will vanish, and finally how the texts themselves upon which these pillars are based will be lost. This last stage, that of the demise of the texts themselves, begins with the following passage:

> The study of the texts will also disappear along with all three Piṭakas. First, the seven Abhidhamma texts will become corrupted and lost. First the *Paṭṭhāna* will disappear because people who know it will not be found. Then the . . . [other Abhidhamma texts as well as] . . . the Suttas will vanish. . . . Even if people who know them still exist, the texts won't be preserved and there won't be people who practice them. Thus the teachings will totally

> disappear from these people. In this way, the Abhidhamma will vanish, the Suttas will vanish, and the Vinaya will become corrupted and will vanish. . . . (MS, 179–180)

And furthermore, once even the *Patimokkha* and *Pārājika* have disappeared because people who know them can not be found, the following disturbing scenario will unfold:

> When a king will desire to hear the Dhamma, he will not be able to find someone in the kingdom who knows the Dhamma. Thus the king will have one thousand pieces of gold put in a bag, then in a box, and then put on the back of an elephant. He will have drums beaten, banners waved, and a search conducted throughout the land and in all the towns. His man will proclaim, "Whoever is able to preach the Dhamma, who knows even a simple four-line verse [from it], come and claim this gold, and preach to us!" The king's man will search all over but will find no one who knows the Dhamma, or even a single verse, so he will give back the gold to the king. Thus at this time the knowledge of the texts and thereby the doctrine of the Buddha will be lost. (MS, 181)

The moral of the story (MS, 181–182) is that people from good families who want to reach *nibbāna* should study (*lao rian*) vigorously and should be taught (*sang søn*) according to the Pali commentaries that have been handed down from generation to generation (*süp paramparā*) since the Buddha's time.

This future scenario, replete as it is with references to the oral tradition, tells us that such a tradition and medium were viewed by the authors of this text as crucial for the survival of the religion. The texts are said to die out when people who know them by heart can no longer be found. There is no deference whatsoever to the possibility that written copies of the texts could exist and be revived by future generations (as has in fact been the case in the real world). We must conclude that the prophecy gives little heed to written texts because of the oral orientation of the MS and the lived environment of its authors.

CONCLUSION

The CDV and MS as a whole speak little about writing, for their concerns are clearly elsewhere. I have suggested that the CDV has stylistic, formal, and discursive features that locate it within a largely oral milieu, even though the CDV as we have it in Pali was in fact written. The MS, which is largely contemporaneous with the CDV, also has a marked concern for oral aspects of Pali textual transmission that is evident in its narratives of both the distant past and the future. The JKM mentions writing marginally more often than the MS and CDV in its narration of the past history of Buddhism, but even then, this is only in connection with Burmese and Sinhalese agents. Thus there is little doubt that in Lan Na during the first quarter of the fifteenth century, just prior to the Golden Age, writing played a minor role in the transmission of Pali Buddhist texts, a role that was matched by ambivalent attitudes towards it, if not total disregard.

According to all the historiographical sources, during Cāmadevī's time, writing was neither highly revered nor commonly used as a medium for the transmission of Pali texts. The existence of writing is mentioned before Cāmadevī, but the Tipiṭaka is nevertheless quite explicitly said to have been transmitted orally by *bhāṇaka*s. Bodhiraṃsi gives the impression that writing at this point was used for official communication but not for transmitting the canonical texts. The fact that no accoutrements such as libraries are ever mentioned in the CDV, even in fairly detailed monastic inventories, further supports this impression. I have also shown that writing features in another work by this author in the same capacity that it does in the CDV—for official communication only. The question is, were these views merely functions of the author's world, or did they genuinely reflect the situation as it was at the time of Cāmadevī?

Appealing to external evidence stimulates some interesting hypotheses. I have said that there is little evidence to suggest that vernacular texts were written down during Bodhiraṃsi's time and that even Pali manuscripts in a Lan Na script were probably in their infancy at this time. However, I have also demonstrated that Mon epigraphy paints a somewhat different picture. Inscriptions from Cāmadevī's era exist that include many passages from Pali texts as well as references to texts being kept in honorable positions. If these do represent a culture that employed and exalted writing for the transmission of the Buddha's Dhamma, then it would seem that by Bodhiraṃsi's time, written culture had actually experienced a decline. It is possible that the various Thai authors characterized the world of Cāmadevī as one with a strong oral tradition and little or no written religious culture, not because this was necessarily the case, but because theirs was so constituted, and they could not therefore conceive of anything otherwise. No doubt in many instances such an error was not the fault of the final redacter but of the earlier bards who transmitted oral tales upon which chronicles such as the CDV were based—tales that did not mention literate culture because their tellers were unconcerned with it.

Writing did, however, have a more significant impact in the cultural life of Lan Na shortly after the CDV was composed, thanks in large measure to yet another forest-dwelling ordination lineage that was brought from Sri Lanka. The efflorescence of the Golden Age may have been a result of this relatively more prominent role of writing among the elite, and is, therefore, the topic of the next chapter.

3 Golden Age, Golden Images, and Golden Leaves

The previous chapters have shown the ambivalent attitudes that existed towards the medium of writing in Lan Na prior to the Golden Age of Buddhist culture. Turning to the Golden Age itself, which commenced towards the beginning of the fifteenth century in Bodhiraṃsi's time and lasted for over one hundred years, this chapter continues to outline the literate culture of Lan Na in broad historical and social perspective.

Three main chronicles produced during or shortly after this period serve as the sources for much of the information in this chapter: the MS from Wat Suan Døk, the TPD from Keng Tung, and the JKM from Wat Pa Dæng. The JKM was written by the monk Ratanapañña approximately a century after the CDV at the height of the Golden Age of Pali learning and culture in Lan Na. Most of the text was completed in 1516 CE, with two final sections added in 1518 and 1528. Ratanapañña, as previously noted, resided at a monastery where scholarly *araññavāsī* monks preserved the Sinhalese dispensation that had been brought there circa 1430 CE by Thai monks who had studied and been reordained in Sri Lanka.

Many monasteries in northern Thailand bear the name Wat Pa Dæng, meaning Redwood Forest Monastery, such as those at Chiang Sæn, Phayao, and Keng Tung[1] and were established by monks of this *araññavāsī* order from Chiang Mai. As Penth points out, there are no redwood trees in the vicinity of Wat Pa Dæng in Chiang Mai (JKMI, 225), which leads one to suspect that it was not named after the area in which it was located, but, in an established pattern of monastic nomenclature, was probably named after another monastery to whose lineage it originally belonged.[2] The namesake in this case was Wat Pa Dæng in Sri Sajjanālaya, which according to Sukhodaya Inscription 9, was founded by Lüthai Mahādharmarāja I in 1359 CE (JKMI, 237). Dhanit Yupho, who helped Coedès prepare his JKM text, states that there are in fact forests in this region that contain the redwood tree (Epochs, 118, n. 2).

To make the development of the various monastic groups of Lan Na clear, it is necessary to turn briefly to the history of Wat Pa Dæng at Sajjanālaya, and to provide more details about Sumana, the Sukhodaya monk who founded the first Sinhalese dispensation. Recall that in 1355 CE, Sumana went to Rāmañña to study with the Sinhalese *araññavāsī* Udumbara Mahāsāmī, by whom he was then ordained. In the JKM, King Lüthai Mahādharmarāja of Sukhodaya wants to implant a more orthodox form of the religion at Sukhodaya and to find a monk who is qualified to enact the monastic rituals (*sakalasaṅghakammaṃ kātuṃ samatthaṃ bhikkhuṃ* [JKMp, 84]). The king therefore sends for Sumana to come back to Sukhodaya and builds the Ambavana Monastery for him, thereby establishing the Sinhalese forest-dwelling *araññavāsī* order in Sukhodaya.

In 1361 CE the monk Sumana comes to Sri Sajjanālaya and on his way is led to a powerful relic by a deity. Sumana brings the relic to the city and shows it to the king, who is impressed by it and, honoring it, invites Sumana to stay at the recently built Wat Pa Dæng (JKMp, 85). Although Sumana does not stay at the monastery long, we can assume that he would have been able to ordain enough monks while he was there to initiate it into the Sinhalese forest-dwelling sect to which he now belongs.

Hearing that there is a great and learned monk of the Sinhalese order in Sukhodaya, King Kilanā (Kü Na) of Lan Na, also wishing to establish the order in his kingdom, sends for Sumana. After some difficulties the king manages to bring Sumana to Lan Na. During the construction of Wat Phra Yün, Sumana stays in Haripuñjaya with the relic that he found on the way to Sri Sajjanālaya. Inscription 9 from Sukhodaya corroborates the JKM account in saying that in the year of the cock, which can only be CS 731 (1369–1370 CE), Sumana went to the north (EHS, 590).

In the JKM, in 1371 CE, Sumana is brought to Chiang Mai and the great relic is enshrined in a *cetiya* at the newly built Wat Suan Døk, thus establishing that monastery as the first one in the Chiang Mai area to be affiliated officially with the Sinhalese forest-dwelling order. As I have shown, it is very unlikely that Sumana brought written texts with him, and I will present further evidence for this below.

Several decades later, in 1423 CE, a group of monks from northern Thailand and the surrounding regions made a pilgrimage to Sri Lanka where they studied for four months according to the JKM and for five years according to the TPD, but were by all accounts ordained into the Sinhalese forest-dwelling order under the Saṅgharājā, called in the JKM Mahāsāmī Vanaratana. These monks then ordained numerous monks on their journey back to Lan Na, their enthusiasm being so great that in an operation more befitting the Coast Guard, they supposedly even ordained two monks whose boat they boarded in mid-ocean. Many of them eventually settled at Wat Pa Dæng in Chiang Mai, and from there spread their ordination throughout the region.[3]

There were, then, actually two injections of the orthodox Sinhalese Buddhist ordination into Lan Na in just over half a century—one by Sumana and the other by a group of monks based at Wat Pa Dæng in Chiang Mai. It appears that although both main Sinhalese Buddhist centers in the Chiang Mai area, Wat Pa Dæng and Wat Suan Døk, were instituted under Sumana, only the former was later fortified by the learning and ordination practices of the group that actually traveled to Sri Lanka. Theravāda ordination traditions are strictly concerned with lineal descent and genealogy, and consequently the two monasteries ended up fostering two similar, but separate ordination lines: the "forest order" (*araññavāsī*) of Wat Pa Dæng and the "flower-garden order" (*pupphārāmavāsī*) of Wat Suan Døk.[4] As Premchit and Swearer report, the new order of *araññavāsī*s

> followed a different *vinaya* than the Wat Suan Dok Order of Sumana. They did not cover their alms bowls with their robes, nor did they carry staffs. They also objected to the practice of accepting money, owning property and rice lands. (Premchit and Swearer 1978, 27)

Unfortunately, these differences led to a considerable amount of rivalry and tension between the orders. The MS tells us that "controversy between the two groups became heated and the king was called upon to resolve the dispute" (Premchit and Swearer 1978, 27). King Sam Fang Kæn, favoring the more established Suan Døk group, defrocked the recent arrivals from Sri Lanka and drove them out of Chiang Mai.

When this king began to lose his hold on power, he was deposed by his son, Tilaka, who soon became the most celebrated king of Lan Na, reigning over the kingdom at the peak of its power and extension. Tilaka was supported by the new *araññavāsī* group during his rise to power, and therefore he established them as the main group in Chiang Mai and expanded their central monastery of Wat Pa Dæng. Numerous monks were reordained into this fraternity and it flourished; affiliated monasteries can be found over much of Lan Na, extending north even into the Shan areas, one of which produced an important vernacular chronicle, the TPD.

The TPD from Keng Tung that I am using was translated by Saimöng Mangrai from the Khön language, a very close relative of the Yuan of Lan Na and the Tai Yai of the Shans, and is taken from a manuscript dated CS 1232 (1870 CE). All known versions of the TPD are host to a particularly large number of problematic passages, and their chronology differs by a few years from other major chronicles (JKMI, 226). As is the case with all the chronicles, it is also difficult to assign an accurate date to the original composition, but the bulk of the contents relate to events between the ordination in CS 769 (1407 CE) of Ñāṇagambhīra, who was to be a leader of the monks who went to Sri Lanka and became an influential monk in the area, and CS 945 (1583 CE), which is the last date actually enumerated in the TPD (182).[5]

The monastery of Wat Pa Dæng lies near Keng Tung (Chiang Tung in Yuan and Khemaraṭṭha in Pali), which is about 300 kilometers north of Chiang Mai, in the Shan region of what is today Burma. Keng Tung was under the influence of Lan Na for some time, and an inscription from 1451 CE explicitly says that the ruler governed on the authority of Chiang Mai (EHS, 750). In 1523 CE, however, a dynastic dispute led to the strengthening of ties with the upper Shan states that were in the orbit of the Burmese, at the expense of relations with Chiang Mai (Griswold 1959, 59).

The monastery is named after the monastery of the same name in Chiang Mai, reflecting its close association with the *araññavāsī* fraternity centered at Wat Pa Dæng of Chiang Mai. The chronicle records many disputes between monks of the *araññavāsī* and *pupphārāmavāsī* orders in Keng Tung, disputes which not only shed light on the different characteristics of these closely related orders, but also on the specific media through which texts were deployed to settle these disputes.

Recall that along with the *araññavāsī* and *pupphārāmavāsī* orders in Lan Na there was another, older order, the *nagaravāsī* or city-dwelling monks, which did not have an explicit connection with Sri Lanka, but was what remained of the early Mon orders. It can be surmised from the following reference to it during the eleventh century reign of King Ādicca at Haripuñjaya that the JKM tradition believed that the *nagaravāsī* order predated the arrival of the Sinhalese dispensation: "The king worshipped that place along with the entire order of city-dwelling monks (*sakalanagaravāsikehi bhikkhusaṅghehi*)" (JKMp, 79).

Penth has accounted for all the monks ordained in the JKM, and attributes 235 ordinations to the forest order, 370 to the city-dwellers, and 1,011 to the garden order of Suan Døk. Considering that the JKM is a text produced by the forest order and thus is likely to have focused more on their proceedings, it is clear from these numbers that the Wat Pa Dæng *araññavāsī* order was an elite group whose penchant for strict practices and scholarly analysis of texts was not matched or welcomed by all (JKMI, ix). Although the Wat Pa Dæng order was the most scholarly and literate, and held writing in the highest esteem of any of the monastic groups, even their opus—the JKM—while making it clear that written religious literature was available at that time, chooses to focus on cultic items such as Buddha images and reliquaries instead of books. We are left with the impression that while a literate culture most certainly existed among the Buddhist elite of the time, it was marginal to the bulk of monastic activity.

It is useful to acknowledge from the outset that the JKM, which was produced almost a century later than the CDV during the height of the Golden Age, itself exhibits features of both oral and written media and ought not to be considered strictly a product of a literate world. The first passage in the JKM that actually mentions writing names the MV specifically as the root text for this episode and contains some clues about the form of the sources for the JKM. The CDV, in contrast, while maintaining that much of the information was garnered from earlier tales, never mentions the names of texts wherein other versions can be found. In the JKM account that I am referring to (JKMp, 58), King Duṭṭhagāmiṇī of Lanka (r. 101–177 BCE) finds an old inscription on a gold plaque (*suvaṇṇapatte lekhaṃ disvā*) in a casket. It prophesies that 140 years in the future, King Duṭṭhagāmiṇī will cause certain buildings to be erected. The king is much impressed by the fact that his name is foretold and does indeed erect a large palace (*pāsāda*). The JKM tells us that it is said in the MV and other works (*Mahāvaṃsādisu vuttam*) that the king studied a painting of a heavenly mansion and then built the palace based on those plans. The measurements of the palace in the JKM account are exactly the same as those given in the MV (1908, 27.24–27), but curiously, the central feature of this story—the text of the actual golden letter found by the king—differs in the two texts.

> *Anāgate cattālīsādhikaṃ vassasataṃ atikkamma Kākavaṇṇatissassa rañño Duṭṭhagāmiṇī Abhayo nāma putto idañ c'idañ ca kāressati* (JKMp, 58).
>
> In the future, with the passing of 140 years, the son of Kākavaṇṇatissa, named King Duṭṭhagāmiṇī Abhaya, will establish this and that.
>
> *Chattiṃsasatavassāni atikkamma anāgate Kākavaṇṇasuto Duṭṭhagāmaṇī manujādhipo idañ c'idañ ca evaṃ ca kāressati* (MV 1908, 27.6–7)
>
> In the future, with the passing of 136 years, the scion of Kākavaṇṇa, Duṭṭhagāmaṇī, lord of men, will establish this and that thus.

The two versions might be consequences of different manuscript traditions, but it is also possible that these are examples of the interface between orality and literacy. In the world of oral literature, the gist of a story is often more important than a word-for-word iteration. Parry's famous statement that "the oral poem even in the mouth of the same singer is ever in a state of change" (quoted in Finnegan 1977, 73) sums up this phenomenon succinctly. Thus, living in a primarily oral world, the author of the JKM would have brought even to his written sources an oral ethos that could allow him to alter certain details and still in good faith claim that he was quoting an earlier text. It is possible, in this more nuanced understanding of the intertextual process of reading and interpreting that a Lan Na intellectual would have engaged in, that the author rounded off the number of years found in the prediction for aesthetic or other personal reasons, without feeling that he was betraying his source. [6]

DEBATES BETWEEN THE ORDERS

Debates between the flower-garden and the forest-dwelling orders are the subject of a large portion of the TPD, and these tell us not only about the differences between these two groups but also illuminate some salient points regarding the position of writing at the time. An unusual example that assigns remarkable powers to writing can serve to inform us of the degree of rivalry that may have been current among the monastic orders. In the TPD, a procedure is described that was used to help solve a dispute between the garden and forest orders around the middle of the sixteenth century. The ruler of the area

> caused to be inscribed on a palm leaf the name "Bra Indamolī" and the name "Ñāṇagambhīra" on another palm leaf, and, the two sides having been made to declare solemn resolves, [the two palm leaves] were dropped into the fire mass in front of the Lord's image of Vat Prahmai Hrokhong there. At that moment the palm leaf with the name "Bra Indamolī" inscribed, when dropped into the fire, was burned without anything remaining. The palm leaf with the name "Ñāṇagambhīra" inscribed the fire did not burn, remaining normal as of old. Thereupon high officials and the populace hooted and shouted at the *bhikkhus* of Yānggong [flower-garden] sect. As for the *bhikkhus* of Pādaeng sect, at the conclusion of the affair, the lord of the earth had people beat victory drums and send them to their monasteries. (TPD, 170)

The trial by fire, during which someone suspected of wrongdoing is thrown into a fire, is a well-known form of primitive justice. If guilty, the accused will be consumed by the flames and thus meet their well-deserved end, but if innocent, they will emerge from the fire unharmed. Most people turned out to be guilty. Anyone familiar with the South Asian cultural universe would of course immediately recognize the trial of Sītā for possible infidelity in the Rāmāyana as the most famous example of such a case. It is not unlikely that due to the influence of Buddhist moral principles, instead of people being thrown into the fire, their names would used as stand-ins. The question then arises as to the nature of the relationship between the monk and his written name. Was the power of this monk somehow transferred to the palm leaf through the writing of his name upon it, or was there perhaps some deity who rescued the palm leaf from the flames? No clear indication of this is given in the passage, unfortunately, although perhaps if a deity was responsible, this would have been stated in the text. It is important to highlight the distinction here. If a deity intervened, then the written words themselves would not bear anything more than the denotative power that all written symbols possess. If, however, the words themselves bear the power to retard the flames, then this would be a rare example in the literature of northern Thailand of what can best be described as magical powers being attributed to writing in a Buddhist context.[7]

The subject of magical, apotropaic, or other hieratic powers inhering in objects in Hīnayāna Buddhism has had a long and controversial history, which has been discussed at length in particular by Gregory Schopen,[8] who points out that modern scholars in their rationalistic and textually centered interpretations of Buddhism have tended to disregard the epigraphical and even literary evidence stating that it was commonly believed that relics, *stūpas*, and other cultic items were invested with fantastic powers beyond the mundane ability to remind one of the Buddha's teachings. In fact, he concludes that according to numerous sources, it appears that "relics were thought to retain—to be infused with, impregnated with—the qualities that animated and defined the living Buddha" (1997, 160).

Could, then, the writing of Ñāṇagambhīra's name onto the leaf be thought of as having some of the attributes that his relics might later attain? While there is a noted absence in Thailand of stories such as this one, where power is attributed to the written word, there is a plethora of similar accounts in the literature of relics protecting a person or place, emitting beams of light, splitting rocks, and so forth. While the author may have had such a process in mind, this lone example does not provide enough evidence to say with assurance what other roles beyond the denotative can be attributed to the written word in this text. The very fact that this incident is recorded, however, suggests that those responsible for the production of this chronicle, namely, the newest forest-dwelling order, did have more elevated views of writing and the wide range of possible uses to which it might be put, when compared with other groups at the time in whose chronicles no such incidences are ever reported.

A dramatic episode that occurred according to the TPD in CS 945 (1583 CE) supplies key evidence suggesting that written Buddhist texts were used at this time for scholarly debate. A conference is held between the forest and garden fraternities on the subject of exactly when to commence the rains-retreat, and this culminates in a public debate on the issue to which the rulers and laypeople are invited on the condition that they do not interfere. When the monks arrive, the leader of the *araññavāsī*s asks one of the *pupphārāmavāsī* monks why he has arrived late, but the monk does not understand the wording of the question. Then the forest monk chides him, saying that if he cannot even understand a question in his own language, how can he be expected to debate points of the Dhamma (TPD, 185–187)? The flower-garden monks are quite embarrassed by this exchange. "Each lord carried away his volumes of the Dhamma with which he had hoped to debate, and all ran away. Afterwards Bhikkhus of the Pupphārām Sect were even more jealous of the Nattārām [Forest] Sect" (TPD, 189).

This is the only text of Thai provenance that I have come across describing the use of written texts within a debating environment. This is among the last events narrated in the TPD, and no earlier passages mention any similar uses of written texts. As we have seen, both the Pali and Thai historiographical traditions were subject to the thematic and stylistic constraints common to literary genres of Asia. While the rules governing the production of these chronicles were less strict than those constituting, say, the genre of *kāvya* as articulated in the *alaṃkāraśāstras*, there were nevertheless strong expectations about what constituted appropriate material. One can also get a sense of an author's concerns by a statistical analysis of how frequently he chooses to include different topics. The inclusion of a reference to the books used to support the monks' arguments attests that details about the media used by monks to support and transmit Buddhist teachings could have found their way into the text and would not have been constrained by either genre considerations or the author's personal style. The fact that this literate debate comes so late in the chronology, therefore, is in keeping with the notion that before this time, turning to books in such circumstances was far less common than turning inward to memory. The later date of this incident also puts it shortly after Burmese influence would have begun to have been felt in earnest in all walks of life in this region, and as it happens there is very good evidence that precisely these kinds of debates were conducted in Burma not orally, as we know they were, for example, in Tibet (Klein 1994, 5–6), but rather with the help of written documents.[9]

The SV from Burma includes a long discussion of a major dispute that infected the Saṅgha for many years concerning the way that the robes were worn. The account includes information about how written texts were deployed in the context of a legalistic debate and specifically how their contents were weighed in relation to other factors. Beginning about a century after the debate in Keng Tung, the followers of Guṇābhilaṃkāra in Burma—called the Ekaṃsikas—went on their alms rounds with one shoulder uncovered, thereby distinguishing themselves from the rest of the monks—known as Pārupanas—who always entered the villages with both shoulders covered. The author of the SV condemns the Ekaṃsikas, saying that their opinions are not seen in the canonical, commentarial, or other texts (SV, 119). The use of the word "seen" (*dissati*), instead of "heard," suggests that the texts being scrutinized are in written form.

In the SV the dispute continues on and off for the better part of a century, but is quite convincingly resolved in 1784 CE when an Ekaṃsika monk by the name of Atula sends a letter to the king proclaiming that the *Cūlagaṇṭhipada* says that novices should enter the village for alms with the upper robe on only one shoulder:

> Having come to a firm conclusion through the statement in the *Cūlagaṇṭhipada* to the effect that novices should enter a village only after having put the upper robe onto one shoulder at the time of entry, and having fastened the girdle, he sent a letter into the presence of the king. (SV, 135)

The king then decides to call the monks together and has Atula debate with them. Atula proceeds to make his argument and shows the monks the appropriate reading in the text (*Cūḷagaṇṭhipade āgatapāṭhaṃ dassetvā* [SV, 135]). The Pali is unmistakable here and provides a clear glimpse of an episode of engagement with written texts. The text that Atula uses is not very well known, and he thus has to produce it in order to convince his opponents that it exists at all and that he is not just making it up. Atula says that the text is to be found in his hand at that very moment, *Idānāyaṃ gandho amhākaṃ hatthe saṃvijjatī* (SV, 136), and he shows it to the other monks, clearly believing that it is only by seeing the text that the other monks will be convinced of his interpretation. But when they take a good look at it, they realize that the text is not by the respected monk Moggallāna, to whom Atula had attributed its authorship, but rather by someone else. Atula's plan backfires as the monks scold him for misrepresenting the text and decide that the doctrine of the Ekaṃsikas is false.

While this event is supposed to have occurred two hundred years after the episode in the TPD, it is only one piece in a pattern of Burmese engagement with written texts. In Chapter One I mentioned that Buddhaghosa, in a fifteenth-century account from Burma of his life, witnesses an altercation between two women, which he promptly records in writing for use in clearing up the matter, figuring that he will be asked about it in the near future. Writing was used from early on in Burma as the most important vehicle for evidence in legal and religious arenas, and it is therefore quite possibly due to Burmese cultural influence that written books were brought into the debate in Keng Tung.

These examples of the debate and the trial by fire show that there was very real hostility between the different monastic groups, providing strong reasons for each to want to highlight their own views and achievements in their respective chronicles. The subtly and not-so-subtly different treatments given to the important symbols and instruments of the religion such as relics, images, and texts in works such as the MS, TPD, and JKM are conscious attempts on the part of each fraternity to place their lineage in a position that appears favorable according to their respective convictions and concerns.

THE MISSION TO SRI LANKA AND ESTABLISHMENT OF THE *ARAÑÑAVĀSĪ* ORDER

The event that most strongly shaped the early part of the Golden Age is the second introduction of the Sinhalese *araññavāsī* dispensation (JKMp, 91–95), as well as the Sinhalese style of reciting and, possibly, writing. If, as the translator Jayawickrama holds, the JKM account tells of the learning of writing, it is one of the only times that the study of writing per se is specifically outlined in any of the Pali historiographical texts that I considered. In the JKM, in CS 785 (1423 CE), twenty-five elders from Chiang Mai and another eight from Kamboja decide to travel to Sri Lanka, where they believe the Buddha's teachings to be flourishing, out of the desire to bring back the monastic ordination current on the island. Before actually being ordained in the Sinhalese order, they study there:

> *Laṅkādīpe pavattitaṃ akkharapaveṇiñ ca tadanurūpaṃ padabhāṇañ ca sarabhaññañ ca uggahetvā* (JKMp, 93).
>
> They took up the tradition of *akkharas* used in Lanka, and the method of reciting the words and the *sarabhañña*[10] in conformity with it.

Unfortunately for our purposes, the term *akkhara* may refer to both written and vocalized syllables, as it means literally "that which is indestructible," i.e., the smallest possible phoneme *or* grapheme. Significantly, the term *akkhara* is used in the Tai languages to denote "script," and this meaning may have prompted Thai authors composing in Pali to associate it with the written rather than the spoken word. Furthermore, the fact that the *akkhara*s studied are specifically referred to as those employed in Lanka is suggestive of an orthographic system, because while each region had its own script, they all shared the same phonological theory.

As one might expect, the story is not quite so simple. It seems that there is very little evidence of Sinhalese writing on any manuscripts or inscriptions in Lan Na, which would be anticipated following Jayawickrama's translation of *akkhara* as "orthographic system." If the monks who brought the Sinhalese ordination to Thailand also learned the Sinhalese style of writing, then there should be some traces of texts written in this script in Lan Na, but this is not the case. To date, only one item, a Buddha image, has been found with any Sinhalese writing on it; Sinhalese writing has been found nowhere else in Lan Na.[11] It is not surprising, then, that Penth, a paleographer, argues that the monks studied phonetics and pronunciation, not writing (JKMI, 115).

According to the JKM, these monks, after studying, gained the higher ordination and then returned to Thailand, passing through Ayudhyā and Sukhodaya on their way back to Chiang Mai. They are not said to have brought any texts back with them. Because this is one of the seminal events in the history of the monastery at which the JKM was produced, surely if these monks had brought back some canonical texts, this would have been featured in the chronicle.

The TPD sheds light on the issue of the media employed by these monks through its inclusion of information not given in the JKM about the nature of the problems that the mission to Sri Lanka was supposed to rectify. Starting at paragraph 37, and extending to paragraph 53, Ñāṇagambhīra examines and disputes the ordination as it was found in Chiang Mai at the time. His complaints are very technical and deal almost exclusively with the grammatical and phonological fitness of the texts recited at the *upasampadā* ordination ceremony. For example, he saw that they were using *Buddhāṃ* instead of *Buddhaṃ* and their pronunciation of *saraṇaṃ* neglected the retroflextion of the *ṇa* (TPD, 37).[12] Such concern with the sounds of the Pali words in ritual and liturgical settings has always been of prime importance in the Buddhist world and is an expression of its oral foundation. An episode related by Nidhi Aeusrivongse illustrates that this was still the case even in the eighteenth century: "Rama I is recorded as having been asked by monks whether ordination of Laotian novices was valid as the Laotians pronounced Pali 'incorrectly' in the ordination ceremony" (1994, 73).

Ordinations were not traditionally viewed as valid if there was any reason to believe that any part of the ceremony—the enclosure in which it took place, the texts recited, the qualifications of those officiating—was flawed. It is important to stress the degree of anxiety that monks would have felt with regard to the fidelity of their ordination. As Griswold reminds us:

> There was always a risk that some flaw which might have occurred centuries ago would invalidate an entire succession without anyone being aware of it; and the only way for a monk to be certain of avoiding it was to retire to lay life, and then be re-ordained, with the most orthodox rites, by a chapter of monks whose own succession was unassailably valid. (1975, 6)

With this in mind, we should not be surprised that in order to learn more about the Kammavācā ordination texts, Ñāṇagambhīra travels hundreds of kilometers south to Ayudhyā to question monks there. They discuss their texts with him, saying "Our guru has handed down [the texts] thus" (TPD, 38) and suggest that if he is still in need of further help, he should go to Sri Lanka, which he does, along with an entourage. He discusses the problems with the head of the Saṅgha, covering details such as incidences where *ka* should be *kkha* (45) and where a word has too many morae (48). This particular passage of the TPD conveys the sense of an exchange based on oral texts. No manuscripts are scrutinized, although there are ample opportunities to do so.

A statement about the origin of these problems adds further strength to the likelihood that the Kammavācā texts in question were borne orally. In a possible snub directed at the *pupphārāmavāsī* monks, the blame is laid squarely upon Sumana in the TPD (53). The Sinhalese head monk accuses him of adding "made-up words creating perversity not in accord with good grammar." According to the TPD characterization, then, Sumana must have altered and then transmitted the ordination texts orally. Had he been armed with manuscripts that were written correctly, he would have had to have gone through the trouble of writing new ones that were incorrect. If indeed Sumana caused the problems, then the only reasonable explanation is that they evolved in an oral context and were due to his insufficient memory skills and ignorance of certain aspects of Pali grammar and phonology.

In the TPD account, unlike that in the JKM, upon leaving Sri Lanka around 1425 CE, Ñāṇagambhīra requests a Bodhi tree sapling, a Buddha image, *and* the Tipiṭaka.

> Having resided after a duration of five vassā of study of the Dhamma, [Ñāṇagambhīra] asked for the Sāsanā together with Mahābodhi [saplings] and an image of the Lord and the Three Piṭaka. (54)
> When the brayā learned that Lord Mahāñāṇagambhīra had brought the Sāsanā, the Mahābodhi tree, an image of the Lord, and the Three Piṭakas to repose in the city, the brayā was exceedingly delighted and made people dismantle an old royal pavilion and re-erect it as a monastery for him to live in. (59)

It is extremely difficult to see how such a seminal event could have been omitted by the author of the JKM, if it actually occurred, for this could have served to link the Pa Dæng textual tradition directly to the fount of Theravāda orthodoxy that was Lanka and thence to the Buddha himself. In light of this possible motive, and in view of its lone appearance here, it is possible that the contents of this shipment were altered by the author of the TPD to include the Tipiṭaka. Such an addition would have been meaningful because the *araññavāsī* monks were placing an increasing amount of importance upon written scriptures as symbols of the religion.

I believe that the monks did not physically bring copies of the texts from Sri Lanka, which would, after all, not have been usable by the vast majority of monks back in Lan Na, who could not read the Sinhalese script. Rather, the monks brought the knowledge of the importance of writing and an appreciation for the technology of manuscript production, but not manuscripts themselves. Pali manuscripts based upon the knowledge acquired in Sri Lanka combined with existing traditions inherited largely from the Mon were produced in the Dhamma script shortly thereafter, and these monks then spread them to various locations in northern Thailand. This is also supported by von Hinüber's contention (1983b) that a Lan Na recension of the Tipiṭaka exists that does not simply reproduce the Sinhalese or Burmese tradition. A full comparative study of a wide range of Lan Na and Sinhalese manuscripts would need to be carried out to make any final pronouncements about the relationship between the two, but von Hinüber has examined two versions of the *Sagāthavagga* from the *Saṃyutta Nikāya* that are highly suggestive. A manuscript written at Chiang Sæn in 1602 CE and another written at Lampang in 1549 CE both have an extra three verses at SN II, 15, which are not present in either the Burmese or Sinhalese versions, and there are numerous minor orthographical and other features that are found exclusively in these texts (von Hinüber 1983b, 81). He concludes that

> it might not be too far-fetched to think that we really can find traces of the Chiang Mai Council in the Thai tradition. . . . the hope is growing and seems to be well-founded now that more material still hidden in *Wat* libraries in North Thailand, when brought to light, will help to re-establish an old and truly Thai Pali tradition. (88)

If a full copy of a Tipiṭaka recension was brought from Sri Lanka and simply transcribed into northern Thai letters, surely the Lan Na texts written shortly thereafter would reflect more strongly this redaction.

Whether or not actual texts were brought back from Lanka, what most assuredly was imported from the island was the Sinhalese attitude towards the written word, an attitude that the monks who had studied there would have imbibed. By that time writing occupied a conspicuous position in Sri Lanka, which was, of course, the very site where the Tipiṭaka was first written, around 70 BCE (MV 1908, 33.100), and a strong tradition of Pali manuscript production remained there, as suggested by the MV. In the seventh century, to mention one early example, King Kassapa II is said to have sponsored the production of a considerable segment of Pali literature: "Appointing a monk from Kaṭandhakāra who was living at the monastery of his brother, he had him write down all the canonical texts with their compendiums" (MV 1925, 45.3).

Following a low ebb of Buddhism on the island, King Vijayabāhu I also had texts written down, according to the MV. In the chronicle, after bringing in learned monks from Burma, he has them not only perform many ordinations, but also recite the canon with its commentary (*piṭakattayaṃ ca bahuso kathāpetvā savaṇṇanaṃ*) to help strengthen Buddhism in Sri Lanka (1925, 60.7–8). After building the Temple of the Tooth and establishing monasteries and performing other meritorious deeds, the king has the Tipiṭaka copied and donates it to the Saṅgha (*piṭakattayaṃ likhāpetvā bhikkhusaṃghass' adāpayi* [60.23]).

The MV recounts the construction of two libraries[13] shortly after the unification of the monastic orders present in the island under the twelfth-century king Parakkamabāhu I. Whereas only five libraries are mentioned in the whole of the JKM, 128 houses for books are built in a single chapter of the MV (1925, 79.80).

In chapter 81 (MV 1927, 81.40) the thirteenth-century king Vijayabāhu III gathers *laymen* (*upāsake*) together who have good memories, and they write down in books what they know about the doctrine. They are paid one gold *kahāpana* for each division, demonstrating that the king felt that the transfer of oral knowledge into written books for safekeeping was a project worth paying good money for.

Later, Parakkamabāhu II (1234–1269) is faced with a dire situation and chooses to rectify it by importing texts from India. "Thinking 'Theras who know the texts are rare in this Island,' he had all the books brought from Jambudīpa and having many monks train in those texts which dealt with all the subjects such as philosophy and grammar, he made them into attentive monks" (MV 1927, 84.26–30).

By the end of the thirteenth century written manuscripts had undoubtedly eclipsed oral transmission as the primary vehicle for religious texts. In the late thirteenth century the king Bhuvanekabāhu I "gave to the learned scribes of the Dhamma books much money and having all three Piṭakas copied by them, preserved them all over in the monasteries of Lanka. Thus the lord of men caused the development of the canonical texts" (MV 1927, 90.37–38).

Note that here the transmission and dissemination of the texts is specifically linked to the delivery of written manuscripts to various places. This section, moreover, was actually written in the fourteenth or fifteenth century and thus embodies sentiments held by contemporaries of Bodhiraṃsi, author of the CDV, whose world we can now see was very different. Just over a century later, Parakkamabāhu VI

> had the magnificent three Piṭakas together with their commentaries and subcommentaries copied and caused a summary of the teaching of the Buddha to be made. He also granted villages and the like to the scribes, so they could copy day by day the books of the true Dhamma. (MV 1927, 91.27–28)

Land grants in Thailand are often made to monasteries and are intended for the monastery in general or for the support of a particular Buddha image and sometimes for a library, but never for the support of scribes themselves. This highlights how important literary activity and its agents were deemed to be in Sri Lanka at this point.

There is, then, little doubt that the time spent by the Thai monks studying in Sri Lanka would have exposed them to a very different approach to writing, one which saw it as an important, desirable and indeed useful vehicle for the preservation and transmission of Pali texts—an approach that they took back with them to Thailand.

TRANSMISSION OF THE SĀSANĀ THROUGHOUT LAN NA

The TPD (69) agrees with the JKM in stating that the monk Somacitta brought the ordination to Keng Tung but places the event in CS 804 (1442 CE), whereas in the JKM it occurs in CS 810 (1448 CE) (JKMp, 96). According to a local inscription, on the other hand, at some point between 1434 and 1443 CE, the monk Khemamaṅgala studied with and was ordained by Dhammagambhīra, one of the leaders of the mission to Sri Lanka, and then consecrated the first *araññavāsī* monastic boundary (*sīmā*) in Keng Tung (EHS, 748, Face 2: ln. 10–15). The inscription also says that Dhammagambhīra[14] brought the religion and the Vinaya to the Thai countries, which may refer either to the tradition of monastic discipline or specifically to written texts from the Vinaya Piṭaka—unfortunately the context does not allow us to make a definite assignation.

The narrative in the TPD of the bringing of the Sāsanā to Keng Tung (here called Müang Khemaraṭṭha) commences in the year CS 803 (1441 CE) and yields a surprising amount of information about the different dynamics of the oral and written forms of the teachings. A demon has been haunting a golden palace, so monks from nearby are invited to recite the Dhamma to cleanse and protect the premises. This does not help, so monks from Chianglæ are invited to recite, and although the haunting is diminished for a short while, it soon reappears and continues for ten years. In the narrative, word of this comes to Mahā Ñāṇagambhīra, who sends five monks to perform the recitations properly and get rid of the demon once and for all. When they arrive, they are greeted by some local boys: "The boys playfully practiced reciting ordination Dhamma according to what their fathers had taught them. When Lord Somacitta Thera heard [the recitation] he told them, 'Your Dhamma recitation is not word-perfect'" (TPD, 71).

The boys then return home and aver that perhaps these monks really know what they are doing because they are sensitive to even minor problems with the recitation of sacred texts. This suggests that effective power was deemed to reside in the words themselves but only when pronounced properly. Note, too, that the boys learned the recitation from their fathers and not from texts. Unfortunately, it is unclear from this passage alone whether the monks think the boys intone the wrong words or whether they utilize the correct words but *pronounce* them incorrectly.

For the actual purification ritual we are again in the realm of the power of the spoken word. The head of the delegation, Somacitta Thera, recites *suttas* for three days and nights. This finally drives the demons away for good, and the following year, when there is a great flood, the monks are invited to recite the *Ratana Sutta*, which reduces the volume of the waters.

After this the ruler of Khemaraṭṭha invites the group of monks to bring their guru Ñāṇagambhīra to spread the Sāsanā. At this point we are told of the transmission of written texts when the monk agrees to come and brings the Sāsanā and the Piṭaka Dhamma (TPD, 81). That the Piṭaka Dhamma refers here to the texts themselves in manuscript form is suggested in the next paragraph, which tells that large building projects, likely including libraries, were initiated in order to strengthen the religion in the region:[15] "The elder sister queen constructed the great library providing Yāngjôn, Yāngman with twenty thousand paddy fields and five houses of Yāng people. The younger sister queen constructed the inner library[16] . . . " (TPD, 82).

In the *araññavāsī* chronicles such as the TPD and JKM, we often find it said in sections about the transmission of the Sāsanā that the ordination tradition itself is brought before the texts are transmitted, which come later with important monks, and after this libraries are built to house the texts. In the JKM, most instances of religious transmission also involve the establishment of a Buddha image or relic. This whole process cements the religion in the areas in question by laying the ground for its constituent monastic, literary, and cultic institutions. In the chronicles such as the CDV and the MS, which were produced by other groups not affiliated with the new Sinhalese *araññavāsīs,* the establishment of the Sāsanā comes about primarily through the ordination of new monks and the establishment of relics or Buddha images, and need not culminate in the transmission of written canonical texts and the construction of libraries. The evolution from an oral, personally transmitted culture to a more concretized, literate one is not highlighted in these latter texts.

EARLY LITERATE CULTURE AT KENG TUNG

The TPD sketches the lively literate culture that was developing through the efforts of the *araññavāsī* monks at Keng Tung. As time goes on, the newly established ordination lineage flourishes and many people are ordained by Ñāṇagambhīra as the monastery grows in size and prestige. Even isolated tribal people come to learn at this monastery.

> Many hill people came down to take the Sāsanā back to every hill and mountain. Some of them came down to study and learn correctly and thoroughly the study of the Dhamma, its meaning, the letters of the alphabet, the canon and grammar (*pariyatti attha akkhara byañjana pāḷi sadda*), and returned home to teach pupils and disciples. (TPD, 100)

An interlude about the duties of various villagers from the area includes the duty to set up the *ādhāra dhamma* (a stand upon which palm-leaf manuscripts are placed for preaching and reciting) on the part of the residents of Muang Küy (TPD, 137).

Shortly after the building of Wat Pa Dæng in CS 819 (1457 CE), the monastic author of the TPD orders that "if any part of the *vihāra* becomes dilapidated, call the monastery people to come and work, including [repairs to] the buildings, *cetiya*, *vihāra*, outer library, inner library" (TPD,123).

Later in the TPD, two Piṭaka pavilions are described (148), which indicates that there was both the need and the desire to expend resources on a number of structures whose main purpose was to house books. It is likely that this was a time during which ever more libraries were being built, as it is about a generation after the time of the CDV, a period which I have shown was at the beginning of manuscript usage in the Lan Na Buddhist world. The first library (*hø tipidok*) in the region that the MS attributes to a Thai person (a Mon library is mentioned earlier) was erected at Wat Suan Døk in the 1460s by a powerful laywoman named Mün Dang who apparently was a government official at Lampang (MS, 172). Thus we can say that the people living during the second generation of functional Pali literacy amongst the Thai were early promoters and supporters of the building of libraries to house the increasing collection of manuscripts. Monks at a stronghold of the *araññavāsī* order such as Wat Pa Dæng were keen to insist in texts such as the TPD that the libraries be maintained, whereas in the MS, from Wat Suan Døk, the only force behind the construction of the library that is mentioned is a ruler.

In fact it is often people with political rather than religious power who have had the most unambiguously positive attitudes towards writing. How did King Tilaka, who ruled Lan Na at the height of its power during the middle of the fifteenth century, approach writing? A section in the TCM, an early nineteenth-century vernacular chronicle based on older sources,[17] tells us about this. A certain brave warrior, Mün Ma, who had done no wrong gets into a fight with Røi Ngua:

> Ngua wrote a letter saying that Mün Ma was disloyal, and was revolting against the king. Then Røi Ngua ordered minor officials to steal the seal of Mün Ma to stamp the letter. He then took the letter and left it in the palace, north of the Pæn Gate. A group of swordsmen found it and presented it to King Tilokarat. The king had the letter read, demonstrating that Mün Ma was disloyal, so he had Mün Ma taken off to be killed. Only later did he learn that he was blameless. King Tilokarat was very contrite, and issued the order that henceforth anonymous letters would not be read, which is still the rule. (TCM, 5.06–07)[18]

This suggests that the king himself initially had an attitude towards writing that was similar to that seen in the *Buddhaghosuppatti*, examined in Chapter One. There, when Buddhaghosa witnesses an altercation between two women, he promptly records the event in writing for use in clearing up the matter, demonstrating that oral testimony, even that of an eyewitness, was seen as inferior to a written account. However, in the TCM story, circumstances dictate that the trust in anonymous written documents be curtailed. It is likely that this later sentiment parallels the attitudes that many people actually had towards written Pali canonical texts—that in the absence of an author(ity), they should not be used. Rather, they should be read (or recited by heart) by someone present, namely, a monk, who could represent the author or the tradition and thereby vouch for its contents. The outcome notwithstanding, it is notable that it is a king who at first seems to be most comfortable trusting the written word. This is the same king who is held by Thai tradition to have sponsored the eighth Buddhist Council, during which the Tipiṭaka was edited and written down by learned monks at Chiang Mai. Unfortunately, the extant sources reveal little more about the textual culture during this king's reign.

A GOLDEN COPY OF A PIṬAKA

Libraries are featured in the JKM, but first appear almost half a century later than in the TPD, during the reign of King Tilaka's grandson, Bilakapanattu. Bilakapanattu was by all accounts a devout Buddhist who engaged in many acts of piety and sponsored numerous building projects for the religion. It was during his reign from 1495–1526 CE that Pali culture in Lan Na reached its zenith. The first library that appears in the JKM is constructed by royal decree at Pubbārāma (Eastern Monastery), and in a great ceremony in CS 863 (1501 CE) Bilakapanattu installs a golden copy of a Piṭaka in that library.

What may be that library is still standing in the *wat* today, where a modern plaque says that a golden copy of a Piṭaka used to be housed there. It now contains a Buddha image, and there is no physical evidence of its past history as a distinguished library. Unlike most of the other libraries in the region, this building is not elevated on poles to protect the books from vermin, although if it was built specifically to house a golden text, then this would not have been a concern, for mice, unlike people, do not hunger after gold. There is no further mention of this golden book in the JKM, nor do I know of external evidence indicating what became of it. Examining the Pali, we learn some further details about the treatment of this artifact:

> *Bilakapanattādhirājā Pubbārāme attanā kārāpitassa akkharamandirassa suvaṇṇapiṭakassa mahāmahaṃ katvā* (JKMp, 104)
>
> King Bilakapanattu made a great festival for the golden Piṭaka of the library which was established by him at the Eastern Monastery.

In this case the word for library is *akkharamandira*, which translates literally as "house for letters." The text itself is called a golden Piṭaka, which technically refers to one of the three sections of the canon, but there is no indication as to which section it was or whether it was written on pure gold leaf or on palm leaves that were only gilded. Its production was regarded as an important event because of the festivities associated with it (*mahāmahaṃ*), but there is no further mention of what happened to this unique text, nor are its origins or the method of its production discussed. Presumably it would have been both spiritually and physically very valuable, and one would expect the fortunes of this golden book to have been duly chronicled somewhere, especially when one considers the attention given to the careers of so many Buddha images. In contrast, the section that immediately follows the description of the golden text pays great attention to a festival surrounding the installation of an image at Wat Suan Døk and includes such minute details as the quality and color of the silk used to make the monks' robes

(JKMp, 105). In fact, lengthy narratives surrounding Buddha images and other relics—but never sacred books—abound in the JKM. For example, an account of the king of Ayudhyā says that he

> invaded the city of Khelâṅga with a large armed force . . . and captured from the Setakūṭa "White Spire" Monastery a Buddha image called Sikhī, "flaming," and withdrew. Interrupting (the story) here, the origin of the Buddha-image called Sikhī should now be narrated. It is said that there was a black rock on the western bank of the river not far from the city of Ayojjhā. . . . (Epochs, 155)

The absence of such a narrative about the golden Piṭaka allows us to draw only one conclusion—a negative one—about the importance even of unique manuscripts, to say nothing of common ones, to the people of Lan Na at this time, especially given the fact that the author of the JKM seems to have been more interested in the components of literate culture than many of his contemporary religious professionals.

It is instructive to compare this episode to the story of a very similar artifact produced five centuries earlier in Sri Lanka. In the tenth-century, King Kassapa V has the Abhidhamma written down on gold tablets:

> The king of Laṅkā had the Abhidhamma recited. Having had the Abhidhamma written on gold leaves and then having adorned the *Dhammasaṃgaṇī* book with various jewels, bringing it to the middle of the city and having it placed in the upper house, he bestowed honor upon it. Giving the position of *Sakkasenā* to his own son, he urged him to care for the books of the Dhamma. (MV 1925, 52.49–56)

Each year the king holds a great festival in which the books are carried through the town on the back of an elephant with much pomp and placed in a pavilion on a cushion for relics, where they are worshipped (*maṇḍape dhātupīṭhasmiṃ patiṭṭhāpiya pūjayi*). This affair is also mentioned in a contemporary inscription from Anurādhapura made at the behest of Kassapa (EZ, 1: 52). Housed in a splendid temple and marched through town every year, the golden book was venerated as a cultic object, which points to the deference paid to writing and clearly indicates that Sri Lankans at this time held writing in high esteem.[19]

In comparing the MV episode to the account of the golden Piṭaka found in the JKM, one is stuck by the brevity of the latter and is forced to conclude that while the practice of making golden texts did sprout up in Thailand, it did not achieve anything like the wide acceptance or cultural depth that it did in Sri Lanka.

THE LITERATE WORLD OF BILAKAPANATTU

King Bilakapanattu, who sponsored the golden Piṭaka, went north to the city of Jayasena (Chiang Sæn) in CS 877 (1516 CE) and, according to the JKM (Epochs, 154), built great monasteries and *cetiya*s there, organized the ordination of many monks, and also donated his own royal pavilion to be used as a library for the Tipiṭaka at the Mahārattavanārāma. This monastery was affiliated with the Wat Pa Dæng of Chiang Mai, which shows that libraries were becoming a more prestigious and integral part of at least the *araññavāsī* monastic complex at this time, through the support of the king.

The JKM goes on to recount a visit to Chiang Mai by the rulers of the cities of Nāya and Jayakaṃsa with their retinues, who are all made to pay homage to the three orders of monks, the three Piṭakas, but most especially to the Sinhalese Buddha image (JKMp, 115). The king has them make a pledge in the midst of the Three Jewels and then drink. Thus we see that although the Buddha image is considered the most important object of reverence, above even the monks and the canon, the canon is still an artifact worthy of worship. The use of the phrase "in the midst of the Three Jewels" (*tiṇṇaṃ ratanānaṃ majjhe*) suggests that the visitors were honoring an actual physical text that was present in the audience hall. This would also indicate that there was a copy of the canon at Wat Phra Singh, where this audience took place, which is reasonable because of both the importance of this monastery, which houses one of the most revered Buddha images in the region, and the fact that it still today has a library that contains a significant number of early palm-leaf manuscripts.

Thereafter, we are told of some renovations that occur at the Mahābodhi Monastery (Wat Chet Yøt), in 1517 CE:

> That great edifice which the Emperor Tilaka, the Universal Monarch Siridhamma erected of yore at the Monastery of the Great Bodhi to deposit the Three Piṭakas which he had had cleansed of scribe's errors *(piṭakattayaṃ akkharaṃ sodhāpetvā)* by appointing great Elders versed in the Three Piṭakas (to the task) (*tipiṭakadharamahāthere uccinitvā*), on account of the dilapidated condition of that edifice (*mandirassa jiṇṇatāya*), the King converted into a li-

brary the ancient "City Spire" (*porāṇaṃ nagarakūṭaṃ rājā akkharamandiraṃ kārāpesi*) whence his (great-) grandfather Siridhammacakkavatti, his father the king, and himself exercised their authority. He conducted a great festival of honour by making forty great elders versed in the Three Piṭakas recite the Three Piṭakas (*tipiṭakadharamahāthere tipiṭakam kathāpetvā mahāmahaṃ akāsi*) from the eighth day of the bright fortnight of the month of Māgasira, the day the event of his converting the "City Spire" into the library housing the Piṭakas took place, up to the full moon day of the bright fortnight. (Epochs, 164–165; JKMp, 115)

From this passage we can conclude that the council sponsored by Tilaka[20] culminated with the production of written copies of the Tipiṭaka, which were deposited into a library. It is not clear from the site as it is today where this building may have been located.[21] That the oral tradition was still very much alive at this point is evinced by the fact that forty monks recite the Tipiṭaka. The verb *kath* usually means reciting from memory. The fact that the monks involved are specifically said to have been selected for their knowledge and were *tipiṭakadhara*s suggests that in cases where the written texts were unreliable, the memory and learning of these monks was deemed to be sufficient to correct them.

Significantly, the edifice containing documents as important as the revised canon from the eighth council was allowed to become dilapidated after less than fifty years. It is striking to compare how the library must have been constructed and treated with the seemingly endless accounts of gold being gilded onto image houses and *cetiya*s. The very next passage tells how, for example, a nearby *cetiya* was covered with gold and the finest silk, and the Great Relic of Haripuñjaya was encircled with a wall of 100,000 pieces of gold.

The next section in the JKM (Epochs, 165) includes an important aside about the author Ratanapañña's own circumstances. He says that during the two years that he was working on the JKM, he was often disturbed because the work on the pavilion at Wat Pa Dæng, where he was living, was not yet complete. When the pavilion is finally completed, at a cost of over 100,000 gold pieces, the chief monk of the Mahābodhi Monastery, where the council was held, takes up residence there. Since he is not reordained, this tells us that the Mahābodhi Monastery, which was then well outside of the city, must have been part of the new *araññavāsī* lineage. This provides more evidence that monks from this order were the most concerned and involved with written culture and scholarship during the Golden Age of Lan Na.

There is also a strong possibility that the important Wat Phra Singh, though located within the bounds of the city and thus not formally a forest monastery, had some affiliation with the *araññavāsī* monks, and this may account for its significant manuscript collection. It certainly is associated with Sri Lanka through the fact that it is referred to in the JKM as the Sīhalārāma (Sinhalese Monastery) and contains an image that local tradition holds to have come from that island. This does not in itself, however, indicate any institutional affiliation because the image, if it really is from Sri Lanka, would have arrived long before the *araññavāsī* monks traveled there. What is more telling is the fact that not only did Bilakapanattu, who favored the Sīhala *araññavāsīs*, choose Wat Phra Singh as the site for an important fealty ceremony, but that he also held the funeral for his daughter there in 1522 CE (Epochs, 182). Furthermore, according to the JKM, a year later he invited important monks headed by the Mahārājaguru from Wat Pa Dæng to recite texts at Wat Phra Singh and to dedicate the merit to his daughter. This monastery, then, was clearly a main royal monastery and would no doubt have had many cultural and political transactions with monks from the favored order, if indeed it was not in some way formally associated with them.

THE ORAL WORLD OF BILAKAPANATTU

While libraries were being built, Pali texts written, and some monks were becoming more acquainted with the written word, a lively oral culture was still persisting. In the JKM, when the new chief monk from the Mahābodhi Monastery is actually installed at his new abode, 120 monks are made to recite (*kathāpesi*) the *Maṅgalaparitta, Dhammacakkappavattana* and the *Mahāsamayasutta*s, an event that occupies eighteen days in the month of Citra CS 880 (1519 CE)(Epochs, 166). The monks also have some novel stanzas recited (*gāthāyo bhaṇāpesuṃ*) (Epochs, 168), which have apparently been altered by scribal hands over centuries of textual descent.[22]

This case can give us a better understanding of the semantic field of the word *bhāṇa*. It is surely not a coincidence that this section recording the stanzas is riddled with more mistakes and ambiguities than any other in the JKM. In fact, Coedès did not even translate this section because he considered it too corrupt. This is what we might expect if the author recorded the lines based only on hearing them rather than having access to a written copy. Perhaps he heard the recitation, and since it was a new text apparently composed for the occasion, he had no recourse but to quickly record what was being said or try to fill in any gaps as he best remembered what he heard.

This, then, should be considered as further evidence that the word *bhāṇa* in the JKM is a technical term that denotes oral recitation from memory, as opposed to reading. This episode concludes with what may be a furtive complaint about the quality of the voices of the monks who recited these verses (which would have made it hard to hear exactly what they were saying). Ratanapañña tells us that "at the conclusion of the speech of benediction they selected just eight monks with a deep resonant voice and capable of distinctly articulating consonantal sounds (*sarasampanne vyañjanavuddhikosale*) and made them recite the Mahāmaṅgalaparitta" (Epochs, 171). One gets the sense that the hapless author implies that it was a pleasure to finally hear monks who *could* enunciate properly, after having to decipher poorly articulated verses.

In that same year the king consecrates the golden Sīhala image and listens to the *Mahāvessantaranidāna* that he has had written (*attanā likhāpitaṃ*) (Epochs, 176). It is not clear exactly what this text is. It may be a version of the *Vessantara Jātaka* itself, in which case the term "written" would indicate that it was copied down at the behest of the king.

After listening to this text, the king and his retinue then hear a disquisition on the Dhamma called the *Buddhavaṃsa* (*Buddhavaṃsaṃ nāma dhammapariyāyaṃ suṇiṃsu* [JKMp, 121]). Later, when he installs the Kamboja image at the Mahābodhi Monastery, he brings thirty-six monks who are *tipiṭakadhara*s and listens for over a week to a discourse on the Dhamma known as the *Cariyapiṭakaṃ*. Although Pali texts were regularly committed to writing by this time, then, they were still generally displayed and communicated orally. The duties of a monk as depicted in the JKM include a copious amount of reciting, mostly from memory, but also from books. It is important to emphasize that each instance of recitation was an event of some significance. The monks would be honored both ceremonially and materially; not only would they sit on elevated platforms and be treated like kings themselves, but they would also usually receive generous *dāna*. It is easy to see why, therefore, they would value and defend this aspect of their vocation. They may have perceived a threat in the increasing reliance upon written manuscripts, which could, after all, in theory be read by anybody.

COPYING PROJECTS UNDER BILAKAPANATTU

In the Haripuñjaya National Museum an inscription from Wat Phra That declares that Somdet Bophit Maharat built a library (*phra dharma mandira*) for the canonical texts (PSC, 3: item 71). The text includes many details about the building, the financing, and the deference paid to the library and scriptures:

> [Inscription begins with a horoscope and the date, given as CS 862 (1500 CE), the year of the monkey, the first lunar month]
> Somdet Bophit Maharat the king of the land of Phing, known as Chiang Mai, who follows the ten principles of kingship together with his mother, having great knowledge and unadulterated faith in the teachings, in order to root them well in Haripuñjaya and ensure them a solid legacy, that they should shine forth for five thousand years and engender faith, do hereby make a royal donation. Its aim is to enable the seven jewels to be continually brought to honor the *cetiya* of the Great Relic, the chief in the land, every month and year without end.
>
> The king and his mother declare that the meaning of the Dhamma is lofty and great. Their hearts are not satisfied with merely ruminating on the nature of Truth, and therefore they built a library for the scriptures covered with gold leaf and gilt floral patterns that will be as astounding as Indra's palace. When finished, the king will get people to copy the Dhamma texts, which are the Buddha's words memorized in 84,000 sections, as well as other important texts such as the commentaries and subcommentaries totaling 420 books in all. There will also be a Buddha image made. When finished, the king will bring all these things and put them inside the library. The whole project will cost 200,000 units of silver . . .
>
> A permanent endowment fund is to be set up, with the interest used for betel to honor the scriptures. Another endowment is to be used to purchase rice to put in a silver bowl to honor the scriptures.
>
> The royal sponsors also get revenue from 2,000,000 rice paddy fields to pay for twelve families including their children and grandchildren and great-grandchildren. 500,000 goes for rice to honor the Dhamma, 500,000 goes to the master of the library, and ten people get 100,000 each. [The twelve families are then listed].
>
> The two royal sponsors have decided on the following command: the paddies and people of this group are for the support and protection of the library and for its upkeep in the future. No one may involve them in any secular work or use them for this and that. . . . Thus the king, whose heart is pure and devoted to the teachings of the Buddha, wishes to establish and protect them here always in order to get unparalleled benefits from this good deed for us always.

> Through this beneficent royal intention, let the king and his mother get two kinds of riches, both inner and outer. Let them achieve fame, glory, and victory, let there be no one who can gain the upper hand over them. . . . Let them be intelligent and wise, that they may understand the entire meaning of the Dhamma and be able to preach and teach all of it. In the future, let them secure well-being and glorious attainments beyond measure, let them arrive at the great cessation and enlightenment which are the ultimate ends.
>
> The king and his mother offer part of the inestimable royal merit from this deed to [the king's] father and grandfather and grandmother, and the host of gods such as Indra, Brahma, Yama, the guardians of the four corners, and the local spirits, that they may rejoice and help to preserve the teachings of the Buddha in this place forever.

The king can be none other than Bilakapanattu, who, as I have just said is also characterized in the JKM as particularly inclined towards literate culture and its accoutrements. August Pavie (1898, 281) records another inscription about the works of Dharmarāja Bophit from Wat Lamphoung, which he says is located ten kilometers southwest of Chiang Mai.[23] In the inscription, his queen establishes a monastery called Tapodārāma for one hundred monks that she has invited, and the king donates numerous rice fields and families for the upkeep of the monastery. We are then told that 153,530 pieces of silver were expended for the making of the Buddha image and manuscripts, and 182,170 were disbursed for the *wat* itself. For other *wat*s in the area, 513,810 pieces of silver were spent. The merit thus gained is dedicated to all the people of the kingdom. Regrettably, how much was spent on the Buddha image and how much on the manuscripts is not indicated.

The JKM provides still more details about the copying projects instigated by this king. In CS 882 (1521 CE) King Bilakapanattu "had the woodwork of the library at the Great Rattavana Monastery, housing the Piṭakas which had been redacted in writing, completely renovated" (Epochs, 175). In this passage we see that there was a copy of the Tipiṭaka at Wat Pa Dæng and that the library was perceived as being worth renovating.

In the year CS 883 the Tipiṭaka was written down at Wat Pa Dæng, probably by a group of Chiang Mai officials, which would be significant because they would probably have been laypeople at the time, although that does not in any way preclude the possibility that all or most of them were monks at some point (JKMp, 122).[24] Regardless of who the scribes were, we are now left with the impression that the monastery where the JKM was produced was the only one in the Chiang Mai area housing no less than two series of canonical texts. Because the bounty of two canons must have strained the resources of the library, and possibly to spread out the books in case of disaster, the next year the king establishes another library at Wat Pa Dæng (JKMp, 125). Whether this would have been another edifice, and whether it was intended to replace or supplement the existing library, is not clarified.

Let us take stock of the canonical literature that may have been available in the Lan Na capital region around the time of the JKM. Three of five canonical collections were located in what we know to be *araññavāsī* monasteries: Wat Pa Dæng (Chiang Mai) had two libraries and two sets of the Tipiṭaka, and the Mahābodhi Monastery had one set. The other monastery that probably had a set was Wat Phra Singh, which had a strong affiliation with the *araññavāsī*s because they performed monastic rituals there, and which in any case was a central royal monastery and thus an important center of religious authority. The fifth significant collection would then be the somewhat mysterious golden Piṭaka at the Pubbārāma.

Were there many other canonical copying projects in the region that are not recorded in the JKM? The JKM certainly leaves the impression that other monasteries did not have significant collections of Pali manuscripts. If the important Mahābodhi Monastery, where the wisest monks in the region had gathered in council to edit the canon, could barely marshal the resources to maintain its library housing the original copies that came out of this great project, one would be hard pressed to envision lesser monasteries having any significant holdings, *if* one were to base one's assumptions on the scenario as depicted in the JKM. Furthermore, while the other *araññavāsī* historiographical work that I have been focussing on, the TPD, mentions libraries and canonical texts in the far north at Keng Tung, they feature hardly at all in other chronicles produced outside this order. A final but highly significant piece of evidence requires going back to the lengthy inscription cited above about the library built at Wat Phra That in Haripuñjaya. This is one of the older monasteries in Lan Na, having its origins during the Mon hegemony sometime prior to the twelfth century (JKMI, 247–251), and the inscription is the longest one yet discovered from the period that contains details about the establishment of books and a library. The centuries-old monastery had plenty of time to build a library if it had had canonical texts that needed to be housed, yet the inscription gives the impression that no library was located on the premises until the time of the inscription. There was, however, some strong *araññavāsī* influence that reached this monastery about fifty years prior to the building of the library, in the form of none other than Mahāthera

Medhaṅkara himself, one of the leaders of the group of monks who were reordained in Sri Lanka. In 1448 CE, the JKM tells us, King Tilaka constructed a consecration pavilion at Wat Phra That and invited this monk to be honored and given a new title reflecting the royal favor that he had attained (Epochs, 136). It is also worth noting that besides the library and the canon, Wat Phra That Haripuñjaya was one of the largest recipients of donations of all kinds, ranging from gold and silver to utensils given by Bilakapanattu throughout his reign. Like Wat Phra Singh, it was a royal monastery that no doubt would have maintained the close connection to the *araññavāsīs* that was initiated fifty years earlier by King Tilaka and Mahāthera Medhaṅkara. It seems unlikely, then, that there were many other monasteries at the time that held copies of the Tipiṭaka but were not affiliated with the *araññavāsī* order either formally or through involvement with the circle of royally favored institutions. Certainly no such monasteries are mentioned in the chronicles or inscriptions.

The best way to fortify these conclusions is to look at the colophons from extant manuscripts made during the period under study. If the *araññavāsī* monks of the new Sinhalese lineage really did have a more intimate relationship with writing, one would expect this to become evident through the remaining record of their efforts to actually produce manuscripts. Therefore it is important to determine what percentage of monastically sponsored manuscripts were the fruit of this group. While this is admittedly difficult to ascertain, because the affiliation of the sponsors is not always mentioned in the colophons, a few educated guesses can nevertheless be put forward. I have collected the colophons from a significant portion of the known Pali manuscripts from this era, of which forty-seven were sponsored in some way by monks. The sponsors of four of these manuscripts are described as *araññavāsī* monks in the colophons themselves,[25] but there are a number of other monks who very likely belonged to this group as well. One manuscript, for example, was made to be put in Wat Pa Da Luang.[26] As the word *pa* means "forest," and is found in the names of many monasteries in the *araññavāsī* lineage, it is quite probable, although not certain, that this monastery was part of that lineage. Another was made for Wat Mahāvana, the "Great Forest," also suggesting a monastery in the *araññavāsī* lineage.[27] Two were sponsored by monks with *pa* (forest) in their titles, which was perhaps a Thai equivalent to the title *araññavāsī*.[28] One was made at the behest of the Saṅgharājā in Chiang Mai in 1517,[29] who in all probability was Saddhamma Saṇṭhira, the abbot of Wat Pa Dæng who was favored by King Bilakapanattu (Epochs, 160). Thus it is very likely that at least nine of the forty-seven manuscripts sponsored in whole or in part by monks were sponsored by *araññavāsī* monks.

A much greater number can be attributed to this group if we take into consideration the following factors about a region known as Tha Søi, where the largest number of extant sixteenth-century manuscripts were produced. A manuscript was sponsored by Mahā Pa Ñāṇamaṅgalo for Wat Srī Puñ Tha Søi in 1542 CE, and if this monk was a forest-dweller, which seems very likely from his name, then it is probable that the monastery to which the manuscript was donated was of this lineage as well. Von Hinüber (1990, 64) points out that a colophon says that the Mahāsaṅgharājā of Pa Luang Basjharam went to Wat Srī Puñ and made a manuscript for that monastery, further suggesting that there was some institutional connection between forest monasteries and Wat Srī Puñ. If this is the case, then another manuscript that was donated to this monastery can be attributed to forest-dwelling monks.[30]

It is possible to extrapolate even further and assume that the title *Mahāsaṅgharājā* would at this point have been given in the Tha Søi region, as in Chiang Mai, to a monk from the new *araññavāsī* order, for this was the order favored by the royal power of the day. Two of the three Saṅgharājās mentioned in the colophons are, in fact, specifically identified as forest-dwellers (von Hinüber 1990, 71). Thus one could, with a fair degree of confidence, attribute all the occurrences of a monk with such a title to this order. In this case, six more manuscripts could be added to the list.[31] Javanapañña, a Tha Søi monk who sponsored at least three manuscripts,[32] became a Saṅgharājā later in his life (von Hinüber 1990, 70), and thus although his name is never followed by the title *araññavāsī* in the colophons, it is likely that he, too, belonged to this order. A final point is that certain names were more likely to have been adopted by monks from the new Sinhalese *araññavāsī* order than others. For example, two names found among the monastic sponsors of the colophons examined above are Medhaṅkara and Ñāṇagambhīra.[33] These are the names of the leaders of the group of monks that went in the 1420s from Chiang Mai to Sri Lanka and were reordained in the Sinhalese forest-dwelling tradition. Upon their return to Chiang Mai, there was enough tension between them and the other monastic orders to have led to their expulsion from the city for a period before returning triumphantly under the wing of King Tilaka. It is thus not only unlikely that monks in other orders would take these names, but is instead probable that these would have been name choices for monks ordained into the lineage founded by these men.

Thus, arguably twenty-two out of the forty-seven manuscripts, or 46.8 percent of those sponsored in whole or in part by monks were made by individuals with some affiliation to the new Sinhalese *araññavāsī* order headquartered at Wat Pa Dæng in Chiang Mai. Penth has found that of the ordinations mentioned in the JKM, only 23 percent were of monks from this order (JKMI, ix). Since the JKM was written by an *araññavāsī* monk, this monk would presumably have focused more on matters concerning this order, and therefore the true proportion of monks ordained into this order was surely even less than this amount. It would then appear that the proportion of manuscripts sponsored by these monks was at least twice that of their representation within the Lan Na Saṅgha. Of the five named monasteries at Tha Søi, at least three seem to have been affiliated with the forest-dwelling order, namely, Wat Srī Puñ, Wat Pa Mai, and Wat Pa Luang Basjharam (von Hinüber 1990, 66). Another monastery, Wat Srī Un, inasmuch as it was affiliated with the Saṅgharājā Javanapañña, may also have been connected to this order. This, then, would account for the particularly large number of manuscripts extant from this area while also strengthening the impression garnered from the chronicles that these monks were central to the support and expansion of literate culture in Lan Na.

Furthermore, the Tha Søi and many other old manuscripts were found in the library of Wat Lai Hin in Lampang, a monastery whose main structures were built in 1683 CE under the aegis of Kesārapañña, an *araññavāsī* monk, and the name of which, Lai Hin, means Stone Forest Monastery (von Hinüber 1996a, 36).

> Kesārapañña seems to have been a keen student of Buddhist texts . . . therefore it is tempting to think of him as the collector of the older Pāli manuscripts dating from the late 15th to the early 17th centuries. However that may be, during Kesārapañña's time Vat Lai Hin seems to have enjoyed a certain reputation for the manuscripts it possessed. (von Hinüber 1996a, 37)

Again we see that literate modes of Buddhist life were more central to the *araññavāsī* culture than to that of other monastic orders.

ORIGINAL WORKS IN PALI FROM LAN NA

A number of original works were produced in Lan Na during this period, ranging from popular tales to cosmological treatises, grammatical texts, and commentaries on the Abhidhamma. These have been dealt with in some detail by Coedès (1915), Saddhatissa (1989) and von Hinüber (2000). Besides Ratanapañña, two of the more learned and productive authors about whom something is known are Sirimaṅgala and Ñāṇakitti. Sirimaṅgala was active during the first quarter of the sixteenth century, and his best-known works are the *Vessantaradīpanī, Cakkavāḷadīpanī* and the *Maṅgalatthadīpanī*. Ñāṇakitti was active for several decades, starting probably in the 1480s; he authored a comprehensive grammatical treatise and commentaries on Vinaya and Abhidhamma texts. Neither author is referred to as *araññavāsī* in the colophons associated with their works, but there is clear evidence that they were strongly affiliated with this group, if not formal members of it. Sirimaṅgala is described in the SV as *pattalaṅkatherassa vihāre vasanto* (living in the monastery of the monk who arrived from Lanka). In extant colophons he is said to have worked at Wat Suan Kuan, near Wat Phra Singh in Chiang Mai. Two old copies of the *Cakkavāḷadīpanī* still exist,[34] one dated CS 900 (1538 CE) and the other from about the same time, both of which were sponsored by Mahā Saṅgharāja Candaraṃsi Araññavāsī. This is the only premodern Pali work from anywhere in Asia that is extant in a traditionally made manuscript that was likely copied during the lifetime of the text's author. As it was sponsored by an *araññavāsī* and chosen out of the hundreds of possible titles in the Pali corpus, it is evident that the author had close ties to this group and that its leader wished to promote his work. The *Cakkavāḷadīpanī* is an examination of the various divisions of the Buddhist cosmos and is largely a compilation of quotes from canonical and commentarial sources; it displays little ingenuity but certainly a deep familiarity with obscure passages from a great swath of Pali literature. The *Maṅgalatthadīpanī* is a text still widely used in Thailand as part of monastic education because of its copious summary information about key elements important to Buddhism, such as generosity, discipline, learning, and concern for others. Saddhātissa (1989, 43) cites a text (which I have not been able to trace) called *Vajirasārasaṅgaha* that was written, according to the colophon that he saw but unfortunately did not reference, by Sirimaṅgala in 1535 at Mahāvanārāma (the Great Forest Monastery), which may be a reference to Wat Pa Dæng itself.

Ñāṇakitti lived at the Panasārāma and flourished a few decades before Sirimaṅgala; he may even have taken part in the eighth council sponsored by Tiloka in 1477. The king himself is said to have given him a room in which to work at a monastery whose name translates as the Jackfruit Tree Monastery (von Hinüber 2000, 124). There was, then, a close connection between the king, who supported the *araññavāsī* order, and this monk. In his commentaries Ñāṇakitti occasionally confronts variant readings, for which he uses the term *pāṭhā*.[35] This is the Pali equivalent of the English word "reading" and is the standard word used in Pali to denote written texts. Ñāṇakitti most certainly was an outstanding intellect with a keen grasp of grammar and a wide but deep range of knowledge pertaining to Buddhist literature and doctrine. He quotes not only from canonical texts, classic commentaries, and chronicles, but also from more recent and obscure subcommentaries such as *Khuddakasikkhāporāṇaṭīkā* and *Vinayatthamañjūsā*. He is even aware of some texts that Buddhaghosa also quotes in his great commentary on the Vinaya, the *Samantapāsādikā*. As von Hinüber is quick to observe, this provides evidence of the strong connection that certain monks must have had with Sri Lanka, where these texts were in part still known (von Hinüber 2000, 133–134).

Von Hinüber also has an important insight into the motivations that may have driven this textual production (2000, 134ff). Many of the first subcommentaries (*ṭīkā*s) were produced in Sri Lanka during the monastic reforms undertaken in the twelfth century under King Parakkamabāhu in an attempt to clarify the monastic rules and thus leave posterity with a clearly articulated program for future orthodox monasticism. Ñāṇakitti, just a couple generations removed from those intrepid monks who had initially gone to study and be reordained in Sri Lanka, lived during a period in which King Tilaka wished to bring the practice of Buddhism in Lan Na more in line with the Sinhalese interpretation of the religion that could ultimately be traced to Parakkamabāhu's "purification." Ñāṇakitti's commentaries were on Vinaya and Abhidhamma literature, which, unlike the more narrative Suttas, are precisely where the most contested areas of praxis and doctrine were located. Commenting upon them would have helped to lay the groundwork for the renewal of orthodox Buddhist practice as desired by the *araññavāsī*s; a further detailed study of his commentaries would be of great value for the history of Buddhism in the region. Despite all of this, Ñāṇakitti is relatively unknown not only in the larger Theravādin world but even in Thailand, where manuscripts of his works are very rare. How different the popular practice of the religion was can be demonstrated by some of the other literature from this time that seems to have been produced in Lan Na and for which manuscripts are plentiful. I refer here to the *Māleyyadevatheravatthu* (Collins 1993) and the *Paññāsa Jātaka* (Jaini 1983), which both include stories culled from the folk tradition with only a thin veneer of Buddhism overlaid. They will be discussed in more detail in Chapter Six.

ROYAL SUPPORT FOR MANUSCRIPTS

All of the manuscript copying projects mentioned in the JKM and inscriptions were initiated by kings, queens, or other rulers. Only on manuscript colophons themselves are monks sometimes named as sponsors of these items.[36] This suggests that most copying projects occurred not so much out of a need for monks to have more study copies, but out of the desire of the king to establish his Buddhist credentials, make merit, and demonstrate the interconnection between his authority and the religion. That the communicative utility of the scriptures for scholarly monks was eclipsed by certain ideological components is seen by the fact that while oral recitation of individual Suttas is mentioned numerous times, all JKM accounts of writing Pali canonical texts tell of making at least a "Piṭaka" and usually the "Tipiṭaka." The only possible exception to this is the case of the king having the *Mahāvessantaranidāna* written (Epochs, 176), but the genre Nidāna may just as easily be a vernacular as a Pali text. The idea of the canon,[37] conceived of as a whole system that embraces all of the teachings and maintains them within its bounds, appears to have been central to the copying projects sponsored by the kings. These projects were not intended just to supply needed books, but by replicating the entire body of the Buddha's words, the kings symbolically subsumed the religion within their domain. Here, written books served a crucial iconic role in which they stood metonymically for the teachings as a whole.

Such behavior accords well with what we know of neighboring Burma,[38] although there, in concord with the more developed state of writing in general and the higher esteem bestowed upon it, the practice was part of a more elaborate and developed tradition:

> Newly crowned Myanmar kings were compelled by tradition to commission a set of the Tripitaka for presentation to a monastery or enshrinement within a pagoda. Scrupulously following ancient precedent, a temporary building was constructed for the monks and scribes. Ink for the text . . . was obtained by burning the robes of the parents of the monarch, a form of filial piety practised by the royal family. The ashes were then mixed with water, resin of the *tammar* (*Azadirachta indica*) and the gall of the *ngagyin* fish (*Cirrhina morigala*) which ensured a glossy finish. (Singer 1991, 137)

The finished product was greeted with great festivities that were held for seven days. It is clear that this project was intended to solidify and legitimize the monarch's claim to power and to show that as he controlled the canon, so he could and should control the nation.

The multivalent issues at play in the case of Thai royal sponsorship of the Tipiṭaka revolve around the complex interdependent relationships obtaining among the king, the Dhamma, and the Saṅgha. Righteous (*dhammika*) conduct plays an important role in legitimizing the sovereignty of the king, as seen by such things as the frequency of the epithet "Dhammarāja" in Sukhodaya inscriptions and the admonition in the traditional Thai law codes, the Thammasat, for the king to rule according to the ten rules of kingship (Ishii 1986, 44–45). Frank Reynolds has said that "[t]he king's rule had to be carried out in the service of the Dhamma. The king was responsible for maintaining the integrity and purity of the canonical Dhamma . . ." (F. Reynolds 1971, 197).

The Dhamma that helps to justify kingship must, in turn, be upheld, and this task has traditionally been fulfilled by the Saṅgha. Because the Buddha himself is gone, his words (which serve as the basis for the Dhamma) survive only in the Tipiṭaka, transmission of which is maintained by the Saṅgha. "The proper function of the Order . . . its actualization, preservation, and transmission of the Dhamma, and its maintenance of effective discipline, served as a sign of the legitimacy of the established order and the merit and piety of the reigning monarch" (F. Reynolds 1971, 186–187). However, the Saṅgha, because of the restrictive nature of the monastic rules, must be supported by outside interests, which throughout Thai history have been headed by the king. Thus an interdependent web takes shape:

> Legitimated by the Dhamma, the king secures the following of the people. The Dhamma, on the other hand, must be transmitted by a pure Sangha; the Dhamma's survival is guaranteed by the purity of the Sangha. And the purity of the Sangha is manifested in the correct observance of the precepts by its members. Laity then voluntarily fulfills its duty to support this Vinaya-observing community. Historically, the support lent by the king, the "supreme defender of Buddhism," liberated the monks from the burdens of daily subsistence and allowed them to sustain an unworldly lifestyle in accordance with the precepts.
>
> The "Buddhist State," defined as a state structured such that the king supports the Sangha, the Sangha transmits the Dhamma, and the Dhamma legitimates the monarchy, can be considered to be typified by Thailand. (Ishii 1986, 46)

Given these relationships, the king, in sponsoring the copying of the Tipiṭaka, provided even more immediate support for the Dhamma than through his maintenance of the Saṅgha. The king may also have been particularly supportive of this new technology of writing because it afforded him a much more reliable and predictable degree of control not so much over the contents of the canon but over the authority that it represents. In having a physical copy of the scriptures made under his auspices and placed in a royally sanctioned location, the king could establish a more stable connection to the Buddha and his Dhamma than through royal support of the monks. Dissent between monks and kings was always a possibility, which, even if rare, could theoretically erupt at any time. The written scripture took the unpredictable human factor out of the process; the king may have felt (rightly or wrongly) that he would never have any trouble or challenges from a mute book.[39]

It is clear from various sources that rulers had in fact been promoting writing from early on and were interested in integrating it into the workings of the polity. We first encounter the use of writing in the TCM, for example, in an episode in which Ai Fa sends a letter (*nang süa*) to King Mangrai in the year CS 643 (1281 CE) telling him of the desire of the people of Haripuñjaya to have him come down and rule them instead of their current king (TCM, 1.4). Tilaka, too, has also been portrayed as being favorable towards the written word.

Some of the strongest evidence for the relationship between rulers and the written word comes from the large number of legal texts found among extant manuscript collections throughout Lan Na and Thailand in general.[40] The tradition holds that Lan Na law was initiated with the code of King Mangrai (Wichienkeeo 1996, 31). A leading scholar in the field tells of her impressions:

> The 19th century manuscripts which we collected from the book depositories of monasteries contain material from the Mangrai dynasty period. From my study of the texts I deduce that in those days Lanna legal procedures used both written and customary laws. The written laws can be divided into three types: traditional Buddhist ethics, royal decrees and royal judgements. (Wichienkeeo 1996, 33)

While it is daunting to reconstruct exactly how written legal texts were used in the Golden Age and earlier from the thousands of extant nineteenth-century manuscripts, their sheer number suggests that they are built upon a long-existing tradition of written legal texts. Furthermore, legal passages occupy a very large proportion of inscriptional space from early Sukhodaya

(Huxley 1996, 119), suggesting again that the idea of writing down laws was an old one that enjoyed strong support from rulers. It is not difficult to understand why kings would have wished for their laws to be written down—in order to lay the infrastructure for a secure and organized polity, the legal continuity of which would as it were extend their will into the future.

It is clear, then, that rulers had for some time appreciated the utility of the written word and therefore would have been more prepared to sponsor its deployment for the transmission of religious texts as well. Other lay and monastic groups might have been less inclined to use this technology simply because, among other reasons, it was unfamiliar to them. Of course, elite monks would still have been involved with the production of legal texts as both scribes and consultants since many of the laws were based on Buddhist practice and principles; but these monks, as we are beginning to see, were more the exception than the rule.

MONASTIC ATTITUDES TOWARDS WRITTEN SCRIPTURES

Towards the end of the JKM (JKMp, 127), we finally see a clear example of the transmission of the Tipiṭaka in Lan Na through the transport of the scriptures in written form. In CS 885 (1523 CE), the king sends the monk Devamaṅgala with his followers and a Tipiṭaka consisting of sixty volumes (*pakaraṇa*) to the king of Dasalakkhakuñjara (Luang Prabang). This is a distinctly different way of spreading the Dhamma than the way it was done by Cāmadevī, who went to Haripuñjaya with 500 monks described as *tipiṭakadhara*s. The monks in 1523 CE do not themselves have to know all the texts by heart, but rather they accompany written copies almost as ancillary features. Now we can begin to see why some monks may have resisted the growing reliance upon writing and displayed their ambivalent attitudes in their historiographies: writing was poised to usurp their important and prestigious role of bearers and upholders of the canon. The monks did not have access to some of the most important sources of power—the ability to physically punish and materially reward. However, they did possess a virtual "monopoly of access to the public mind," as John Galbraith describes the nature of priestly power (1983, 174). It is easy to see that they would have viewed books as a threat to their absolute dominion over Buddhist texts and thereby their enormous influence on the minds of the faithful. This is not to say that they necessarily foresaw the eventual revolution of individual engagement with religious texts and the advent of lay meditation and study groups that has characterized much of the Theravāda Buddhist world over the last century, for that required the further innovation of print. However, the possibility of others reading the texts was now present in principle and would have had an effect on the metonymical identification of the monks with the words of the Buddha and ultimately with the religion itself.

Many of these sentiments can be understood very well by people today whose occupations are likely to be overshadowed or overtaken by new technologies. Indeed, the monks had good reason to feel this way, as Mahinda Deegalle, who has chronicled the decline of the *bhāṇaka* tradition in Sri Lanka, has shown. Building on the work of Goonesekere, Godakumbara, and others, he attributes in large measure the demise of this tradition to the use of writing, which gradually rendered the cumbersome *bhāṇaka* system of oral transmission obsolete (1997, 437).

Another possible reason for apprehension on the part of some monks stems not so much from the exigencies of sociocultural capital and political power, but rather from the textual encounter itself. Some monks may have been more attuned than others to the aural aspects of religious literature. These add a rich dimension to the texts—a dimension that is lost when they are transposed onto paper or palm leaf. William Graham (1987) has argued that the very way a text sounds when chanted or read—what he calls the sensual aspect of a text—is an important part of the experience of the text. Many monks may have agreed experience is greatly impoverished when texts are read silently and privately. Before Graham, McLuhan posited that the oral mode of communication is more open than the visual, which tends to direct one's thoughts in the same manner as it directs and dominates the eye (1962, 37–39). One can do and experience many things while listening, but when reading, one must be focused on the task at hand to the exclusion of all else. This, believes McLuhan, initiates a process of individuation that moves one away from the oral "tribal" world. While McLuhan was the first to express these ideas in such an explicit manner, it is not impossible that many premodern people intuited the type of changes that might arise from the introduction of writing on a large scale. Fearing a denuding of the Buddhist cultural world as they knew it, they may have therefore opposed the introduction of written texts.[41]

CONCLUSION

The Golden Age of Lan Na was a dynamic time in the history of northern Thailand. There were several monastic orders vying for power and influence, scholars producing learned Pali texts of various genres, and kings continually expanding their dominion both politically and religiously. While written copies of Pali texts were available to some extent, many were kept in libraries largely as symbols of royal power rather than as scholarly tools. Most people, including monks, engaged the texts in an oral environment. Even those monks who returned around 1430 CE from the *araññavāsī* mission to Sri Lanka and served as the catalysts for the Golden Age of Pali in Lan Na had extensive oral knowledge of the Dhamma and did not necessarily bring manuscripts back to Thailand. However, the transmission of written canonical texts does feature in the JKM account of Anuruddha of Burma and then later in the account of the transmission to Dasalakkhakuñjara. But even when written scriptures are mentioned, they are not given nearly the position of prominence that is accorded to Buddha images or *tipiṭakadhara* monks by the author of the chronicle. Nor do the people of Lan Na in general seem to exhibit great reverence for such worthy objects; the library containing the scriptures that were redacted at a great council in the region quickly became dilapidated, perhaps because donors thought their money was better spent elsewhere.

It must be emphasized, however, that for texts produced within the cultural orbit of northern Thailand, the JKM and the TPD actually grant writing a relatively *prominent* position. This can best be attributed to their positions as products of the newest *araññavāsī* order brought directly from Sri Lanka. The monastery where the JKM was written is said to have had two libraries on the premises, and the council that produced the first fully redacted written Tipiṭaka in a northern Thai script was convened at another monastery belonging to this order. The TPD, while focusing largely on questions of pronunciation in the context of the Kammavācā texts, turns its attention to writing in the context of the strengthening of the Sinhalese version of the Sāsanā in the region. There are several references to libraries and even one to a stand upon which the manuscripts would be placed in the preaching hall. It also imputes a degree of magical power to the written word as demonstrated through the trial by fire of two written names. The CDV, on the other hand, does not in any way allude to the use of writing for the transmission of religious texts and the MS has only marginal allusions.

Different monastic groups, besides having different ordination lineages and varying interpretations of Buddhist precepts and practice, apparently had different attitudes towards writing as well. Writing was probably the least integrated into the textual practices of the older order of "city dwelling" monks to which Bodhiraṃsi belonged. Writing played a more important role in the first Sinhalese *araññavāsī* order (later known as the *pupphārāmavāsī* or "flower-garden" order) brought by Sumana but was more utilized and revered by the monks in the second *araññavāsī* order, which was brought about a generation after the CDV was composed. Each succeeding order also seems to have had a stricter interpretation of Pali canonical texts than the prior one. Even the account in the partisan MS itself of the conflict between the *pupphārāmavāsī* and *araññavāsī* orders allows that the latter, rival group was stricter in its interpretation of the monastic code, condemning such practices as the acceptance of money and land. This elicits the question of whether there might be a connection between how the texts were communicated and how they were interpreted. In this case a stricter interpretation of religious codes seems to have arisen in concert with more extensive usage of written versions of the texts in question.

4 The Text in the World

Scribes, Sponsors, and Manuscript Culture

How were written Pali texts in Lan Na produced, stored, and retrieved in the fifteenth and sixteenth centuries? While seeking to provide a window onto the manuscript and scribal culture of historical Lan Na, this chapter also seeks to provide a snapshot of what the life of a scribe, donor, or reader might have been like. In doing so, it looks at one of the most important sources for information about this topic—the Pali manuscripts themselves.[1] Although manuscripts constitute the living remnants of historical Pali Buddhist literary culture, they have until recently been overlooked by scholars in the field, who considered them merely the raw data from which to construct critical editions of Pali texts. The remarks of John Dagenais about European manuscripts apply equally well to those from Southeast Asia:

> . . . manuscripts exist, not as "vehicles for readings" to be discarded in the process of edition-making, chopped up into lists of variants and leaves of plates, but as living witnesses to the dynamic, chaotic, error-fraught world of medieval literary life that we have preferred to view till now through the smoked glass of critical editions. (1994, xviii)

The features of manuscripts that I examine below, while usually overlooked, can nevertheless offer up a wealth of historical information. Scribal colophons, for example, generally record such basic data as the title of the work, the date on which the manuscript was completed, the name of the sponsor, the monastery where it was made, as well as more culturally illuminating details, such as the reasons for making the work, the living conditions of the scribe, and sometimes the remuneration provided to the scribe.

The environment in which a manuscript was situated will be fleshed out by looking at writings in the margins, as well as interlinear corrections and other markings. Certain metatextual features can teach a lot about manuscripts. The condition of the leaves themselves, the quality of the writing and calligraphic embellishments or other ornamentation, and the caliber of the wooden protective covers (*mai prakap*) all contribute to a better understanding of the career of these texts.

The manuscripts from the north of Thailand constitute the oldest extant cache of Pali manuscripts from Southeast Asia. The earliest available Pali manuscript in the Lan Na Dhamma script is a fragmentary Jātaka dealing with previous lives of the Buddha (SRIcat-16; 17; 18; 19); it comes from Wat Lai Hin and bears the date CS 883 (1471 CE). There are at least two other manuscripts dated before CS 912 (1500 CE), a copy of the semicanonical *Milindapañha* from 1495 CE[2] and the Abhidhamma text *Yamakapakaraṇam* from 1497 CE (Lai Hin: SRI 04–025). There are some manuscripts that are attributable to the late fifteenth century, but they are not precisely dated. Coedès mentions a copy of the *Sāratthappakāsinī* commentary on the *Saṃyutta Nikāya* in the National Library in Bangkok from 1440 CE and a *Yamakavohāra* at the Siam Society from 1487 CE, but modern scholars have not been able to trace either of these (von Hinüber 1990, 57). Thus at least eleven extant manuscripts from the fifteenth century and over a hundred from the sixteenth century, of wide-ranging provenance, afford a glimpse of a variety of early styles.

Lan Na manuscripts have been cataloged in a number of accessible ways, thanks largely to the efforts of an ongoing project started in 1971 at the Social Research Institute (SRI) at Chiang Mai University that has microfilmed and numbered thousands of Pali and vernacular manuscripts, often in situ.[3] Unfortunately, in all cases the current repository of the manuscript may have nothing whatsoever to do with its original provenance. We cannot therefore get a truly accurate impression of the differing manuscript cultures of various areas unless the region or monastery of origin is mentioned in the colophon, which is not often the case.[4] The National Library in Bangkok, the Siam Society, the Royal Danish Library in Copenhagen, and the Otani University Library in Japan all have significant Thai manuscript collections that I have considered as well.

As mentioned in Chapter Two, the number and condition of manuscripts from the fifteenth century suggest that the tradition of writing Pali manuscripts in the Lan Na script did not commence until that century. Further evidence of this is that the very earliest manuscripts have short colophons, giving only the most vital information, but as the manuscript culture expanded after the first quarter of the sixteenth century, the writing of colophons flowered into a more developed and involved art.

The early stages of manuscript production also coincide with the return of the delegation of monks who went to Sri Lanka in 1425 and were reordained as *araññavāsīs*. Although Bodhiraṃsi did write down his Pali CDV about a decade prior to this event, there is little doubt that the production of significant numbers of Pali manuscripts emerged out of the enthusiasm of these monks who had tasted the literate environment of Lanka. Myriad other religious projects were undertaken in the Lan Na kingdom at this time, including the construction of large edifices such as the Wat Phra That in Lampang and the Chedi Luang in Chiang Mai as well as the adaptation of the Tipiṭaka into the vernacular through bilingual didactic texts called Wohan and Nisrai (Nissaya).

The Thai rulers began to lose power to the Burmese in the middle of the sixteenth century, and a few decades later manuscript production waned. Many present-day repositories that contain dozens of examples from the sixteenth and nineteenth centuries have only one or two from the period 1620 to 1750 CE, during the Burmese occupation. The *Mūlapaṇṇāsa Sutta* (SRI 07–04–001) from CS 1009 (1647 CE), which is kept at Wat Phra Singh, for example, is written in a poor, inelegant hand. The awkward look of the letters, most likely a sign of scribal inexperience, renders it very difficult to read and represents a low ebb of the scribal arts. The manuscript has all the hallmarks of having been written by someone who did not have the opportunity to practice this art sufficiently and thus it fails to live up to the standards set by more experienced hands. There is even an *a* missing at the beginning of *arahato* in the introductory panegyric, *Namo tassa Bhagavato rahato sammāsaṃbuddhassa*.[5]

The characteristics of the manuscripts made during better times before the Burmese conquest tell a significantly different story. In particular, notions about the relationship of monks and laypeople to manuscripts may at first glance be transformed when seen through the lens of these artifacts themselves. Whereas in the JKM there are only a few occasions of laypeople copying the Tipiṭaka, such as King Anuruddha and the officials known as Biṅgasenā, over 90 percent of the manuscripts that mention the name of the scribe identify him as either a monk or a novice. Furthermore, about half of the sponsors appear to have been monks. These bare facts should not, however, be regarded as negating the statements I have made, based on other sources, about the indifference to writing on the part of the general monastic population. The other literary and inscriptional sources cover a very wide range of social, religious, and political history, of which literate and manuscript culture is just a small part. The manuscript colophons, on the other hand, are concerned solely with details that have some bearing on the lives of the texts or their makers. Anyone engaged in making or sponsoring manuscripts would no doubt have felt that they were important. Thus the information in manuscript colophons is preselected for a literate bias. Statements found therein can not be considered random samples of general social attitudes towards writing, and we would surely be shocked to find a scribe confessing that he sees no point to his labors.

About half of the extant early manuscripts were sponsored by monks and the other half by laypeople of some means or by rulers with varying degrees of power. This does not indicate, of course, that half of all monks were interested in supporting manuscripts, but only that there was a group of religious, constituting an unknown proportion of all monks, that was involved in the making of half of these manuscripts. Furthermore, a large proportion of manuscripts sponsored by monks may have survived because fellow monks put more care into their maintenance.

MANUSCRIPT STORAGE

In the older monastic libraries the manuscripts are usually kept in boxes (*hip*) of up to a cubic meter in volume. These are often stacked and require a few people to lift the topmost box down to ground level if its contents or those of the one below it are to be accessed. Within the boxes there may be a number of manuscripts piled on top of one another, rendering it extremely difficult to access a particular manuscript.

These boxes are usually made from wood and may be painted, lacquered, or inlaid with depictions of the life of the Buddha or other religious themes, as well as with floral designs. In northern Thailand the attractive, highly ornamented boxes stand in marked distinction to the rather plain palm-leaf manuscripts that they contain, although the northern Thai boxes never reached the degree of ornamentation boasted by the lavish central Thai manuscript boxes.

Most extant boxes are from the nineteenth or twentieth centuries, and neither the Chiang Mai National Museum nor other northern museums possess any made before the end of the eighteenth century.[6] One might be tempted to blame this sad state of affairs on the excessive humidity and hungry rodents and insects of Thailand. However, as these boxes were specifically intended to protect the manuscripts, one would expect that they would be at least as durable as the manuscripts themselves. Had they been in common use since the early years of manuscript production in Thailand, at least some specimens would have survived from that era. There are manuscripts from the early sixteenth century in excellent condition, testifying that there is always a chance that a delicate artifact can escape the ravages of time. Should not an item designed to forestall these very forces have much greater chances of survival? Why, then, are there no *hip* that are more than two centuries old? The answer must be that *hip* were not generally employed until manuscripts came to be considered important enough to warrant such protective treatment.

European accounts of the region permit us to make some conjectures about the preservation of manuscripts before the earliest extant manuscript boxes. In their reports of life in Siam in the last two decades of the seventeenth century, the European travelers and diplomats Engelbertus Kaempfer, Nicolas Gervaise, and Simon de la Loubère mention the use of books and manuscripts in monasteries and at court several times, but they have little to say about monastic libraries or manuscript repositories. While these observations were made in the central region of Thailand, they are at least suggestive of what might have been the case a century earlier in the north. In his chapter on the pagodas of Siam, Gervaise (1989, Pt. 3: Chap. 10) identifies a variety of structures found within the monastery compound, including the monks' cells, meeting halls, image houses, and even lavatories, but he does not mention any libraries. In describing a monastery in Ayudhyā, Kaempfer notes a building with a floor that "was cover'd with heaps of large palm leaves, being the remains of their Pali, or religious Books, which when they grow old and worn out, are here laid aside in this manner, as in a sacred place" (1998, 58).

While a burial chamber for sacred texts was a well-known institution in the medieval Mediterranean world, largely in the form of the Jewish *genizah*, I have not heard of any such buildings in Thailand. I have, however, seen buildings in monastic compounds that I was told by the resident monks were "libraries" in which the manuscripts were lying in heaps on the floor covered with dust. When Louis Finot went to Luang Prabang in the early twentieth century, he, too, was struck by the disorganization of the monastic libraries (1917, 2). It is not impossible, then, that Kaempfer mistook a disorganized repository of manuscripts *in use* for a *genizah*-type building. Even if what he saw was a chamber for discarding leaves, one might expect them to be discarded in boxes of some sort in death if they were so kept in life, in order to avoid the ignoble fate of being consigned to the mercy of vermin and filth.

On the other hand, some colophons from Lan Na manuscripts *do* specifically tell us that boxes were being used in the mid-fifteenth century. For example, a *Dhammacakkaṭīkā* (MF 80.054.01E.031–041) from CS 923

(1562 CE) has the following colophon: "*Dhammacakkaṭīkā* sponsored by Dhammacinda who lives in the village of Rat Yuak. Made to be kept in a golden box in Tha Søi. Made in the year of the cock 923."

Von Hinüber points out that many manuscripts from Tha Søi,[7] from which many of the oldest manuscripts come, specifically say that they were made to be kept in a golden box:

> Moreover, four manuscripts can be attributed to a monastery in a quarter of Da Sqy called *pa hmai* "new woods": *kap pa hmai da sqy* or *kap hrid gam pa hmai*. The expression *hrid gam* "golden box," which is found in the following manuscripts with the exception of the *Vimanavatthu* commentary, evidently corresponds to *hid dharrm* "box for keeping the Tipitaka." Here it seems to be used in the same way as *ham pitak* "library" discussed earlier. At the same time it is typical for the *pa hmai* manuscripts. (von Hinüber 1990, 66)

Rather than upsetting the thesis that manuscripts were generally not kept in protective boxes before the Burmese conquest, von Hinüber's evidence may be the exception that proves the rule. It is surely not a mere coincidence that there are far more old manuscripts from this region than any other. Surely these very golden boxes must have favored the preservation of these manuscripts. As discussed in Chapter Three, there is also reason to believe, based on the nomenclature, that the *pa hmai* or "new forest" region was inhabited by *araññavāsī* monks from the new Sinhalese forest-dwelling lineage—precisely those monks that I have been arguing would have been most concerned about the preservation of manuscripts.

The manuscripts from Tha Søi also sometimes include references to libraries. For example, one of the oldest dated manuscripts found in northern Thailand so far, a *Milindapañha* (HH-04) from CS 857 (1495 CE), possesses a colophon with a reference to the library in which it was supposed to be kept: ". . . made for the scripture hall of Tha Søi." Tha Søi is an area, and not, insofar as we know, a monastery. It is unclear whether there was perhaps one library that all the monasteries in this area may have shared or whether there was just one monastery in the area at this time, so it did not have to be singled out by name. Since no monastery is named, it is possible that it was a new settlement at the time, with just one monastery (Hundius 1990, 66). If so, it is interesting that a library has already been built at this point. All of the earliest references in colophons to the fact that the text is supposed to be put in a library come from the Tha Søi region.

There is inscriptional evidence for the existence of libraries in the early sixteenth century in several areas, notably Phayao. In terms of institutional affiliation, it is very interesting that Wat Pa Mai, one of the early monasteries possessing a library according to these Phayao inscriptions, has the same name as a monastery in Tha Søi to which the largest number of early manuscripts trace their origins. Perhaps further research will lead to the location of Tha Søi within Phayao.

It is also relevant that the only reference to a *hip* that I came across in a nineteenth-century colophon comes from an *Ānisaṃsa* manuscript (MF 84.135.01I.039) that praises the writing down of the Dhamma. It states that the text was sponsored by various women with their children and grandchildren, who also made the box for it. In this case there is little doubt about the attitude of the makers towards writing, which furthers the thesis that the boxes go hand in hand with an exceptional degree of respect for the manuscripts.

One final curious point in connection with the care taken to preserve manuscripts is that it is not uncommon for colophons to state that the scribe wrote during the evening or the night. This was forbidden in European scriptoria because to do so required a lamp or candle flame, which could burn or otherwise damage the precious manuscripts. In Lan Na, such a restriction seems not to have been in place.

MONASTIC LIBRARIES

Unlike other aspects of manuscript culture, monastic libraries feature quite prominently in early inscriptions from Lan Na. One inscription from an unknown location in Chiang Rai (PSC, 4: item 87) includes the earliest reference to a library, one that was built in CS 850 (1488 CE). It says that fifteen families and 600,000 cowries worth of rice paddy fields were donated to a monastery in Chiang Sæn in honor of the king's mother and children, as well as teak wood with which to build a *vihāra* and library (*hø pidok*). An inscription from Wat Chiang Man in Chiang Mai that deals with the history of the monastery and the region in general up to CS 943 (1581 CE) also makes reference to a library (EHS, 716). It says that in CS 933 (1571 CE) the *wat* was rebuilt, including a *cetiya*, *vihāra*, *uposatha* hall, and a library. The term used for library is *pittakaghara*, which in Pali means "a house for the scriptures," certainly a reasonable appellation for such an edifice.

It is impossible to say what these early libraries looked like. They may have been small wooden buildings that were either raised on poles or on more substantial brick and stucco bases like the largely nineteenth-century examples that now dot the region. The various techniques of elevating the libraries, and sometimes even of surrounding the support poles with water, were attempts to prevent hungry insects and small animals from obtaining easy access to the delectable palm leaves upon which the texts were written.

Several early inscriptions that mention libraries occur in the region of Phayao, about fifty kilometers northeast of Chiang Mai. They date from the turn of the sixteenth century. In CS 858 (1496 CE) (LNI, Phayao 89) Mahāsāmī Sīlavisuddha built Wat Ban Pan, along with the *uposatha* hall and a library for the scriptures. An inscription (LNI, Phayao 8) dated CS 859 (1497 CE) says that when Wat Pa Mai was built by monks led by Mahāthera Madhurasa acting on behalf the governor Chao Lø Davasricula, the queen donated five families to the scripture hall (Face 1: ln.13), as well as other donations of twenty families to the Buddha image, five to the *uposatha* hall, and 200,000 cowries of rice each for the monastery and the Buddha. Another inscription, dated CS 865 (1503 CE) from Wat Ban Døn (LNI, Phayao 10), says that seven families were bought by the Mahāsāmī Ñāṇadevaguṇa for the monastery, and a total of 550 pieces of silver was spent on officials to oversee the library/scripture hall and 2,400 pieces of silver was procured in order to take care of a Buddha image and the scripture hall (Face 2: ln. 6), of which 700 went to the scripture hall.

An inscription dated CS 868 (1506 CE) from Wat Visuddhārāma in Phayao is now kept at the National Museum in Chiang Sæn (IHP, Lamphun 22). According to this inscription, a whole series of people were involved in the initiation of the project. The inscription begins, after the date, by saying that Mahāswāmī Srī Vimalabodhiñāṇa, who is the ruler (*adhipati*) of the Great Red Forest (Pa Dæng Luang), got the *mahāthera* Jayapāla Ratanapaññā to ask permission from the king Mahādharrmarājādhirāja to erect this inscription in the monastery to help the Buddhasāsanā last for 5,000 years (Face 1: ln. 3–7). A few lines later, it says that the ruler of Phayao took ten families to take care of the Tipiṭaka. At the end of the second face we are told that the monk Sinpraya paid 200 in silver for the people who were to protect the canonical texts as well as relatives of the monks, and none of it was to be used to do household or civic work but only to help protect the *mahāthera* and the canon as ordered. Several families are donated to take care of the library at Wat Sri Umong Kham between Phayao and Chiang Rai in an inscription dated CS 865 (1503 CE) (PSC, 4: item 105). At the end of this text it says that if any of the people who are supposed to protect the Buddha and the Piṭaka are not satisfied with this task, then the price of that person should be used to buy another to replace him.

Why are there so many references to libraries in early Phayao inscriptions in particular? Since these inscriptions all come from a short time span, it can be inferred that there were governors and important monks in Phayao at the time who were particularly interested in the written word. In assessing the attitudes towards any cultural materials, especially ones that involve relatively new technologies, one cannot overlook the predilections of individual agents who may, for various (often unknowable) reasons, have inclined towards some technologies rather than others. These particular rulers may have realized the many benefits both to themselves and to the religion of having a strong collection of physical manuscripts well protected in libraries. It is easy to see that some individuals may have wanted to build libraries to preserve manuscripts for posterity, for merit making purposes, and to unlink the success of the religion from the vagaries of monks' memories. The monks, for their part, may have been following the lead of the rulers but may also have had faith in the power and utility of written scriptures to ease their lot and strengthen the religion.

The ruler of Phayao at the time was known by the title Chao Si Mün. He was the successor to his close relative Yudhiṣthira, a learned king who lived just before the period of the inscriptions under consideration. Perhaps sensing strong local support, the king and queen of Chiang Mai, who were closely related to the ruler Chao Si Mün of Phayao, were also particularly active in the sponsoring and maintenance of libraries in Phayao. They can be identified as Bilakapanattu and his wife who feature prominently in the JKM as supporters of religious literature, as well as in other inscriptions from the Chiang Mai-Haripuñjaya area. There is a Pali inscription about Yudhiṣthira that may shed some light on the culture he tried to establish. This inscription, now kept at the National Museum in Bangkok (IHP, Krung Thep 93), was found on the base of a Buddha image at Wat Pa Dæng Luang Døn Chai Bun Nak in Phayao and is dated 1398 in the *mahāsakkarāja* (1476 CE).

> In the year of the monkey 1398, the month of māgha on the fifth day of the waxing moon, a Sunday, the highest nobleman, a tipiṭakadhara, the younger brother who rules[8] named Lord King Yudhiṣthira, who was a righteous king in the lineage of the great heroes, made this image of the perfect Buddha out of 14,000 units of gold for the purpose of (honoring) the most perfect Buddha.[9]

Of interest is the use of the term *tipiṭakadhara* to describe the king, for the term, of course, has different connotations when applied to monks. This king features in many inscriptions from Phayao and is generally regarded in them as being quite well versed in the Buddhist texts. By being extolled as endowed with this knowledge, which would have rivaled that of the best monks, the king is trying to make it known that he himself upholds the Dhamma, that he is not completely reliant upon the monks for this aspect of his legitimacy. Not only, then, was he aware of the political expediency of not leaving the Dhamma solely in the hands of monks, an awareness that would have made him quite receptive to written texts, but he also was likely concerned with the maintenance of the texts for religious reasons. No ruler would invest the time required to learn numerous texts by heart if he were not sure of the ultimate importance of keeping these texts alive. He would thus probably have cultivated an environment that encouraged the production of written scriptures for their utilitarian value.

There is another possibility that is highly pertinent to my hypothesis. If we look at the names of some of the monasteries and people involved, it appears that monks from the same new Sinhalese lineage of forest-dwellers that was centered at Wat Pa Dæng in Chiang Mai may have been prominent players in this particular arena. The name Wat Pa Mai, as I have said, means the "new forest monastery" and may very well indicate that it was connected to this monastic lineage. An even stronger argument may be made in the case of the inscription from Wat Visuddhārāma (IHP, Lamphun 22) in which the monastery, which has a library, is connected to Mahāswāmī Srī Vimalabodhiñāṇa of the Great Red Forest (Pa Dæng Luang). This monastery must surely have been affiliated with the Red Forest Monastery of Chiang Mai. Thus it is likely that half of the monasteries in this region at this time with libraries were influenced by the scholastic and literate inclinations of the monks who had gone to Sri Lanka about seventy-five years earlier to be reordained into what they felt was a more orthodox form of the religion. Furthermore, the JKM records that King Yudhiṣthira removed the important Sāvatthī Sandalwood Buddha image from one monastery and had it placed instead in Wat Pa Dæng Luang (Epochs, 179–180), an act that suggests the king chiefly supported this monastery and hence the Sinhalese lineage.

There is also a particularly strong statement about the queen's attitudes towards writing in an inscription from Wat Phra Kham in Phayao (IHP, Lamphun 10). On face 3, lines 15–20, it is recorded that the order was given for a *paṇḍita* to compose a pleasing text that was to be inscribed onto the stone *sīmā* markers in order to establish the text firmly at the monastery for 5,000 years until the end of the religion. Although it is implicit in the very act of carving words into stone, the sentiment that an inscription on stone will exist far into the future does not often appear in the actual inscriptions themselves. This points, therefore, to the possibility that those responsible for this particular inscription were consciously aware of the particular advantages of writing in a stable medium, and this in turn may help to explain the number of libraries mentioned in other contemporary inscriptions.

Libraries, then, are incontrovertible evidence not only for the existence of a manuscript culture, but also of an accompanying climate of respect for these texts. The word for library in all the epigraphy seen so far involves the word *piṭaka* in some way. Thus although the libraries may have contained texts other than the canonical scriptures, the scriptures were viewed as being the libraries' raison d'être. One wonders if such structures would have been built to house only nonreligious works, or if, indeed, the term for library necessarily has anything to do with its contents. In general, we are not told anything about the specific manuscripts housed in these libraries. What texts were they? Were they really, as the term for library implies, Pali canonical texts?

An inscription from Chiang Rai (LNI, Chiang Rai 37) might have offered some answers to the above questions, but it is unfortunately very fragmentary and undated. Judging by the orthography, the editors of LNI attribute it to the mid-sixteenth to seventeenth centuries (21–23 BE), sometime after the Burmese conquest. It seems to list some Pali texts accompanied by some numbers, but there is no indication as to the meaning of this list. It may refer to the contents of a library, with the numbers representing either the number of copies of that text in the library, or possibly the number of fascicles comprising each text, or even the divisions within the texts themselves.

I am not aware of any other similar inscriptions in northern Thailand. However, a number of library inscriptions in Burma catalog the contents of the building and look very much like this inscription. One such inscription from 1442 CE says that the king of Taungdwin and his wife, a sister of Kyocvā, the former king of Ava, commenced the building of a monastery at Pagan. The king's wife obtained the money to copy the Tipiṭaka and ancillary texts by selling her hair (Luce and Tin 1976, 214). The inscription ends with a long and detailed list of the books copied, as well as their cost and the names of scribes. The titles are laid out in a manner similar to that of the inscription at Chiang Rai, except that the Burmese list is much more extensive, with close to three hundred titles, including canonical, commentarial, grammatical, medical, and astrological works. This represents a very substantial collection for that time and was specifically intended for the use of monks. Standing in marked contrast to the evidence in Thailand, the doners' desire to make merit does not feature in the inscription (although it was surely a consideration in the initiation of such a project), but instead the utility of the texts for the monks is highlighted. In fact, the Chiang Rai inscription, which was produced during Burmese suzerainty, may have been influenced by Burmese archival practices.

We can see, then, that while libraries were certainly built and utilized from as early as the mid-fifteenth century, it is difficult to ascertain exactly how the monks and rulers would have known what texts were being kept in the building. Perhaps the monastic custodians or those persons deeded to the monasteries to take care of the libraries kept written or memorized records of their contents. But as we will see, exploring the interiors of the small library structures still extant does not clarify matters.

JUDGING A BOOK BY ITS COVER

Once one gets access to the libraries and then past the unwieldy manuscript boxes, other obstacles still come between the user and the manuscript itself. The palm leaves are generally sandwiched between two protective wooden boards called *mai prakap*. Unfortunately for the researcher, these boards also cover the title page, but often do not bear the titles themselves, necessitating the process of untying and removing them in order to be able to see the title of the text.[10] These boards are usually made from teak, a very durable and water-resistant wood, and may be lavishly embellished with lacquer or gold leaf and traditional Thai designs or coated in simple red lacquer.[11] Sometimes a cloth has been wrapped around the boards for further protection. This suggests that the manuscripts in question were not intended to be available for easy reference in the way that books in a modern library are; rather, keeping them safe seems to have been foremost in the minds of their guardians. One aim of the ongoing cataloging project at the SRI is to affix plastic tags with the catalog number and title of each text for easy identification. Such an endeavor demonstrates a modern approach to manuscripts as sources of important and necessary textual information that should be carefully ordered and stored for easy reference—an approach that contrasts sharply with the intentions of premodern manuscript custodians.[12]

A number of later manuscripts have wooden title markers known as *mai lap*. Like the modern tags, *mai lap* help to overcome some of the problems just mentioned, but they are not seen in connection with any manuscripts from the Golden Age. Von Hinüber has, however, seen an old manuscript of

Saṃyuttanikāya (1996a, 43) with what can only be described as a table of contents on the cover leaf, saying that "the first chapter called *Naḷavagga* ends on folio *ki*."

There can be little doubt that early premodern texts were employed very differently from modern, systematically archived texts. The lack of an efficient retrieval system accords with the idea that many manuscripts during the Golden Age served a largely iconic function as a symbol rather than a source of the Dhamma. Those manuscripts in circulation for discursive purposes must have been separated somehow from the confusing mass of manuscripts in storage.

Once a manuscript has been found, the protective boards removed, and the title identified, the next problem is to ascertain whether the leaves are in order. The fascicles are held together by a string that is usually fed through one of two holes that are found a few centimeters from either end of each leaf, but this string has more often than not been broken or rotted away since the manuscript was first composed. It is not uncommon to find fascicles with leaves strung out of order or with no string at all. Of course, if the manuscript was made primarily to make merit and kept by custodians with a low level of literacy at the bottom of a box as an iconic representation of the Dhamma, then the order of the pages would not make much difference. On the other hand, nonsequential pages could also be the result of usage so heavy that the binding strings keep breaking and the leaves, when hastily restrung in preparation for the next ceremony or study session, keep getting mixed up.

ORNAMENTATION AND MARGINALIA

Northern Thai palm-leaf manuscripts are devoid of ornament or illumination, save for a small flourish, called a *gomūtra*, sometimes found at the beginning or end of sections. There is a substantial difference between these and some of the manuscripts found in neighboring Burma. The most ornate Southeast Asian manuscripts are the Burmese Kammavācā ordination texts, which are usually painted with cinnabar and gilded with gold or silver and then written upon in a rich black ink or lacquer.[13] Even in the case of these richly decorated texts, the earliest examples from the fourteenth century have only the text and no marginalia, but by the seventeenth century a number of exquisite patterns had emerged which characterized Kammavācā ornamentation (Singer 1993, 98–99). Moreover, because of the extensive gilding, these texts have tended to last a lot longer than the raw palm-leaf manuscripts.

A clear trend towards greater ornamentation is discernable in Burmese manuscripts over time. In the nineteenth century, brass and copper sometimes replaced leaves as the material out of which the pages were made (Singer 1993, 102). The covers and margins, too, became increasingly more decorative and must have been of significant cost to the patrons. The situation in Lan Na is quite different. Although the written word does seem to have increased in importance in northern Thailand after the Burmese period, there is no sign of this in the physical appearance of the Pali palm-leaf manuscripts that I have seen. Minute orthographical variations aside, a palm-leaf text from 1900 CE could easily have been written in 1500 and vice versa. The folding paper books (*samut khoi*), especially those from central Thailand, are far more likely than palm-leaf manuscripts to bear illustrations and other ornamental designs.[14] Interestingly, even after these paper books came into general use in Lan Na in the nineteenth century, they were very rarely used for Pali texts. No doubt the *samut khoi* were far more illustrated than palm leaves partly because of their larger size, which created a much more welcoming surface area for these additions. However, we must not let utilitarian considerations overshadow the ideological elements implicit in the division of labor among the different writing materials employed in Lan Na. There is a marked note of conservatism in the Pali palm-leaf manuscripts that suggests that the northern Thai literary community wished to preserve their traditions from any outside influence. Indeed, except for very minor transformations, the script has remained the same for over five hundred years. A person trained to read the script from a twentieth-century manuscript would be able to read the earliest examples available.

Perhaps illustration and illumination were viewed as a Burmese or other foreign incursion into Thai literary space. This might be tolerated in non-sacred texts, but not in manuscripts containing what the Lan Na people believed were the Pali texts redacted at the eighth council convened under the great king Tilaka. Noncanonical texts, if written in Pali, might have been kept without illustration by extension. The degree to which conservative attitudes have influenced the approach towards different media in the realm of religion in Thailand is illustrated by a story related in the writings of Prince Wachirayan, who was the patriarch of the reformist Thammayut order during the reign of Chulalongkorn. In his travels to outlying areas in 1899, he noted that monks were not reading printed books that were being distributed by the government because they believed that this form of communication was inextricably linked with Christianity (Jory 2000, 365). There was a simple equation in their minds of palm leaf with Buddhism and print with Christianity, to which we might add that in the north the equation included "unillustrated" as a qualifier for "palm leaf." The question remains, however, as to why the early Lan Na manuscripts from the Golden Age that set this trend were devoid of illustration or any other significant ornament. Does this reflect a low regard for written texts themselves? Were they not viewed as items of cultural, artistic, and spiritual value in and of themselves—items to be beautified and extolled? While a lack of beautifying ornamentation alone could reflect utilitarian concerns and does not necessarily indicate ambivalence toward an object, when coupled with the unimpressive chirography seen in so many examples, it is highly suggestive that written texts did not have the highest cultural value. In the Thai world, as in much of Asia, the ornamental beauty of an object is, in fact, very much a sign of its importance. Other cultic or cultural items are not similarly unadorned (Ginsburg 1989, 96–100); on the contrary, they are usually quite lavishly decorated. But perhaps the writing is so beautiful that there was no need for further ornamentation?

The Lan Na Dhamma script itself has an elegance that emerges through its well-rounded characters, but quite unlike Chinese or Arabic writing, the Lan Na script does not possess a true, self-conscious calligraphic tradition (Ginsburg 1989, 10). There is no appreciable difference between what can be described as a foundation script[15] and the fully developed hand that an expert scribe might employ. I was struck in many cases by the poor quality of some of the handwriting, which often consists of shaky lines and ill-formed ligatures as well as unevenly sized characters. The general impression one gets upon viewing northern Thai manuscripts is one of surprising carelessness and inattention to the potential beauty of the script itself. This is highlighted further when one compares these texts with medieval chirographic Buddhist texts from Bengal (Pal 1988, 85), Nepal (Pal 1988, 104), and Tibet (Pal 1988, 156), as well as Christian texts from Europe (Camille 1992, 34).

A further surprising finding was that far from being lavishly appointed, leaves that had previously been used for one text have sometimes been recycled. The recto of the first leaf of a *Dhammapada Gāthā* (SRI 19-04-039-00) contains some lines from another text: "*bhaso asattaṃ sugataṃ buddhaṃ tamahaṃ brūmi brāhmaṇaṃ yassa gati na jānanti devā gandhabbā mānusā khīṇāsavaṃ*," and the last page of a vernacular northern Thai text has some lines in Pali: "*ekam samayaṃ bhagavā sāvatthiyaṃ viharati*." The apparent willingness to use discarded leaves from one text for another even though these leaves were fairly plentiful (they literally grow on trees) suggests that aesthetic considerations and notions of purity were of secondary importance in the making of these manuscripts. The use of discarded leaves from a Pali canonical text for a vernacular text also suggests that texts were not subject to a strict triage by which resources would be directed towards Pali texts before vernacular ones.[16] Both of these examples are from the nineteenth century, but there is little reason to believe that such recycling would not have occurred during the Golden Age as well.

The marginal markings that I have encountered in northern Thai manuscripts have been limited to the title and perhaps date of a work written on the side margins of some leaves. There are also numerous interlinear corrections that are most often written in ink or lacquer, but are also incised into the leaves just like the main text. What are completely absent are any marginal comments by readers to note their own thoughts about the text, such as are evident, to pick just one of many possible examples, in a copy of Aristotle's *Physics* from the thirteenth century (Camille 1992, 23). Thus what Martin has said about Renaissance European readers, that "the literati often read with pen in hand and became their own glossators, sprinkling the margins of the works they read with annotations" (1994, 362), cannot be said of contemporaneous Thai readers. Nor is there any verbal or pictorial evidence in the margins of differing points of view, as is often found in medieval European manuscripts. Margins, as Michael Camille has so eloquently argued, offered a space for parodying, subverting, and questioning texts that led to an "irreverent explosion of marginal mayhem" (1992, 22). Such "images on the edge," a sure sign of a lively engagement with the texts, are not seen in any of the Pali manuscripts that I have examined.

It may be, however, that ideas, comments, and notes that might otherwise have found their way onto margins were recorded in the Nissayas, the oldest written vernacular texts that we have, with some dating to the sixteenth century. These texts developed over the years as resources for supporting the study and preaching of Pali texts. They consist of disjointed grammatical and doctrinal explorations of Pali pericopes lifted from various sources.[17] "*Nissaya*s," says McDaniel, "do not read like sermons, stories or instructions. They are supports for those who have to read and explain Pāli texts to an audience" (2003, 377).

These idiosyncratic compositions were not supposed to stand alone but rather were intended to help explain Pali texts to the monks and make it easier for them to deliver their message to the faithful. In this sense they function very much like the marginalia of European texts, recording thoughts about this or that passage, emphasizing words or phrases deemed to be of particular importance, and glossing difficult words to remind the reader of their meaning for next time. Perhaps, then, the work of the margins was done by these little-studied texts.

THE COPYING PROCESS

We can learn something of the copying process from information in the margins and in colophons. The first, basic question is whether scribes in the Golden Age were copying texts from other manuscripts laid out before them or whether they were writing down texts that they or others had memorized. It is important to keep in mind that an oral tradition was still alive well into the fifteenth century. I have also already pointed out that the Lan Na manuscript tradition did not commence until shortly before the date of the oldest extant manuscripts, that is to say, the middle of the fifteenth century. This raises the question, therefore, of the nature of the sources for these first-generation manuscripts. Were they made from Mon, Burmese, Sinhalese, or other exemplars, or were they composed from memory?

Let us explore this last possibility for the moment. We are fortunate to have examples of Pali texts that were, it seems, produced from memory, and these can help us to conceive of what written texts might look like if they were based on oral sources. I refer here to a group of early inscriptions known as "heart-letter verses" (*khatha huachai*), found quite frequently on images and plaques in Thailand. One example is a Pali inscription from Chiang Rai (LNI, Chiang Rai 11) that was found on a Buddha image at Wat Døn Yang. It dates the installation of the image to 2024 BE (1480 CE) and includes the following passage in Pali:

> *Pathamaṃ sakalakkhaṇamekapadaṃ dutiyādipadassa nidassanato samanī dunimā samadu sanidu vibhujje kamatopathamena vinā*
>
> The first word contains the marks of the first (noble truth). There is a division of the others showing (the noble truths) in terms of *samanī dunimā samadu sanidu* without the first term accordingly.

We can see here the chief characteristic of these "heart-letter verses," namely, that the first letters of key terms are strung together in various ways to form easily recalled, short phrases. Each of the four words *samanī*, *dunimā*, *samadu*, and *sanidu* contains syllables from three of the Four Noble Truths. So, for example, *samanī* has the ***sa*** of *samudaya,* (the origin of suffering), the ***ma*** of *magga* (the eightfold path leading to nirvana), and the ***ni*** of *nirodha* (the cessation of desire leads to the cessation of suffering), and *samadu* encapsulates ***sa****mudaya,* ***ma****gga,* and ***du****kkha* (existence involves suffering).[18]

Other such heart-letter verses include an encapsulation of the Abhidhamma that takes the form *cicerūni (**ci**tta, **ce**tasike, **rū**pa, **ni**bbāna)*, and the Vinaya is found as *āpāmacupa (**Ā**dikammika, **Pā**rājika, **Ma**hākhandaka, **Cu**lakhandaka, **Pa**rivāravagga)* (Penth 1997b, 496). The premise underlying these texts is that the benefits of reciting even the abbreviated titles of longer central Buddhist texts produces merit similar to having read or heard the entire text.

Some oral features of these inscriptions emerge through an analysis of similar heart-letter verses. On the pedestal of a Buddha image from Wat Kesa Sri, which Griswold believes is a product of the early sixteenth century,[19] is a verse written in Sinhalese characters that is the only example of this script in use for an inscription in northern Thailand (Penth 1997b, 499):[20] "*Paṭhamaṃ sakalakkhaṇamekapadaṃ dutiyādipadassa nidassanato samani dunimā samudū sanidū vibhije kamato paṭhamena vinā.*"

There are a few vowels that differ between this and the version from Wat Døn Yang, although they clearly are supposed to be the same text. Penth's directory of inscribed Buddha images from Chiang Mai (1976) includes five further items with heart-letter verses, all of which are from the last half of the fifteenth century, save one, number 19, from 1519 CE. They, too, differ in small ways from each other and from the two already presented. What appears in Penth's list as item no. 1 is: "*Paṭhamam sakalakkhaṇamekapadaṃ dutiyādipadassanidassanato samanī dunimā samadū sanidū vibhājekamato paṭhamena vinā.*"

Although item no. 6 is identical to the above text, items no. 3 and no. 19 differ from item no.1 in commencing with *padamasakalakkhaṇam*. Item no. 5 is completely devoid of any of the nasal *m*'s called *anuśvāra*s and includes a long *ū* in the second heart-letter word "*dūnimā.*" Thus of the six heart-letter verses examined above, only two are identical, while the rest contain orthographical differences such as the replacement of *ṭha* with *tha* or even *da*, varying vowel lengths, and even different vowels.

There is little doubt that this type of inscription is intimately tied up with oral transmission. Not only is the text clearly intended as a mnemonic device, but many of the earliest dated images include such a verse, while few are found on later images, when the impact of writing had become more strongly felt in the region. This leaves one wondering whether the discrepancies can be attributed to the oral aspects of these texts. Originally they were probably memorized by monks and even laypeople in lieu of memorizing the full text of the Noble Truths, the Vinaya, or whatever is represented by the heart-letters. When the sponsor had an image made, he or she (there is evidence of images with heart-letter verses being made by male and female laypeople as well as monks) may have wished to enrich the item with the power of these verses that they had remembered. Then, when actually inscribing it, either the scribe or the person dictating was unsure of exactly how to spell some of the words. It is easy to see why vowel lengths and similar sounding letters might get confused in such a situation. These are precisely the linguistic features that are most easily misconstrued in an oral context. When listening to the recitation of a text without the benefit of a written text to follow, it is often difficult to differentiate between such things as vowel lengths or voiced and unvoiced consonants.

These types of mistakes can also be seen, for example, in a 1339 CE inscription from Phræ that is the second-oldest inscription in a Tai language.[21] It commemorates the making of 11,108 clay votive tablets stamped with an image of the Buddha and begins with the following Pali dedicatory passage:

> *Vanndetamanujaṅṅ s...mahannaṭaṅrattanattaya (yaṃ pava) kkkhāmi mahādānaṅṅ sunātha (sādha)vo* (EHS, 772).
>
> I honor the great Three Jewels. I will explain this great donation so listen well.

The spelling here is quite irregular and suggests that the Pali in this region at this point was mostly known from oral, not written sources. The errors are not those that one would expect from a written culture, whereas inaccuracies such as the replacing of *ṃ* with *ṅ* are easily explainable in an oral context because of the high degree of phonological resemblance. Furthermore, the number of errors is far greater in these inscriptions than in later manuscripts based on written sources.

While mnemonic devices were employed to remind people of Buddhist ideas, most older manuscripts available to us were still copied based on written sources. A *Saddanīti* from CS 953 (1591 CE) examined by Hundius (HH-12) has a colophon on the verso right margin of fascicle 40 that sheds light on the copying process a few generations later: "The above text was written in the year CS 855."

This tells us that the current copy was executed based on another copy that was made in CS 855, corresponding to 1493 CE. This is the only old manuscript that I know of that says that another manuscript was followed, although there are some more recent texts that speak of an exemplar being used. A nineteenth-century *Cakkavāḷadīpanī* (HH-15) includes a note on the back of the first leaf of fascicle 2 saying that the text was made following the original. A *Cāmadevīvaṃsa* (HH-17) manuscript from the same sponsor has the same declaration written on the cover of the first fascicle (Hundius 1990, 102).

It is unfortunate that we do not know how scribes went about procuring the exemplars from which new copies were made. In the case of medieval Europe, letters were sent from one abbey to another requesting books to be sent to serve as exemplars, and in the thirteenth century early universities began renting out texts in their libraries as exemplars (de Hamel 1992, 35). There are no similar records pertaining to Thailand, but based on the varied provenance of the manuscripts in each library, a lively trade was taking place for this purpose. In cases where numerous copies of the same text are found, it is quite possible that this is a result of some difficulty in obtaining other exemplars. It may have been felt that it was better to make merit by recopying superfluous texts than by doing no scribal work at all.

All this is not to say, however, that memory and oral recitation did not still play a role in the copying process as well as in the communication of texts to the faithful. McDaniel's study of Nissayas has revealed instances where the verses that are quoted and commented upon are hosts to various mistakes. One study of two similar manuscripts suggests to him that

> the source text may not have been present and both authors were merely discussing grammar rules based on Kaccāyana without consulting or relying on the source text. The haphazard, commonly misspelled, and indirect reference to verses from Kaccāyana by both authors suggests the author was drawing from memory rather than examining an actual copy of the source text. (McDaniel 2003, 192)

McDaniel continues with more observations that point to the high degree of oral communication involved in their composition and transmission. While texts of the Nissaya genre existed in an environment more strongly marked by oral features, these observations about orality certainly have some purchase in the world of Pali texts as well. One of the most striking elements in the Nissaya texts is the complete lack of any standardized orthography, which applies not only to vernacular words, but also to Pali words. McDaniel brings up as an example the word *puggala* (person), which he has seen spelled *pugalā, puggala,* and *pugla* in the same manuscript (2003, 333). No doubt *pugalla* lurks somewhere in those leaves as well. He concludes:

> This shows that 1) there was no overarching authority in place which determined what was the proper spelling of different words; 2) that scribes were poorly trained in both vernacular and classical composition; 3) that spelling was phonologically determined and scribes wrote texts that were dictated to them and changed the spelling of words based on what they heard rather than having a standardized way of spelling any individual word. (333)

How long did it take to copy a manuscript? It seems to have taken the monk Javanapañña about seven months to complete a sixteen-fascicle *Suttasaṅgaha* in the mid-sixteenth century, judging by the dates mentioned in the colophons (von Hinüber 1990, 62). The long time taken to complete this manuscript suggests that scribal duties were commonly relegated to a small part of a monk's day. A similar situation is reflected in a commentary to the *Yamaka* (SRI 04–091–06), where the colophon says, "I wrote it little by little with effort in three years" (von Hinüber 1990, 63).

The eight extant fascicles of another *Suttasaṅgaha* (SRI 19–04–008) from CS 1174 (1812 CE) shed more light on the chronology of the making of a manuscript. It took each scribe on average thirteen days to write out each twenty-four-leaf fascicle, resulting in an average output of about two leaves per day—a very small amount, representing perhaps an hour of work. Interestingly, if one scribe were to work on the manuscript at this rate, a complete sixteen-fascicle version of the text would be completed in about eight months—so Javanapañña's productivity 250 years earlier was almost exactly the same.

The above examples suggest that scribal duties were just one part of the many obligations of monks and novices at monasteries in northern Thailand from the Golden Age onwards. They did not constitute a professional class whose sole responsibility was copying manuscripts, but rather spent a few hours each day copying, interspersed among other monastic duties. I have found no suggestion that there were any equivalents in Lan Na to the medieval European scriptoria, in which legions of full-time scribes would spend six or more hours of the day copying manuscripts.[22]

Scribal work was not only part time, but seasonal as well. The dates found in manuscript colophons demonstrate that the work was carried out mostly during the rainy season. The vast majority of dated manuscripts were completed in months nine, ten, eleven, and twelve. The rains retreat (*vassa*), during which monks are not allowed to travel beyond the monastery, usually commences during the tenth month and lasts through the twelfth (Doré and Premchit 1991, 169). The rains themselves sometimes begin early, hence the common appearance of manuscripts made in the ninth month as well. This is an ideal time for the monks to engage in copying work, and thus it is not surprising that most manuscripts were made during this period.

As it happens, manuscripts generally have fewer mistakes and variants than one might expect based on their physical appearance, which, as I have said, sometimes gives the impression of carelessness. What is more, monks seem to have corrected mistakes if they noticed them. One scribe gives us a clue as to how manuscripts were corrected: "Don't correct by using a stylus, but if you want to correct, then correct by using red lacquer and ink" (*Papañcasūdanī* SRI 04–083, cited in von Hinüber 1990, 62).

These kinds of corrections, including the use of a stylus, are indeed seen in extant manuscripts. A *Cakkavāḷadīpanī* (SRI 07–04–24–00) written in the sixteenth century (only eighteen years after the original text was composed by Sirimaṅgala) has corrections both in ink, such as on leaf 19, and inscribed, as on leaf 75. The inscribed corrections seem to be in a hand other than that of the original copyist. A *Pācittiya* from 1560 CE (SRI 07–04–007) and a *Sagāthavagga* from 1602 CE (MF 81.095.01E.055–057) also include both inked and inscribed corrections; a *Visuddhimagga* from 1597 CE (SRI 19–04–32–00) and a *Sammohavinodanī* from 1612 CE (SRI 19–04–31–00) have inked corrections. There are many different ways mistakes are marked, but they usually involve some combination of crossing out wrong letters and writing in new ones above or near the place where they ought to be. Often an *x* marks the spot where the additions should be.

The colophons themselves are not without mistakes. The colophon of an *Aṭṭhakathā Mātikā* from CS 933 (1571 CE) says that the writer hopes to reach *nibbāna* in the presence of Metteyya, spelled Mekteyya. In fact, the frequency of mistakes in many of the vernacular colophons, and in the short Pali phrases found in them, is often greater than in the main text. This is not surprising because the manuscripts were often being copied from exemplars located before the copyist's eyes, whereas the colophons were probably written directly by the copyist from his head. Thus his personal—and often flawed—knowledge of Thai or Pali spelling would have been engaged. These scribes would appear to fall into the class described by Petrucci in reference to medieval Italy as "semiliterates." In arguing for a wide range of reading and writing abilities among medieval European producers of texts, Petrucci suggests that many may have had a low degree of familiarity with reading and writing as integral aspects of discursive culture (1995, 77). He points out that while it seems self-evident that scribes must be literate, the truth is that they can be placed along a very wide spectrum of reading and writing ability, from the merest capacity to imitate the curves and lines of the script of the exemplar, to the ability to produce and understand exquisite texts in many different styles and letters (1995, 78).

The colophons are not necessarily written in the same hand as the text itself. Von Hinüber points out that in the sixteenth century Javanapañña wrote the colophons for some manuscripts that he himself did not copy (1990, 64). Perhaps he had supervised their production. The situation is no different for many of the manuscripts that I saw from later centuries. This gives further support to the possibility that the copyists in these cases were just that—*copy*ists. They may have been trained only to copy and did not have the ability to produce novel text of their own, thus necessitating a more learned hand to produce the colophons.

It is instructive to compare this state of affairs to that of Burma. A story found in the SV of a man wishing to write a book reveals some very different expectations with respect to a scribe.

> Formerly they say in Arimaddana the religion flourished on the strength of learning, memorization, and the like. And in that very city of Arimaddana a monk who had renounced as an old man, who wished to write a book with a stone-writing stick entered the royal residence. The king asked, "Why have you come?" "I have come wishing to write a book with my stone-writing stick." The king said, "Well then, you are an old man and though studying a text with great energy I do not see the possibility of attaining skill in the texts. But if a club having yielded a sprout could grow, if this were so you could attain skill in the texts." After that, going to a monastery, the old man took up writing only what could be measured by a single tooth-stick each day, and making the *Kaccāyana* and *Abhidhammatthasaṃgaha* and other books, he learned them in the presence of his teacher (SV, 77).

When the monk returns to the king to announce that he has attained skill in the texts, the king does not look at examples of his writing, but rather sends him to other monks who question him on his knowledge of the contents of the texts and in particular on grammar. This suggests that the scribal arts were ideally not considered to be independent of an analytical knowledge of the text that one was copying. In this case the scribe was expected to have an intimate knowledge of the text being copied, and was not supposed to blindly mimic what was before him, as often seems to have been the case in Lan Na.[23]

MANUSCRIPT SPONSORSHIP

Who was sponsoring these manuscripts? Is there a discernable difference between the attitudes of various sectors of society towards these items that is reflected in their financial or institutional sponsorship? We would be in a better position to answer these questions if it were not so difficult to penetrate the meaning of the various terms related to the sponsorship of the manuscripts. As von Hinüber laments, "the exact function of an *upatthambhaka* occurring frequently in the colophons is not clear. Nor is it obvious, whether or not *upatthambhaka* designates the same function called *mula* (*saddha*)" (1990, 71). Thankfully, it is at least clear that one important designation, the "maker" of the manuscript (*phu sang*), refers to the sponsor or donor and not to the person who physically made it, namely, the scribe (*phu khian*), because a number of texts speak of a maker as well as a scribe and differentiate between the two.[24]

One of the most general terms for a person involved in the making of manuscripts is *saddhā*, which in Pali means "faith." The etymology of the term suggests that it refers to a person who has faith in the teachings of the Buddha and therefore is driven to produce the manuscript. *Mūlasaddhā* likely denotes the person who is the primary or perhaps the initial sponsor, who either paid or did the most for the project, or who initiated it. Colophons such as the following distinguish this role from that of the scribe proper:

> The chief sponsor (*mūlasaddhā*) was Mahā Kesalavaṃsa from Wat Bandhanamdi in Chiang Mai. He was only the initiator (*ri rang*) who hired someone to write (*khian*) the Nissaya text called the *Ākhyāta* in order to support the teachings of the Buddha. (*Ākhyāta*, CS 1178 (1816 CE), SRI 19–16–009–00, fascicle 3)

Another term, *khlao,* seems to indicate specifically the initiator of the project—the person whose idea it was to make the manuscripts in the first place. A *Cakkavāḷadīpanī* from 1833 (HH-15) says that Kañcana Araññavāsī was the *khlao*, and we are told in more detail in inscriptions that, desiring to have texts copied, it was this monk who went to the king and convinced him to finance the project (Pavie 1898, 367–369). The *khlao* must be similar to the *ādikammasādhaka* whose activities are described in a 1551 CE *Buddhavaṃsa* colophon cited by von Hinüber: "He persuaded many people who want to make merit . . ." (1996a, 55).

I should say here a word about the very idea of monks as donors and initiators. As Schopen (1997, 3–4) has so thoroughly documented, it has been commonly assumed, based on the extant versions of the Vinaya, that monks did not carry or handle money. For example,

> Bühler, in discussing the second or first century B.C.E. donative inscriptions from Sañcī, said: "Proceeding to the inscriptions which mention donations made by monks and nuns, the first point, which must strike every reader, is their great number. . . . As the Buddhist ascetics could not possess any property, they must have obtained by begging the money required for making the rails and pillars. . . ." (1997, 3)

But Schopen then goes on to point out that not only are there many inscriptions that list monks and nuns as donors of caves, implements, and images, but even in the Vinaya itself, the possession of property is listed only as a "minor offense" (1997, 4). Thus, legally or not, monks and nuns have certainly possessed property from the earliest times and have continued to do so throughout the ages, as their appearance in lists of donors in late nineteenth-century manuscripts that I have looked at confirms.

A similar problem relates to the position of monks as initiators of a project and providers of institutional but not monetary support. There is a general tenet that a monk should not directly request what he needs. Craig Reynolds points out that even though many monks in Thailand realized that the canon as it stood at the end of the eighteenth century was imperfect, a council to edit the texts had to officially be convened by King Rama because the monks were not supposed to initiate such things (1979, 102–103). Nevertheless, like the bending of the rules that occurred in the case of property ownership, there was, it seems, a willingness on the part of some monks in Lan Na to overlook the breaking of certain principles in the service of such unselfish goals as spreading and preserving the Dhamma.

Manuscripts were often the fruit of joint endeavors between monastic and lay sponsors, known as "internal" (*bai nai*) and "external" (*bai nøk*) sponsors respectively. For example, a sixteenth-century copy of the learned grammatical text *Saddanīti* (HH- 12) was sponsored by at least three different people. The first group of fascicles was supported by the child of the laywoman Nang Khao Sri and the second group by the abbot Candamūli. Fascicle 33 was sponsored by the monk Mahā Vajirapaññu. This was a well-coordinated project and the various sponsors must have been kept informed of the progress of the writing, yet it is unclear how they actually decided who would sponsor which fascicle.

After examining the sponsorship information in a number of colophons, I have found no statistically significant difference between the number of manuscripts sponsored by monks and nonmonks until the decline of Lan Na cultural production under the Burmese, nor do these ratios change when looking at manuscripts from after the reconstruction. Both periods are characterized, based on the colophon data alone, by a roughly equal division between manuscripts sponsored by laypeople and monks. These findings do not necessarily negate earlier ones in which I suggested that many monastic groups were ambivalent towards the making of manuscripts. First of all, these samples are not large enough to make precise claims, and furthermore the very fact that they have survived hundreds of years through the efforts of concerned monks already suggests that examples donated by monks might be overrepresented. There are, however, strong indications, already presented, that a very large proportion of monastically supported manuscripts were prepared at the behest of *araññavāsī* monks.

THE MANUSCRIPT ECONOMY

We are fortunately able to get some idea of the pecuniary remuneration provided to scribes for their efforts and can therefore compare this with the money spent on building and maintaining other religious objects. The currency system of Thailand remained remarkably stable over the centuries, so it is possible to get a sense of both the absolute and relative costs of various items and projects. Below is a list of the Asian currencies mentioned in this section, along with what is known about their value.

Exact values:[25]

1 *bat* = 4 *salüng* = 8 *füang* = 8 *bi*

Approximate values:

1 *bat* = 9 *ngoen* = 5000 *bia*, also known as cowries
1 *thæp* = 7 *füang* or 3.5 *salüng*
1 Siamese *bat* = 1 Burmese *tical*
1 Ceylonese *kahāpana* > 1 *bat*

Von Hinüber has found several old colophons that mention scribal remuneration and in some cases the outlay for materials as well. For example, a manuscript of the *Mahāpaṇṇāsa* and its commentary donated to Wat Srī Un at Tha Søi and now kept at Wat Lai Hin (SRI 04–20) bearing a date of CS 911 (1549 CE) cost 350 *ngoen* (von Hinüber 1990, 72). Von Hinüber calculates that the whole text probably consisted of about seventy fascicles,[26] and therefore each fascicle would have cost five *ngoen*. Similar findings in other colophons have led von Hinüber to conclude that prices at the time for making a fascicle hovered around four or five *ngoen*, or 2200–3000 cowries, or about half of a *bat* (1990, 72–74).

What do these figures mean? Some practical insight into the economy of the time can be gained by looking at European accounts of central Thailand, which, although not ideal, shed light on what may have been the situation in the north. In 1688 CE, the French diplomat Nicolas Gervaise wrote that when monks in Ayudhyā chant for three evenings at funerals, they are usually each given three *bat* as well as food (1989, 143). Whether this number is accurate or not, it is clear that at least in the central Thai kingdom, and probably in the north too, there was much more value placed upon chanting than the abstruse task of copying manuscripts, which in the north was only remunerated at an average of half a *bat* for a fascicle.

Gervaise also relates that the daily wage given a slave in the kingdom of King Narai was one *füang*, which is one-eighth of a *bat* or half a *salüng* (1989, 88). This is very similar to the average wage given to scribes for copying manuscripts in northern Thailand, which works out to three *füang* per fascicle. If it takes an average of fifteen or perhaps twenty hours to copy one fascicle, and a scribe were to work for six or seven hours,[27] then it would take about three days to copy each fascicle, during which the scribe would receive one *füang* per day. These slaves' wages do not suggest that scribes were highly valued, although of course as monks they would not have had any dire need for the money.

Turning to the prices for food, Gervaise regards it as very cheap that a dozen chickens cost fifteen French *sols* (1989, 73), which is just under two *salüng*. This means that a day's work for a slave or a scribe could buy three chickens at these prices, which if nothing else would be enough to keep them well fed. Once again, all this must be tempered by the understanding that as monks, scribes ought not to have found themselves in the position of having to purchase their daily requirements. The information is presented more to provide some notion of the market value of scribal work and not to outline the living standards of a monk-scribe.

An inscription from Phræ (LNI, Phræ 6) dated CS 859 (1497 CE) tells of the ruler of Phræ who sponsored the casting of a golden image of the Buddha, weighing "three hundred thousand." Although it is unclear exactly what units these are,[28] the editors believe it is about 360 kilograms. If so, then regardless of the exact monetary value of such an artifact, it must have been extremely expensive, well over 200,000 *bat.* This sum is many orders of magnitude greater than that paid for manuscripts. Another inscription from a monastery in Chiang Rai (Pavie 1898, 413) dated CS 862 (1500 CE) provides some prices paid for various items used to provide light. Wax cost 25,760 silver *ngoen*, oil cost 102,500, and candlesticks cost 7,950. Just as was the case in the chronicles, we again see that the making of manuscripts did not command large monetary outlays, especially in comparison with building projects, image making, and other religious activities. This makes it all the more surprising that large copying projects were not, as far as one can garner from the available evidence, frequently and enthusiastically undertaken. A weak or impoverished ruler could have sponsored, at little cost to himself, the making of sacred texts, but it seems that in general they preferred to empty their coffers on golden images than skim them to produce scriptures.

Finally, it is instructive to compare these prices with those in Sri Lanka as recorded in the MV. Specific sums are given on three occasions. In the thirteenth century, 84,000 *kahāpana*s are paid to scribes for writing the 84,000 divisions (*khandha*) of the Dhamma—one *kahāpana* per division (MV 1927, 81.45); in the sixteenth century, 60,000 is spent to honor a Tipiṭaka that is written on 30,000 leaves (MV 1927, 92.13); and in the eighteenth century, a number of *sutta*s are inscribed onto gold leaves at a cost of 9,600 *kahāpana*s (MV 1927, 99.28). Although the numbers of leaves and divisions are conventional and probably do not represent the true numbers involved, they can suffice to provide a very basic idea of the type of costs involved. In fact, if the Tipiṭaka really did occupy 30,000 leaves—a not-impossible figure—then one of these projects would have involved an outlay of two *kahāpana*s per leaf. If the writing of the Dhamma cost a total of 84,000, and the Dhamma here is considered to be roughly equivalent to the Tipiṭaka, then this would have entailed a cost of 2.8 *kahāpana*s per leaf. I have intimated already that that writing appears to have occupied a far more central and elevated position in medieval Sri Lanka than it did in Lan Na, based on such things as the number of references to this medium in the chronicles and the many golden texts made. One would therefore expect that the cost of two or three *kahāpana*s per leaf, or forty-eight to seventy-two per twenty-four-leaf fascicle, would be more than the two *salüng* per fascicle often seen in Lan Na. The PTSD estimates the value of a *kahāpana* at roughly that of a florin, which was the equivalent of forty-eight *sols* or about 1.3 *bat*. A fifteenth-century inscription agrees with these general figures. It says that a garment of gold studded with gems was made at a cost of one thousand *kahāpanas* (Codrington 1924, 198), which tells us that a *kahāpana* had a somewhat higher value than a *bat*, because gold Buddha images are usually priced in the hundreds of thousands of *bats*. Thus based on the MV accounts, the scribes in Sri Lanka received even more *per page* than was presented to scribes in Lan Na for a whole fascicle.

CONCLUSION

Manuscript evidence agrees with the inscriptional and historiographical sources that *araññavāsī* monks ordained into the lineage of those who went to Sri Lanka were among the monastic groups most concerned with producing and taking care of manuscripts. They made golden boxes to protect them and were a driving force in the building of early libraries. We have benefited from their efforts because a large number of manuscripts under their care have accordingly survived. It is possible that others who made manuscripts at this time did not take equally good care of them. While *araññavāsī* monks had a hand in making a disproportionately large number of manuscripts, other groups, as well as rulers and laypeople, did sponsor these items as well.

Scribal work was not remunerated at very high levels relative to other work, although since almost all scribes were monks, they would not have had to rely upon these wages for their survival. Indeed, unlike in Europe, where professional scribes were both religious and laypeople, the scribes in Lan Na were almost all monks and novices who worked only a few hours each day, mostly during the rainy season. Their scribal duties did not supplant their other duties. It is also important to emphasize that manuscripts cost much less to produce than Buddha images and a host of other cultic, merit-generating items that donors might choose to make.

Scribal work itself did not necessarily require a fully literate agent. Not only is the handwriting not aesthetically pleasing in many cases, but the scribes, when not working from an exemplar, tended to make numerous mistakes suggesting a less-than-perfect literacy on their part. This contrasts with the description of a Burmese scribe in the SV where the scribe is expected to have a deep knowledge and understanding of the text he is writing.

The manuscripts are only minimally ornamented, with no marginal commentary and limited corrections, and they are not labeled for the easy retrieval of a specific text. In short, they do not bear the marks of a particularly robust discursive engagement, especially when compared with similar items from other more graphocentric cultures.

It is worth quoting at length a passage by Denise Troll that describes the relationship of scribes to writing in medieval Europe. Although she puts them in overly stark terms, the circumstances she describes are not terribly unlike those that emerge from a close examination of the northern Thai situation:

> Manuscript technology and medieval monasticism constrained the scribes' experience and conception of writing. Writing was not a matter of self-expression or intellection, but a manual labor. . . . The monk was obliged to perform this labor by religious duty. . . . (1990, 111)
>
> The medieval scribes were valuable, diligent . . . and often mediocre talents unaware of their contribution to the transition from an oral to a literate culture. They were writers—what a child would call "copycats"—not composers; more slaves than scholars. . . . Medieval literacy was an institution to preserve what was known, an institution erected on the bent backs of silent, anxious men. More often than not the scribes did not understand or appreciate the intellectual genius they preserved and transmitted. . . . (1990, 118–120)

5 Turning Over a New Leaf

The Advance of Writing

Following the reign of Bilakapanattu, not long after Lan Na had reached its apex, decline began to set in. Taking advantage of this situation, the Burmese conquered Chiang Mai in 1558 and over the next few years brought all of Lan Na under their control. The reasons for the decline of Lan Na are varied, and Penth convincingly lays out some of the basic economic and political parameters responsible (1994, 59). The lavish religious projects carried out by the kings, such as casting Buddha images out of gold and covering *stūpa*s with gold leaf cost money, and in some cases it appears that this was money the kings did not have. In at least one instance the king went so far as to proclaim that eighty units of silver, if given by the king, should be valued as equivalent to a hundred units (Penth 1994, 59, n.11). Inscriptions also give the impression that an enormous amount of land and slave labor was donated to favored monasteries, and these grants were often accompanied by explicit instructions not to allow these resources to be used for any nonreligious purposes. A significant proportion of land, money, and labor was effectively being taken out of the economy and the resulting scarcity led to inflation. By the end of Bilakapanattu's reign, this was beginning to cause tension in the society, which was compounded by serious disorganization in the political arena. As Penth records:

> During the twenty-five years following the death of Phayā Käo [Bilakapanattu], six rulers in succession mounted the throne of Chiang Mai; besides, the country was without a ruler for four years because no agreement in the choice of a new king could be reached, and none of the six rulers ended his reign peacefully: they were either murdered, or deposed, or they abdicated. (1994, 60)

King Ket Chettharat, who succeeded Bilakapanattu, was forced to leave the throne in 1538 due to strife within the privileged political circles that had initially supported him. His son Chai so antagonized the elite that in 1543 he was assassinated, and his father was returned to power. At this point Ket did something that once again angered the generals and ministers and eventually led to his own assassination: he had the *araññavāsī* monks reordained (TCM, 5.30). Reordination is generally done when it is deemed that there was some fault with a monk's original ordination; in this case the ensuing strife tells us that they must have been ordained into another order altogether, most likely because the king had special relations with the receiving order, which convinced him to find some fault with the *araññavāsī* ordination. Until an inscription marking this event comes to light, if there is one, it is impossible to say much more about what happened on this occasion and what reasons were adduced to justify it. However, we can speculate that one of the other orders, probably the flower-garden order from Wat Suan Døk, which was still smarting from its fall from royal favor a century earlier, had gained the trust and confidence of the king and convinced him to challenge the Pa Dæng lineage. The fact that the king was killed shortly thereafter shows how deeply the network of political and religious allegiances was woven into the fabric of society and what the price of upsetting the balance could be.

After Ket was killed, there was no clear successor, and unfortunately divergent interests in Lan Na attempted to enthrone different candidates, including Shan and Lao leaders. The ensuing struggle for power left Chiang Mai and Lan Na in a state of extreme disorganization, which was only mildly alleviated for a few years when most parties were able to agree upon the anointing of Setthathirat, a prince from Luang Prabang with maternal connections to the Chiang Mai royal line. He did not stay long in Chiang Mai but attempted to rule Lan Na from the Lan Chang capital of Luang Prabang, a move which made governing this rapidly unraveling region very inefficient. As succeeding governors attempted in vain to create some political order in Lan Na, the Burmese under King Bayinnaung took advantage of the disarray and conquered Chiang Mai in 1558. They met very little resistance. From there they expanded and took over the rest of Lan Na over the next few years.

BURMESE SUZERAINTY

At first, many Yuan people were pleased to finally have some stability, even if under Burmese military rule, which was not at this point overly harsh. The Burmese, in conjunction with members of the former Lan Na ruling elite, even supported the casting of some Buddha images, and they seem to have attempted to cultivate good relations with the local Yuan through other religious and social projects, including the distribution of Pali manuscripts (Tarling 1993, 72), as well as through the maintenance of Thai elites in some influential positions. The king of Chiang Mai at the time of the siege, Mekuti, was allowed to continue reigning as a tributary of Bayinnaung after the city fell; Mekuti's queen, Visuddhidevi, was installed as regent in 1564 after Mekuti fell out of favor by refusing to join Bayinnaung in a campaign against Ayudhyā.

Bayinnaung was, by all accounts, genuinely interested in maintaining a healthy civil society in Chiang Mai, and according to a contemporary inscription, in 1571 CE he ordered the construction of a new *cetiya* in the venerable Wat Chiang Man as well as a *vihāra, uposatha* hall, and a library (*pittakaghara*) (Griswold and Prasoert 1977, 128). In light of these works, it is not surprising that Burmese tradition holds that when Bayinnaung appointed his son Nawrahtaminsaw (also known as Tharawaddy) to be king upon Visuddhidevi's death in 1579, he called him to his chambers for an important talk.

> He told Nawrahtaminsaw that the kingdom of Chiang Mai, acquired by his power and prowess, was a greater kingdom than Pyay, Toungoo or Inwa; that it was an extensive kingdom with able ministers and courtiers and brave warriors; that it should be ruled justly and its courtiers and retainers supported and protected; that its senior ministers . . . should be treated with respect; and that officials should be prevented from extorting the people and taxes and duties be imposed only in accord with tradition. (Myint 1996, 11)

There are, in fact, poems extant in the Burmese *yadu* style[1] written by Nawrahtaminsaw's wife Hsinbyushinme that express longing for her husband, who was often away on military campaigns. They also reveal her great love and respect for Chiang Mai, the "Victory Land of Golden Yun," as she calls it. The poems speak of the beauty of the city and its surroundings, the fragrance of its blossoms, the grace of its waters, and the glory of its Buddhist heritage.

> Victory Land of Golden Yun, our home
> thronged pleasantly like paradise.
> The clear moving waters flow incessantly,

the forests teem with singing birds . . .
Since my lion-hearted husband marched to war
I guarded my mind and kneeling
before Buddha's representative images
of Phra Kaew, Phra Sing, golden Maha Ceti
and the famous Phra Suthep,
images bright as sun
on western hill-top beyond the city, and within,
with reverence I say my prayers. (Myint 1996, 13–14)

Other former principalities of Lan Na that came under Burmese dominion were also treated with honor and respect. David Wyatt says that the earliest versions of the chronicle of the Chæ Hæng reliquary in Nan were probably written in 1585 when Nawrahtaminsaw stopped there on his way to battle in Laos and, deeply affected by the story of how a relic of the Buddha was enshrined therein, arranged to have it renovated (Wyatt 1994c, 1080).

This picture of a relatively tolerant and productive early Burmese period accords well with what we know from the manuscript record, which suggests that the Golden Age scribal culture was not overly hindered during the first few decades of Burmese suzerainty.[2] Many of the finest examples of Pali palm-leaf manuscripts come from this period. It is only after about 1610 that there is a sudden, precipitous drop in manuscript production—a drop that is not difficult to explain. At this point the people of Lan Na began a series of insurgencies aimed at wresting independence from the Burmese, and the Burmese overlords met these actions with a more systematic program of repression. This era also saw periodic attempts by the Siamese of Ayudhyā to capture Chiang Mai, which were in each case eventually foiled by Burmese might, but not without significant destruction to the once great city. Alliances, the details of which are lost to history, were forged among the different Tai peoples, but they were never successful in driving out the Burmese, who became only more intent on holding the territory. One such episode occurred in 1660, when a report came to Lan Na stating incorrectly that the Burmese capital of Ava had been overrun by the Chinese. Chiang Mai, which at that time had a governor of local Tai extraction who had been installed by the Burmese, requested Ayudhyā that it accept Chiang Mai as a vassal in return for protection from the Burmese. Shortly after Siamese forces arrived, they were beaten back by the Burmese, and Chiang Mai was punished severely for its insolence. Thereafter, the former capital of Lan Na was burdened with a series of Burmese governors who filled the ranks of their forward lines with Tai Yuan men.

The constant war and uncertainty plaguing the region were responsible for population shifts, as people left the cities seeking safer havens or were forcibly ejected by the Burmese. At this point, as Hundius says, "the material and psychological preconditions for cultural and literary productivity must have been severely impaired" (1990, 12), and manuscript production plummeted. These difficult conditions alone may have been responsible for the striking decline in Buddhist manuscript production over the next two centuries, but it is also possible that the Burmese actively discouraged Lan Na manuscript culture.[3]

An antithetical attitude on the part of the Burmese is not difficult to explain. They probably felt that the Lan Na style of writing was deeply intertwined with the independent identity of northern Thailand and that allowing it to flourish would ultimately inspire challenges their rule. The Burmese may have felt that writing was one of the unifying activities around which local dissent could crystallize. After all, the Dhamma script was also known as Tua Müang—local letters. Thus in the minds of the Burmese rulers, cessation of the production of Lan Na Dhamma texts would lead to the disintegration of a strong Lan Na identity and with it the potential for rebellion.

Relations between the government and the Saṅgha may also have been strained, which would help to explain why Buddhist cultural production of all sorts in the region became so anemic. There are at least two known edicts that were enforced around Ava in this period that attempt to limit entry into the Saṅgha, and the Burmese would have had good reason to impose such a restriction in the Tai areas as well (Lieberman 1984, 179–80). Donning the robes was, of course, one of the more effective and acceptable ways of avoiding conscription, and at a time when the army—and a foreign one at that—was made up largely of forced conscripts, this option must have been just as appealing to the Tai as we know it was for the Mon and Burmese at Ava in the 1530s (Lieberman 1984, 110) and the Mon in the Irrawaddy delta in 1593 (Lieberman 1984, 41). At the time of these edicts, the Burmese were having difficulty filling the ranks of their armies because so many eligible men were exempting themselves through entry into the monkhood. The government countered by imposing moratoria on taking monastic vows, and even by purging the existing Saṅgha of anyone suspected of joining to avoid military service. Only those well-known to be of the most pious inclination were allowed to remain in the monasteries, while the rest were given a chance to meditate on the impermanence of life in battle. Before forcibly defrocking a large number of monks in 1637, King Tha-lun warned in a decree that "those who relax in ease and comfort and pretend to be monks, when you die you shall sink inexorably into the Four States of

Woe" (quoted in Lieberman 1984, 110). Even if these steps were not formally taken in Lan Na, news that this was happening elsewhere under the Burmese would have been enough to curtail monastic endeavors.

THE LIBRARY OF WAT LAI HIN

There were, however, beacons of light able to break through the clouds. The *vihāra* of Wat Lai Hin just outside of Lampang was built in 1683 while the monastery was being run by the *araññavāsī* monk Kesārapañña. He collected Pali manuscripts from the late fifteenth to the early seventeenth centuries, perhaps motivated by the loss of literate culture that he perceived occurring all around him. Besides collecting older manuscripts, Kesārapañña himself copied or personally sponsored no less than eleven manuscripts, all of which were mixed Pali/vernacular explanatory texts known as *vohāra*.[4] There are also a number of Pali manuscripts in the Lai Hin collection from the scarce years, such as a *Paritta* from 1677 CE, a *Thūpavaṃsa* from 1722 CE, a *Vessantara Jātaka* from 1714 CE, one *Pārājika* from 1693 CE and one from 1711 CE, a *Pācittiya* from 1716 CE, a *Vinaya Mahāvagga* from 1754 CE, and a *Cullavagga* from 1755 CE.[5] Note that the last five are all Vinaya texts expounding the monastic discipline. It is no wonder that, given limited resources, monks would have chosen to copy these works, because they would be required to reconstitute and revivify the religion in better times. We have seen in previous chapters that the chronicles tended to link the survival and strength of the religion not with the propagation of discourses of the Buddha from the Suttas but rather with the integrity of the monastic discipline and ordination practices. The focus on Vinaya manuscript production reflects this ethos.

GROWING OPPOSITION TO BURMESE RULE

By the eighteenth century opposition to Burmese rule had grown to such an extent that the Burmese decided to divide Lan Na into two separately administered regions. The northern and eastern parts, including Chiang Sæn, Nan, and Phræ, were put under the direct governance of the Burmese capital at Ava and the south, including Chiang Mai, was controlled by military governors as a vassal state. This was not a healthy arrangement for the region, as Penth observes: "By now, Lan Na, impoverished and fractured, and Burma, in the meantime also grown weaker but militarily still powerful, had reached a stalemate where Burma could no longer actively control Lan Na and the latter could not extricate itself from under the Burmese" (1994, 68).

Finally, in 1727, Lan Na was able to achieve some measure of independence under Ong Kham (r. 1727–1759), a Lü prince who was initially installed with the support of the Burmese after he helped them repress a brief uprising in which the Burmese governor of Chiang Mai was killed. Over the thirty-two years of Ong's reign, he gradually built up local support and loosened his ties with Burma to the extent that the area under his influence, essentially the Ping River valley around Chiang Mai, became de facto independent. Ong Kham was succeeded in 1759 by his son, Chan, who was not as successful at statecraft as his father and was overthrown by internal forces shortly thereafter. In 1763 the Burmese were able once again to take Chiang Mai after a lengthy siege, only to lose control about a year later. That the continuing frustration of Burmese regional ambitions removed any reticence they might have had about destroying the material Buddhist culture of their Tai coreligionists is evinced by the harshness of their reconquest of Chiang Mai[6] and the atrocities that accompanied the sacking of the Siamese capital of Ayudhyā in 1767. Numerous Buddha images and *cetiya*s were stripped of their gold and smashed, while most of the Pali manuscripts in Ayudhyā were destroyed. Doubtless the First Noble Truth was constantly on the lips of those unlucky enough to live during this dark period, and when it was over, war, disease, and famine had released tens of thousands from the sufferings of life.

An unnumbered, fragmentary copy of the *Pārājikakaṇḍa* from Wat Duang Di in Chiang Mai provides a glimpse into the difficult circumstances under which scribes were operating at the time. There is no year provided in the colophon, but it is bound with another *Pārājikakaṇḍa* text dated CS 1115 (1753 CE), and looks to be about the same age. On the last leaf of the second fascicle, the scribe writes in Yuan that he is unable to find the words to complete the Pali sentence that he is writing. Perhaps the scribe who wrote this did not have access to any other manuscripts of this text or to monks who might have known the missing words from memory. The hapless scribe simply does not have the resources to check the manuscript.

Another manuscript from this period that reflects the waning of scribal culture is a *Pathamasambodhi* dated CS 1126 (1764 CE) (Otani, 702). The colophon employs very unusual orthography and is particularly difficult to decipher. Words are split at the end of the line, and it is apparent that the scribe did not have a good understanding of what he was writing and was not very well trained.

One of the most remarkable finds has been the discovery of six teak scripture boxes in the Red Cliff Cave in a mountain near the Salween River in Mæ Sariang district in 1968 (Keyes 1970). These boxes contain about 400 fascicles of Pali and vernacular palm-leaf manuscripts written from CS 1000 (1638 CE) until CS 1154 (1792). The cache thus represents a century and a half of textual production from the far northwestern area of Lan Na at what Keyes has called the "frontier" with the Burmese and Shan territories. The large number of texts attests to the industry of the Yuan even while under Burmese subjugation, although the fact that it was finally decided to store the texts in the cave around 1793 CE suggests that the fighting between the newly resurgent Yuan and the Burmese did finally succeed in putting an end to textual production in the area (Keyes 1970, 232).

It was only after the complete devastation of Ayudhyā that the kind of parochial interests, infighting, and constant machinations that had been the hallmarks of Tai alliances were put aside in order to permit a solid alliance of central and northern Tai groups to form a cohesive and coordinated assault against the Burmese and drive them out for good. The Lan Na prince Kawila from Lampang realized that the only way to finally defeat the Burmese was to put himself and his men under the control of the most powerful Siamese army, led at that time by the charismatic king Taksin and his generals Surasi and Chakri, who were drawn from the noble ranks of old Ayudhyā. Kawila seized his opportunity in 1774 when, under the guise of going to challenge the Siamese army marching north from its new capital of Thonburi, he joined them and marched back to challenge the Burmese instead. In early 1775 this joint Siamese-Yuan army drove the Burmese out of Chiang Mai and began the lengthy process of conquering the rest of the region, which ended only when the last stronghold at Chiang Sæn was wrested from the Burmese in 1804. The complete emergence of Lan Na from under the Burmese required a slow but insistent regime of attacks that extracted a heavy toll on both sides. Eventually, however, it produced a strong and fairly cohesive Lan Na in control of its own internal affairs and acting as a neighborly vassal to Siam and its ruler, General Chakri, now known as King Rama I.

THE CHIANG MAI CHRONICLE AND THE RECONSTRUCTION OF LAN NA

The process of reconstructing Lan Na was long and arduous. The key centers of Chiang Mai, Chiang Rai, Chiang Sæn, and Phayao had been severely depopulated, and so people had to be transferred there from other areas, including the Shan, Khoen, and Lü regions, which had escaped the most brutal of the Burmese onslaughts. The most important indigenous source for this period is the TCM.

The TCM, a patchwork text of accretions added over the years, focuses on the fortunes of the capital city of the Lan Na kingdom from its foundation in 1292 CE up to the early nineteenth century. While the last chapter was written in 1828 CE, the earlier ones contain significant portions that date back to the fifteenth century. There are over one hundred different versions of the TCM, many of which have been cataloged by the SRI manuscript project. Here I use the Hans Penth version, which was copied in 1926 and has been translated into English by David Wyatt and Aroonrut Wichienkeeo (TCM, 1998).

Even though the final text that I am working from was written in 1828 CE, fully four centuries after such orally oriented texts as the CDV, it should be kept in mind that there was still a rich tradition of oral histories from which the final redactor of the TCM could have drawn, in a manner not dissimilar to Bodhiraṃsi. Wyatt quotes, for example, a passage about oral history from the journal of British traveler David Richardson in 1834: "A male and two female singers . . . sung a sort of metrical history of the exploits of the Tsoboa and his six brothers, in which the successful insurrection and the carrying off the people from Kein-theu [Chiang Sæn], Kein-toung [Keng Tung] and Mein Neaung [Möng Yòng] by the present chiefs held the most conspicuous place" (TCM, xxxviii).

Wyatt provides us with the few details about the author of the last few chapters, who was also likely the redactor, that can be garnered from the text:

> The author has to have been a local, Lan Na person. Throughout the text, the author displays an exceptional familiarity with local lore, local geography, and even local personalities. The author was not only literate but well-read: he almost certainly was male, having received the traditional education in a period in a Buddhist temple. . . . He sprinkles Pali words liberally throughout his text, though he often mis-spells them. . . . He does not seem to have been a monk, for he is little interested in religious affairs. . . . We might guess that he was a non-royal (non *cao*) minor official, a clerk or someone who had been a clerk. Because he had access to documents that must have been private to the princely family of Cao Kavila, he must have had close relations within that family. . . . (TCM, xxxvii)

The text addresses its audience as "listeners" throughout, indicating that it was expected that most people would come into contact with this and presumably other texts through the oral/aural medium. This assumption is further strengthened by the many early nineteenth-century *Anisong Vessantara* texts cataloged by Coedès (1966, 48–53). These texts are often bound with copies of the *Vessantara Jātaka* and extol the great merits to be attained by listening to this text. In no case do we find any mention of the merit accruing to those who read or write the text. As has been mentioned in previous chapters, even when a text was present in written form, only a few people would actually read it—the majority of the audience would be listening.

Chapter seven of the TCM, dealing with the rebuilding of Chiang Mai under King Kawila at the end of the eighteenth century and with the city's relations with surrounding polities, includes twelve instances of letters (*nang süa*) being exchanged for diplomatic purposes. The sudden and drastic increase in the recorded use of written documents to arrange alliances, warn of impending attack, and placate enemy rulers, is a testament to the growing importance of writing in the daily life of Lan Na society, no doubt in part due to Burmese influence.

A particularly detailed and engaging account of the reception of a letter at the court can be found at TCM 7.29. Here Chiang Mai generals and ministers have gathered together to consider the contents of a letter from the Burmese lord Chøm Hong requesting their friendship: "They summoned the royal astrologers and considered the teachings of the Vedic texts and figured out the *hani* [magical letters] which advised them not to believe what they were hearing." They therefore send a letter back saying that they would like to meet with high-ranking envoys to discuss the matter, which Chøm Hong hears (*trap*) in every detail. He then sends another letter back, and the king listens to it in Chiang Mai. It is clear that although there are written letters being exchanged here, they are being read aloud to the various kings and ministers involved. This is a theme found throughout this text, and in fact there are no instances of a king actually reading anything. Even the two references to the composition of a letter by the king at TCM, 7.45 and 8.14, which are translated by Wyatt and Aroonrut as "wrote a letter," involve the Pali phrase *akkhara katha*, the meaning of which is ambiguous. It could more properly, it seems to me, be translated as "dictated a letter." The world of the TCM, then, was one in which writing was used fairly extensively to record events and mediate governmental and other high-level relations, but in which these written documents were actually conveyed orally in most cases by specialists who would read them.

THE REBUILDING OF LAN NA

The eighth and final chapter of the TCM focuses largely on the revival of Lan Na, starting in 1796 CE, after the long years of conflict with the Burmese and other neighboring states and the reestablishment of Thai rule. There is a glaring absence of concern for what happened to books and libraries in the region during the turbulent times. The TCM says that

> the temples and institutions of Buddhism, monasteries, ubosatha, Buddha images and cetiya were destroyed and dilapidated and falling down in great number, ever since s. 1138, the *rwai san* year (1776), until s. 1158, a *rwai si* year (1796), when the three brother princes came there to reestablish the city and the domain. (8.01)

There is no discussion of the fate of literate culture and its accoutrements, and consequently it is not surprising that the restoration of this particular domain is barely mentioned either. In 1801 CE, after having made numerous auspicious images for the city, "the three brother princes had Buddhist temples, images, stupas and cetiyas, kuti, vihara and *ubosatha* built for the pleasure of the monks, for making merit continuously" (TCM, 7.24).

Libraries or manuscript-making projects do not feature in exhaustive lists such as this, even though there would have been dire need for them at this point because of the destruction of the past two centuries. In fact, TCM 8.01 describes how the city eventually became vibrant once again, replete with good food and drink, all sorts of musical instruments, beautiful palaces, an abundance of monastic requisites, fireworks for festivals, and so forth, but there is no mention of books, libraries, or any features of literary culture. The manuscripts themselves contain admonitions to copy them and store them safely in order to make merit, but, alas, it seems that these sentiments did not cross over into the chronicle and probably not, therefore, into the mentality of the many people who would have heard it narrated.

The first and only account of the making of sacred texts in the TCM version that I have examined is found in a passage telling of the further rebuilding of Lan Na. In 1805 the king orders "the religious teachers to come out and perform their religious duties and preach and study and write and read the scriptures, as the Lord Buddha had instructed" (TCM, 7.44). This passage does not suggest that a major project to rebuild the manuscript collection was undertaken, but only that there was an attempt to get monks to go about their regular duties once again. Reading or writing the scriptures does not play any further role in the chronicle. Rather, the remainder of this passage focuses on an important image, the restoration of which, it is claimed, will herald the flourishing of Buddhism in the area as it was in days of yore.

This spirit continues throughout the chapter. In 1817 CE, Kawila's brother is crowned, and he then issues an order that "everyone should make merit and hear the Dhamma and observe the precepts and heed the preaching, and build temples and monasteries, kuti, vihara, stupa and cetiya, in great glory" (TCM, 8.28). Not only is the making of manuscripts not mentioned in this list of meritorious acts, but people are specifically instructed to *hear* the Dhamma (*fang tham*), which would have been effected much as it is still today by preaching and sermonizing.

It is instructive to compare this narrative to one in the *Mahāvaṃsa* dealing with similarly dire circumstances, but in the thirteenth century in Sri Lanka (MV 1927, 81.40ff). Here, King Vijayabāhu III is deeply upset that so many books have been destroyed by foreign invaders. He gathers together people who have good memories, and they write down in books what they know about the doctrine. They are paid one gold *kahāpana* for each division.

> Thinking "Many books in Laṅkā connected to the true *Dhamma* are destroyed by our enemies," the king became upset and having gathered together learned laymen who were endowed with knowledge and good memory, who were pure and bereft of idleness, and who knew how to write quickly and beautifully, as well as other scribes, the lord of the world had them reverentially write down the 84,000 divisions of the *Dhamma* well. Giving gold coins to them reckoned based on the number of divisions of the *Dhamma* and having made obeisance to the *Dhamma*, he accumulated merit.

In contrast to the Thai chronicle, King Vijayabāhu III is most immediately concerned with establishing a written record and therefore is determined to finance the writing down of Buddhist knowledge into books for safekeeping. The literary is privileged above the oral. In the TCM, almost no space is given to the reconstruction of Buddhist manuscript culture amid the myriad reports of new buildings, roads, restocking of food, and the like. We thus have in the TCM a chronicle produced well into the century that witnessed the first printing of Pali texts in Siam that still does not accord writing a more central position in religious life than many of the Golden Age texts produced over three centuries earlier, although it does play a more prominent role in secular spheres.

As has become clear in previous chapters, it should not be surprising to find that the overall situation is not so simple. An inscription says that King Kawila built a costly library in 1812 CE at Wat Phra Singh in the heart of Chiang Mai, and there are also many manuscripts extant from the Chiang Mai region produced during the decades immediately preceding the composition of the TCM. Again, we seem here to have a disassociation between the material remains and the story as it emerges in the chronicles.

There are very good reasons to believe that revivifying local manuscript production was important for the rulers of Chiang Mai, but that official sponsorship of a grand Tipiṭaka copying project that would have featured prominently in chronicles, such as that undertaken by Vijayabāhu in Sri Lanka, might have been avoided. I am making a distinction here between the creation of a cultural and financial environment amenable to the production of manuscripts, which I believe occurred, and the administration of an extravagant ceremony to produce the scriptures under royal patronage, which I believe did not. While the literary results of both could be similar, the latter could have had unwanted consequences vis-à-vis Chiang Mai's relationship with Bangkok.

The local Lan Na script (Tua Müang) had always been central in the creation of Lan Na identity[7] and would have been even more necessary for the self-definition of the recently liberated region. It is not infrequent that communities coalesce around different scripts, as in the well-known examples of Urdu/Hindi and Serbian/Croatian. In both of these cases, deep cultural meaning is invested in the script used to write very similar languages, and such sentiments surely played a part in the reemergence from under Burmese rule of a Lan Na that was trying to negotiate the hazy boundaries between itself and its more powerful Siamese brethren to the south.[8] Resurgence of Lan Na script would mark both the resurgence of Lan Na from under the Burmese and cultural and political autonomy with respect to the Siamese. The Siamese, for their part, were busy carving out a delicate position for themselves with regards to the European colonial ambitions that were asserting themselves ever more strongly at their doorstep. It is noteworthy that the Siamese eventually decided to tap the well of politico-cultural strength available through the nationalization of the Siamese script. The first step was to transfer the authority hitherto possessed by the Khmer script, which had traditionally been used to write Pali and religious texts in the kingdom, to the central Thai script. This was done through such things as the wide distribution in 1880 of a standard handbook of Buddhist chants in central Thai characters and the printing in 1893 of the Tipiṭaka in Thai script for the first time (Jory 2000, 372).

Besides the importance of stimulating works in the Lan Na script for the strengthening of regional identity, another interesting explanation for the production of Buddhist manuscripts in large quantities during this period has been proposed by Wyatt. Reflecting upon the previous half century, during which the region was ravaged by almost incessant war involving the Siamese, the Burmese, and every principality in the north, he concludes that the unwavering eternal truths of Buddhism must have had extra appeal to the survivors of this dark time. Few people in northern Thailand were living in their ancestral homelands by the beginning of the nineteenth century, so total had been the various expulsions, forced migrations, and resettlement ventures. For those who did not have the comfort of ancient local tradition to ground them, the universal appeal of the Dhamma must have been particularly powerful (Wyatt 1997, 436). I would add to this that the fragility of the oral tradition had been laid bare, which forced people to realize the importance of preserving texts in written form in order to preclude any future complete breaks in the tradition.

There were, then, strong reasons for Kawila and his descendants to wish to rebuild the Buddhist literary culture of Lan Na alongside its physical infrastructure. Such actions would have helped to strengthen their position as rulers able to uphold the religion and would have been a strong expression of Lan Na's unique cultural identity. The question is, therefore, why were no grand, coordinated, royal Tipiṭaka-producing ceremonies held or recorded even though many texts were indeed made (judging by the surviving examples)?

I believe that the answer lies in part with events that had recently taken place in Bangkok under Rama I. A council held under royal auspices to redact and copy the Tipiṭaka was one of the centerpieces of what Wyatt has called Rama's "subtle revolution." It was the culmination of a number of efforts by Rama and his predecessor Taksin to have a definitive version of the scriptures copied in order to improve the acute situation caused by the destruction of countless sacred texts during the sacking of Ayudhyā. The Ratanakosin dynastic chronicle, a royally sponsored work that was compiled and written by court officials and scribes, speaks of the king's interest in promulgating the religious texts and emphasizes his concern for the success of this project:

> In that same year of the Monkey, the tenth year of the decade [A.D. 1788], the king gave his attention to the Buddhist Tripitaka texts, which were the very root of the teachings of Buddha. The king at this time spent a large amount of his royal funds to pay for wages in having the texts written up on dried palm leaves. All of the existing texts available in the Laos or

> Mon scripts were rewritten in the Khom {ancient Cambodian} script. These texts were then kept in a special cabinet at the Phra Monthiantham Library. The king also ordered that the Tripitaka texts be made available for study by Buddhist monks of every temple under the royal patronage.
>
> Then Chamun Waiworanat said to the king that the Tripitaka texts, which the king had spent so much money to have compiled at that time, contained irregularities that actually had been there in the older texts that the new ones were based on. No one had bothered to correct the mistakes. The king, upon hearing this, said that since the Pali texts of the Buddhist Tripitaka contained a great many irregularities, their texts could hardly serve as the basic teaching of the Buddhist religion. Moreover, said the king, there were extremely few people who knew the Tripitaka. Once they were gone the Buddhist texts containing the teaching to be memorized, to be practiced and to be comprehended would soon be in a state of decadence and be of no use. . . . (Thiphakorawong 1978, 152–153)

The Ratanakosin chronicle tells about the eighth council under Tilaka at some length and then remarks that

> from that time on, all the Buddhist monks, high and low, in this peninsula continued to study and recopy the Tripitaka. Noblemen and wealthy people of great faith had the texts recopied in various countries such as the countries of the Thai, the Laos, the Cambodians, the Burmese, the Mon, and in scripts that differed greatly one from another. Variations occurred in these different versions. It was impossible to find a nobleman or clergy who would support the purification and perfection of the Tripitaka as in former times. (158)

In this manner the chronicle builds the case for the importance of the redaction and copying of the texts that will take place under Rama I, hinting not so subtly at the great merit of a ruler with the ability to have these tasks properly executed. It is notable in this context that Taksin had twice sponsored the copying of the Tipiṭaka, fulfilling what Wyatt calls a "customary act of royal patronage of Buddhism" (1994b, 149). The text goes on to tell of the difficult situation precipitated by banditry, war, and the sacking of Ayudhyā, which echoes the situation in Lan Na at the time of Kawila:

> The Tripitaka and all the religious monuments and places there {in Ayudhyā} were completely destroyed. The monks who had kept watch over and studied the Tripitaka were scattered away or died in great numbers.

> There was utterly no one to ward off the enemies. For this reason, the Tripitaka in existence today is not perfect, but has been in a state of decline until this very day. (158)

The chronicle portrays a response to this situation on the part of the Siamese that is much different than the response of the Lan Na rulers. In marked distinction to the scant attention paid in the TCM to the rebuilding of literary culture, the Ratanakosin chronicle tells of a concerned King Rama inviting 100 high-ranking monks to a meeting where they are asked if they believe that the Tipiṭaka as they have it is complete and without mistakes. To this the monks reply that the texts have had defects for a long time, but they have not been corrected because no king could be found to support such an endeavor. The chronicle then goes on to tell of the various arrangements made by the king for the great council, the gathering of the monks and learned laymen at Nipphanaram Temple, near the palace, to undertake the task, and the ceremony marking the commencement of the project. Each monk is given a pen and yellow pigment for writing, and they are divided into four groups to revise the three Piṭakas and the grammatical treatises. It takes five months to complete the task of revising the texts, during which the king "ordered the disbursement of royal funds to pay calligraphers and to give to laymen, monks, and novices who would write down the Tripitaka, which was now purified and perfected" (Thiphakorawong 1978, 161).

> When this was done on dried palm leaves, the front and back covers as well as the frames of each volume were completely covered with gold, and the complete set was to be called the Golden Edition. Each volume was to be wrapped in gold thread fabric and tied with silk threads of five colours. The label was to be made of carved ivory, with inscriptions written with ink. Each of the texts was also to bear a label made of woven cloth, with the title of each text woven in the cloth. . . .
>
> After the Tripitaka was completely bound in the Golden Edition, the entire scriptural collection was placed on a royal palanquin and, with other royal vehicles, carried in procession in a festival in honour of the Tripitaka. (162)

Wyatt emphasizes that

> By his direct sponsorship, and his daily attendance at the convocation to make food-offerings to the monks, Rama I fully associated himself with this

> undertaking and played the role of royal patron of Siamese Buddhism in a highly-visible manner. . . . Few but the most powerful kings had ever dared to attempt [the revision of the canon]. If the task were poorly done, the sponsoring king stood to lose merit and thereby endanger not only his throne but also his kingdom. In sponsoring the Grand Council, Rama I displayed a characteristic confidence in the ability of human minds to meet the delicate challenge of ascertaining and interpreting holy writ. (1994b, 154)

Once the procession ends, the scriptures are installed, with great fanfare, in the Phra Monthiantham Library in the middle of the pond at a temple in the palace compound. The festivities are capped with a fireworks display, which, in a stroke of bad luck, causes a fire in the library. Luckily, government officials are present who brave the conflagration and rescue the pearl-inlaid cabinet containing the scriptures. The king believes that the guardian spirits must have deemed the library to be too low to house such an important artifact. He therefore orders a larger pavilion and library to be built, in keeping with the honor and glory of its contents (Thiphakorawong 1978, 164).

I have presented this episode in detail not only to show the concern for the written word that is clearly evident in the account, but also to demonstrate the extent to which Rama I felt this to be a significant—indeed, even definitive—achievement of his reign. Reexamining the similar situation of cultural decay in which Kawila found himself, we can see that as a loyal vassal of the Ratanakosin court, he would not have wished to upset their relationship by attempting to repeat the feat just performed by Rama I. A formal project to produce the Tipiṭaka under Kawila's direction could have been seen as an effort to usurp some of Rama's glory and merit and could have caused unnecessary tension between the two polities. Furthermore, it would have been a great insult to copy the traditional northern Thai recension when an edition deemed by King Rama to be superior had just been completed at great effort and expense. First of all, Kawila would have had to train a contingent of monks in the Khmer Mul script in which the royal edition was written and then either send them to Bangkok to transliterate the text into Lan Na Dhamma script or bring the texts to the north for the work to be done, two options that were practically and politically difficult. Kawila, having seen and heard about the devastation wrought in consequence of often minor actions, was wise enough to realize that sowing discord of any kind at this juncture would gain little for those who were party to it. The words he spoke to his royal brothers, as recorded in the TCM, tell us clearly about the kind of man he was:

> As for you, lords, all my younger siblings, you must love one another and live in concord like the strands of a rope. Do not quarrel. Help one another. Don't criticize each other. When the elder knows, he helps; and when the younger knows, he helps. When the enemy invades, help one another. Don't betray the Great King {Rama} of ours. (TCM, 8.04)

Therefore he chose to satisfy himself with beautification of the Phra Singh library and cultivation of an environment in which manuscripts could be more easily made but without excessive fanfare.

SOME REPRESENTATIVE MANUSCRIPTS FROM THE ERA

Although there is no evidence of an ostentatious Tipiṭaka production program initiated under Kawila, a large number of manuscripts destined to rekindle Lan Na culture and identity were made during this period under a variety of circumstances, including once again the guidance of *araññavāsī* monks. It is unclear what happened to the forest and flower-garden sects after the sacking of Chiang Mai by the Burmese, but because there are no references to separate groups after this period, it appears that they merged into one forest-dwelling sect carrying the Sinhalese tradition. As Kawila saw with regard to the Siamese, they must have realized that their only hope in these difficult times lay in their amalgamation into one sect that could then carry on the forest tradition.[9]

A forest-dwelling monk was the instigator of a *Niruttisadda* and *Uccāraṇadīpanī* manuscript dated CS 1160 (1798 CE). It has an unusually detailed colophon that provides a valuable window into the way that monks would have learned Pali grammar (SRI 19–04–035–00). The fact that these grammatical texts were sponsored by an *araññavāsī* only confirms the thesis that they were more concerned with literate culture than other groups, contrary to their putative role as primarily *vipassanādhura* or upholders of the meditation tradition. It is clear from manuscript colophons that for at least the first quarter of the nineteenth century, *araññavāsī*s were once again spearheading the manuscript production enterprise.[10]

Colophons from this era are similar in form to the older examples, but one trope in particular is now more noticeable: self-deprecating allusions to the poor abilities of the scribe. These are to be expected as the art matures and people become more critical. The colophon on the verso of the last leaf of fascicle 17 of a *Samantapāsādikā* (SRI 07–04–018) from 1806 CE is worth presenting in full:

> Written while in a happy state at Wat Pua Hong to the south of Sæn Pung gate. My handwriting does not look nice or well proportioned, all of it up to the end. No matter which letters, they are scattered over the lines. I who wrote it all feel ashamed. My humble self does not know Pali words thoroughly. The spaces in between are as large or small as I like, but they follow the order of the original letters. Sometimes I just finished a syllable and lost the line so I didn't know where I was. In the cases where I forgot and erred in putting in the letters, I would like to beg pardon from afar. In case some letters have fallen off the line, as far as one can see, please excuse me; I ask the monk to add them in. I wrote this on this day during the Sakarāja year 1168 by Thai reckoning.

In this rich example we learn that it was expected that monks would read the text carefully and would be in a position to make corrections where appropriate. The scribe also alludes to his difficulty figuring out exactly what the letters in the root text might be and to his inability to keep his vision fixed upon the right line, a phenomenon known to the Latin tradition as *aberratio oculi*. While he notes that other, more learned monks may correct his mistakes later, he does not mention anything about asking someone who knows the text better than he for help clarifying questionable letters. Perhaps the copying was very individual work, or perhaps the humble scribe did not feel it was appropriate to disturb his superiors for such minor matters. There does not seem to have been much supervision of the scribes. They could probably write in any manner they chose, quite unlike in the medieval European scriptoria, which tended to have very distinctive styles that are recognizable by learned paleographic specialists today (de Hamel 1992, 39). This lax discipline allowed a scribe in 1835 CE to write: "The cover pages and letters are not beautiful because I wrote in a reclining position" (*Cūlavagga* [SRI 19-01-019]).

OTHER NORTHERN POLITIES

By the time of Kawila's death in 1813, Chiang Mai had once again become the political and cultural center of the north, but there were other polities, most notably Nan, Phræ, and Luang Prabang, which had separate tributary relations with Bangkok and therefore pursued different policies with respect to the Ratanakosin court. Nan is located about two hundred kilometers east of Chiang Mai and was relatively autonomous for the first few centuries of Thai habitation, repeatedly defending itself successfully against Chiang Mai and other polities. During those years Nan was at pains to maintain its independence, as testified by an early mutual defense pact between Nan and Sukhodaya from 1393 CE that is recorded in inscriptions (EHS, 67–108). The JKM declares that King Tilaka finally conquered Nan after a long campaign in 1449 CE (JKMp, 97). From 1560 CE, Nan, like most of Lan Na, was under Burmese suzerainty, but it managed to achieve some autonomy under governors from Chiang Mai starting in 1727. There were numerous unsuccessful revolts against the Burmese over the next few decades, until the Burmese were finally driven out by the combined forces of Lan Na and the Siamese. In the wake of the Burmese retreat, Nan was established as a semi-independent kingdom in 1774 CE with allegiance to the Ratanakosin court in Bangkok.

The rulers of Nan and the other kingdoms of Phræ and Luang Prabang, while often good vassals of Bangkok, sending tribute and joining them in war when necessary, appear to have been more independently minded than those of Chiang Mai. It is certainly clear that they did not have the same reservations about sponsoring Tipiṭaka projects as did Kawila, because they duly recorded these meritorious deeds in stone and in chronicles for posterity and to gain the admiration of their subjects.

In chapter seven of the Nan chronicle,[11] the many pious works of the first king of Nan during the Ratanakosin period, Attawalapañño (r. 1788–1810 CE), are described and among them is the construction of a library in 1795 (Nan, 7.20). There is fortunately an ornate manuscript box that was also sponsored by this king as part of this same project, and it bears an inscription stating that the king, along with a monk and important people, had the box made in order to store the Tipiṭaka, which constitutes all the sayings of the Buddha (*sabbabuddhavacana*) (CLNI, 5: 75–79). We can see here the hallmarks of a project whose aim is to elevate the status of the chief sponsor in the eyes of his subjects as a powerful upholder and defender of Buddhism.

A few decades later a grand project to make what purports to be all the canonical texts, amounting to 1,103 fascicles (*phuk*), is recorded in an inscription (CLNI, 5: 43–49). It also tells of the celebration and dedication ceremony following their completion in 1837 CE. They were made by the ruler of Nan and his family at the instigation of Mahāthera Kañcana, an *araññavāsī* from Phræ, who took the texts to Phræ to illuminate the teachings there. There is also an inscription at Luang Prabang that talks about this same monk instigating a copying project there. This inscription from Wat Wisun, dated CS 1198 (1836 CE), not only highlights the central role of written scriptures in sustaining the religion, but also tells how much was spent on them (Pavie 1898, 357–359). It is not insignificant that this project was initiated by a monk of the forest-dwelling *araññavāsī* lineage, which I have argued was the most scholarly and literate of the monastic orders.

Wyatt records an oral tradition that Kañcana actually began as an abbot of Wat Phra Singh in Chiang Mai and convinced the king to expand the library there, but for some reason he fell out of favor and migrated to Phræ, where he again commenced his manuscript copying activities. After the library at Wat Sung Men was abundantly supplied, Kañcana moved on to Tak, where he was able to get another project underway before dying and being interred there.

Wyatt has pointed out that this flurry of literary activity was occurring around the same time as a number of ambitious chronicles were being produced in Lan Na. Some have seen this as a last desperate attempt to hold on to the old order before it disappeared in the rush to modernity stimulated by contact with the West (Wyatt 1997, 433). Perhaps the chronicles, manuscript projects, and libraries do constitute a "last stand" of the old order, an attempt to conserve the cultural heritage of the region in the face of inevitable change.

THE COPIOUS COPYING OF KING ANANTA

The final chapter of the Nan chronicle concentrates on the story of a very large copying project, and it provides a detailed list of the texts that were copied. In the year CS 1218 (1856 CE), after going with his retinue to Bangkok for an audience with the king, Anantaworaritthidet is appointed ruler over all of Nan.

> He then observed and reflected upon the infirm state of the Religion of the Buddha, which had to be improved and reformed. Moreover, in piety, he desired to have the Holy Teachings copied; that is, all the Pali and *nipāta* and *nikāya* and *niyāya,* in order that the religion of Gotama should flourish in the future. (Nan, 10.12)

Having decided to strengthen the religion, the king then constructs numerous *vihāra*s and reliquaries at *wat*s all over the province, in effect delineating the area by means of these meritorious works.

> Furthermore, from the very beginning he never ceased to be filled with the essence of the teachings of the Dhamma. Here we will speak of his sponsoring of the [copying of the] Scriptures.
>
> In the year CS 1217, from his Privy Purse he disbursed funds for the copying of all the scriptures. . . .
>
> On Friday, the 2nd day of the second month, he led the princes, officials, and people in a *buddhābhiseka* ceremony and a great celebration. . . . On this occasion when [the ruler] worshipped with offerings there were 189 fascicles presented, each ornamented with shell inlays on the wooden covers, including 5 *bat dok* in 62 fascicles. The monks who received food offerings on the second occasion came from all over the domains of Nan.
>
> In the *ka kai* year CS 1225, the ruler expended funds from his Privy Purse to hire the further copying of the scriptures. . . . This copying was accomplished over eight years, from CS 1225 to CS 1232. Altogether, the ruler, during this third period had 189 texts copied, or a total of 1,251 fascicles. (Nan, 10.14–10.19)

Several other occasions of manuscript production and donation are recorded in this chapter. At Nan, 10.18, the monks are paid 645 *salüng*,[12] to write thirty-four works comprising 434 fascicles, which also amounts to 182 *thæp* 3 *salüng*. Five years later, 56 *thæp* are paid to monks to copy sixty-one texts, or 271 fascicles (Nan, 10.30). When all this copying is done, the ruler has a beautiful library constructed and adorned with gems and gold leaf.

His last large project is described in the following manner:

> On the 7th day of the second month,[13] he invited the scriptures to come to the *mondok luang* at the Sanam Luang, and he prepared the way with music. The next day, the chanting of the scriptures began, continuing to the 14th. On the full-moon day, the ruler led a *buddhābhiseka* ceremony in the ordination hall of Wat Cang Kham, and listened to the six chapters of the *Buddhābhiseka* text. They concluded the next day. This inauguration of the scriptures and dedication of the ordination hall marked another great festival, the seventh. On this occasion, 38 titles were copied, comprising 292 fascicles. (Nan, 10.36)

Among these texts are included most Sutta, Vinaya, and Abhidhamma texts of the Pali Tipiṭaka along with many, but not all, of the commentaries and subcommentaries. There are also numerous vernacular texts, including

Nissayas on the *Dīgha* and *Majjhima Nikāya*s and the *Dhammapada*, as well as many Ānisaṃsa texts, at least one of which, *Ānisaṃsa Piṭaka*, praised the making of copies of Dhamma texts. By this time, then, large, royally sponsored copying projects were viewed, at least by the rulers of Nan, to be essential to the success and propagation of the religion. This attitude, which modern readers might think would be important for the career of any religion, is rarely seen in earlier Pali texts, nor is it apparent even in the TCM, composed only sixty-six years earlier. Equally important is the strong royal approval that underlay this project. As presented in the chronicle, the initiative this time came solely from the ruling circle, and not from monks, which again ties the activities to issues of royal legitimization.

Did manuscript prices change over time? As recorded in the Nan chronicle, Ananta sponsored at least seven large manuscript-copying projects, in which more than 700 texts were reproduced. The chronicle says that in one of the projects, initiated in 1880 CE, 271 fascicles were copied for a total of 56 *thæp* (Nan, 10.30). From fees given elsewhere in this text, we can conclude that there were 3.5 *salüng* per *thæp*. Therefore this project cost about 1.4 *salüng* per fascicle. Another project cost 645 *salüng* for 434 fascicles, or about 1.5 *salüng* per fascicle (Nan, 10.28). At this time there were about 1,600 cowries per *salüng*, and therefore the cost was approximately 2,200 cowries per fascicle, which is, surprisingly, exactly the same amount paid 300 years earlier for this task.[14]

In the colophon of fascicle 9 of a *Paramaṭṭhavibhūsanī* (HH-30) from Wat Chang Kham in Nan dated CS 1231 (1869 CE), the scribe writes that the ruler, in this case King Ananta, paid one *bi*, or about 700 cowries. Importantly, this scribe is one of the very few who are not monks or novices, but rather is a former monk (*nan*). The low price paid for the fascicles of this manuscript may be explained by the colophons: "I did the writing at night time and therefore could not see well, because during the day I had to do my farmer's work" (fascicle 2), and "Living out in the countryside, I lack the skill of writing" (fascicle 5). It appears, then, that this manuscript was made by less experienced hands and was therefore cheaper than average. The remuneration was dispensed not to a monk but to a former monk, which may also have affected its size, if the donor followed the well-known principle that the more deserving the recipient, the more merit accrues to the donor.

The Nan chronicle also gives the cost of numerous other late nineteenth-century meritorious works that we can compare with the prices paid for manuscripts. Building an arched entrance and door frames for a gallery around part of Wat Chæ Hæng, for example, cost 500 *bat*. Hiring an artisan to construct two *nāga*s (mythological snake guardians) cost 2,400 *bat*. The 160,570 clay tiles covering the gallery cost 1,255 *bat* (Nan, 11.1). The entire copying project initiated by Anantaworaritthidet, one of the largest in the history of northern Thailand, entailed copying over 700 titles. At an average of six fascicles per title, this comes to 4,200 fascicles.[15] If the average paid for each fascicle was 1.5 *salüng*, then the total outlay would have been somewhere in the order of 6,300 *salüng* or 1,550 *bat*. This is comparable to the price paid for the clay tiles to cover the gallery of just one monastery. It is a sign of the value given to copying texts that it took an extremely devout king, who is repeatedly praised in both the chronicle and the colophons as being a man of great religious fervor and deeply devoted to the Dhamma, to disperse the funds required to completely revitalize the manuscript tradition of Nan—a task that ultimately cost little more than installing new tiles at just one of the countless royally sponsored *wat*s peppering the land.

The chapter in the Nan chronicle detailing the prices paid for numerous copying projects and explicitly emphasizing the importance of manuscripts for the maintenance of Buddhism is an anomaly among the chronicles that I have examined. Its very existence, however, indicates that if a sponsor wanted to record such a deed for posterity, it would not have been beyond the horizon of a traditional *tamnan* to include it. That such an episode is not found in other places, and that when it is found, it is in the last section of a late nineteenth-century text, gives strong evidence that earlier periods were ambivalent about writing as an act of great cultural value. However, it must be emphasized that this section of the Nan chronicle, coupled with the inscriptions narrating the massive copying projects undertaken in the 1830s and the large number of extant manuscripts from the Chiang Mai region, do show that writing was playing an increasingly central role in the Buddhist culture of Lan Na as the nineteenth century progressed.

POSSIBLE SOURCES FOR THE CHANGING ROLE OF WRITING

Where would new attitudes towards the written word have come from? Did they come from the Burmese, from the flourishing Siamese culture of Bangkok, from Europeans, or from autochthonous sources? There is evidence to support each of these possibilities, and it is not unlikely that a combination of catalysts was responsible.

I have already dealt in passing with the possibility of Burmese influence, which was certainly strong and sustained for a long period of time. As other conquerors have done, the Burmese left their imprint on the architecture and culture of the region, although less so than one might expect based upon the length of their hegemony. Perhaps they spent so much of that time in war that there was comparatively little opportunity to establish deep cultural roots.

During this period, the height of the colonial era, it is fitting to consider whether European influence may have affected the way that written copies of religious texts were incorporated into the cultural fabric of northern Thailand. There is little question of the importance of books to the religious enterprise carried on by Europeans, as is evident even from Thai temple art. I have, unfortunately, not yet been able to conduct a comprehensive survey of the temple murals on the walls of northern Thai *wat*s. These beautiful artistic treasures frequently narrate stories of the Buddha's many lives as found in the Jātaka tales as well as important scenes from other collections of Buddhist literature and from daily life. They were yet another medium through which to convey to the largely illiterate populace the basic ideas of Buddhism. I have not actually seen any murals in the North that include depictions of monks reading from manuscripts, although I have been assured by informants that such exist. Wat Phumin in Nan, renovated between 1867 and 1875 during the reign of Ananta, does possess some murals that depict quite clearly the use of books. Upon inspection, however, one realizes that they are not being used by Buddhist monks, but rather by French Roman Catholic priests (Wyatt 1994a, plate 7). The artist, then, might have actually been using books as a handy sign to clarify that these figures are not supposed to be Buddhist, but Catholic. The historic import of these murals depends upon their accurate dating, which can be estimated based on the subject matter portrayed. While others have assumed that the murals were painted around the time of the renovation, Wyatt believes that they were made about two decades later. He points out (1994a, 25) that the French women are depicted wearing clothing and headgear belonging to the 1880s and 1890s and that, in any event, French missionaries did not reach Nan until that time (31). Thus one of the few murals from nineteenth-century Lan Na in which Europeans are depicted highlights their close relationship with writing and books. However, the amount of influence they could have had on Lan Na before the very end of the nineteenth century is in doubt. While French political and religious missions had reached Ayudhyā in considerable numbers during the seventeenth century, and the Dutch and English had intercourse with Siam in increasing numbers as well, Lan Na remained largely unaffected by this expanding nexus of relations. As Wyatt has said, French influence was not felt in the eastern parts of Lan Na until the 1880s and the first Protestant mission did not open in Chiang Mai until 1867, when Rev. Daniel McGilvary and his wife opened up the "Laos Mission" (Swanson 1996, 31). It need not be added that Thailand is the only country in Southeast Asia, and one of the only in the world, that was never conquered by a European power. All this militates against the idea that heavy European influence led to increased reliance upon and acceptance of the written word in nineteenth-century Lan Na.

The next possible source of influence may have imbibed European ideas about written texts and transferred them indirectly to the Lan Na region. I am talking here of the Siamese kingdom centered at Bangkok during the Ratanakosin period. Lan Na had been a vassal of Siam from the time of its independence from Burma, and political and religious officials went often to the capital to pay tribute, study, and otherwise conduct business. As a matter of course, they would have breathed in the cosmopolitan atmosphere of that great city and would have brought some of its ideas back with them to Lan Na. As Wyatt says, the situation at the time was such that

> conceptions, feelings, values, experience and other "mental furniture" could be widely shared throughout the Tai world. The various institutions of civil, political and economic life, as well as of intellectual and cultural life . . . functioned pre-eminently as channels for communication that made possible patterned behaviour that was more than random—that is, vast numbers of people behaved, because they thought, similarly. (1997, 430)

The Ratanakosin dynastic chronicle includes a lengthy and detailed account of the revision and copying of the Tipiṭaka. The strikingly different position given to the canonical texts in general and the labors directed towards their preservation and reproduction in the Ratanakosin chronicle tells us that writing was viewed differently in the Bangkok environment of the mid-nineteenth century in which it was produced than in contemporary Lan Na, as represented by the TCM. The Ratanakosin chronicle's preoccupation with the details of textual production is truly remarkable when compared with what is found in northern chronicles. It even contains an excursus on the problems that arise when people from different countries transliterate the Pali texts into their own scripts (Thiphakorawong 1978, 157) as well as, of course, giving an account of the councils held under Kings Tilaka and Rama.

The copying projects undertaken by Ananta may have been influenced by those pursued in Bangkok and by the fact that writing was increasing in importance in Siam generally. Coming almost a century after the council convened by Rama I and amid the rapidly expanding use of—and hence demystification of—writing, the idea that Ananta had reached beyond his authority in sponsoring this kind of work would by then not have been an issue.

The question remains, however, as to the extent to which Bangkok itself was driven to promote writing and books through contact with modern Europe. It seems clear that the gradual changes in the social, religious, literary, economic, and political texture of Siamese life in the early Ratanakosin period tended to bring these arenas into harmony with the contours of modern Europe. The success of these changes can be surmised by the fact that Siam was able to navigate the colonial period while maintaining its independence. Less clear are the causes of these changes, for the similarity of the end product notwithstanding, they may have been due just as much to indigenous developments as to the influence of the West. Nidhi Aeusrivongse has convincingly argued that many of these changes arose organically out of a reassessment of Siamese history and traditional cultural sources. He states that early Bangkok literature is marked by several features that were reactions against the old order of Ayudhyā, including increased realism, greater use of folk sources and sentiments, fictional rather than legendary formulations, mundane urban settings, heroes whose merits are not based solely on their high birth, and literary works intended for reading (1994, 69–72).

> Literature, both court and folk, in Ayudhya was "consumed" through listening. Almost all folk literature was aural, improvised and sung by poets. Court literature was recited in Buddhist or Hinduistic ceremonies or melodically recited for listening. The tradition naturally persisted in early Bangkok, but more and more literary pieces were obviously written for reading. It should be also noted that prose became much more prevalent among the Bangkok court writings. A textbook for learning how to read Thai was available for the first time in this period. (Aeusrivongse 1994, 70)

We can see that these literary styles resemble what one might expect based upon European influence, but they also may have arisen based on a thorough reassessment of the Ayudhyān polity that had failed in the face of Burmese offensives. Thus with the unparalleled extent of European power becoming clear, and the necessity of addressing it in some way becoming clearer still, the Siamese looked within as well as without in order to best meet this challenge. The literary and other innovations that ensued should not be seen as simple mimicry of the West, and those practices that were echoed in Nan and other parts of Lan Na should be viewed even less as signs of European influence.

LITERACY IN THE RECENT PAST

While it is important not to simply extrapolate current sociological conditions backwards, it would be remiss not to include some words about Stanley Tambiah's pioneering 1961 study of literacy in the Tai-Lao village of Ban Phran Muan in the northeastern Isan region. This rather remote and unexceptional village is located between the provincial capital of Udøn and the town of Nongkhai on the western bank of the Mekhong, and at the time of Tambiah's study it was home to 182 families totaling 932 persons. While it is not peopled by Yuan, the literary and religious culture is similar to what one might find in villages that were formally part of Lan Na, as is exemplified by the fact that the sacred texts are written in the Dhamma script with only minor local variants. It also appears that at one time it was included in a polity (*maṇḍala*) linked to a Lan Na power center, although the historical record is unclear about this.[16]

Tambiah wished to look at literacy as it existed in the village before the central government instituted modern primary education in the 1930s. He believed, and I think rightly, that one could get a glimpse of the space given to the written word in the years before this reform. Writing in 1961, he said that "some of the literates of the previous era are still alive and play indispensable roles and, more so, because the major agency of literacy in the past—the Buddhist temple—functions intact and undiminished" (1968, 86). His insights provide one of the better means for conveying us back almost to King Ananta's epoch, where we can see that the existence of many manuscripts notwithstanding, Pali literacy remained the province of a small group of elite actors.

Tambiah reminds us that different levels of literacy appear in conjunction with the different functions of the written word and with different facets of the religious life of the village. The Buddhist texts kept at the monastery are largely written on palm-leaf in the Dhamma script and are mostly vernacular Nidāna texts that explain Buddhist doctrine or narrate Buddhist didactic tales and that are often used as sermons. As is the case with other monastic collections in the region, few of the manuscripts are purely in Pali and a number of them deal with non-Buddhist facets of Thai religion such as astrology and the performance of *khwan* rites, which aim to preserve and strengthen the spiritual essence of the human being. While less than what is demanded of the Buddhist monks, a degree of literacy is required to officiate at the *khwan* rites, and those who fulfill this task are usually former monks who have learned the requisite literary skills at the monastery. Those who deal with the spirits, called *phi*, do not in general need to be literate, as their practices consist largely of invoking simple memorized spells and incantations and contacting the spirits through trances. The more literacy is required for a practice—and thus the more associated with Buddhism the practice is—the higher the prestige accorded it in this system. Practicing monks may be involved in *khwan* rites, but they generally try to avoid the *phi* cult, as it is regarded as something that is not condoned by Buddhism. Those involved with the *khwan* rites, on the other hand, are generally actively associated with Buddhism, being members of the temple committee who help to organize festivals, marriage ceremonies, and other rites.

Another important literate figure is, of course, the village headman, who is essentially an administrator operating as a liaison with the district officers. Other than the secular activities of this headman, however, who must occasionally write reports and compile statistics, the primary literate activity was reading both secular and Dhamma scripts, and the secondary activity was copying. Little emphasis was placed on the ability to compose in writing, and it was rarely done.

Since literacy was gained through studying at the monastery, the degree of literacy was essentially a measure of the length of time spent in the *wat*. "The acquisition of literacy, which gives access to ritual texts, is *via* the village temple. The progression of traditional literacy was from *dekwat* (temple boy) to *nen* (novice) to *phra* (monk) to layman ex-monk who functioned as a ritual expert (e.g., *mau khwan*)" (Tambiah 1968, 94). Tambiah points out that most who enter the novitiate or the monkhood do so for a limited time, often as short as three months, and therefore the small number of males, fewer than 20 percent, who remain in the robes for a period of a few years form the truly literate core. They themselves may, of course, have significantly varying degrees of knowledge.

Even though reading and writing played an important role in religious education, at the turn of the century, according to Tambiah's informants, most time was still spent on memorization of texts, without, it should be noted, a corresponding emphasis on comprehension. Moreover, a large proportion of the numerous chants that were required for worship of the Buddha, merit-making, and protection were not lifted from the palm leaves. Rather,

> since they were chanted by monks in the early morning and at night, a newcomer repeats what he hears and memorizes them fairly quickly. . . .
>
> The abbot gives each student the task of learning a set of chants. After about five days, at a common class, each student is asked to recite in turn. The task in question is not merely a matter of learning words but of chanting them according to certain tunes. Early morning before school, or after school in the afternoon, novices and monks practise chants individually in their cubicles.
>
> The fact that Buddhism is aesthetically a musical religion, and that the memorizing of words is closely linked to musical rhythms, gives us a clue to the technique and the way in which novices and monks are in fact capable of memorizing an impressive amount of words in their correct order. (Tambiah 1968, 100)

Buddhist ideas and doctrine were imparted to the laity largely through sermons, but the content was often considered secondary to the manner in which the sermon was delivered. Such things as the quality of the voice, the rhythm of the speech, the fluidity of the sermon, and even its length (yes, the longer the better, believe it or not) were considered important features. Sermons were often based upon stories (*nidāna*) taken from the Jātaka tales, including both the canonical and noncanonical collections, but they also included local tales known only in northern Thailand and Laos that were often only peripherally related to Buddhism. These were mostly read in the vernacular.

> Few village monks are versed in Pali and therefore this specialized learning is infrequent. It is for these reasons that I have argued that the majority of village monks or novices are largely ignorant of Pali (or at least have a shaky knowledge) and therefore of the content of Pali chants and Pali doctrinal texts. While the latter are accessible in local script, the chants cannot be reduced into the words of the local language, for then they would lose their sacredness and their efficacy. (Tambiah 1968, 105)

Tambiah points out that donating texts to the local monastery is considered a merit-making act, but he laments that the palm-leaf texts are gradually being replaced by printed books in the Thai script, and the palm-leaf texts are in danger of being neglected and eventually forgotten.

The situation was not substantially different in the Chiang Mai region itself, where Konrad Kingshill reported in 1953 that

> each temple keeps a whole series of sermons in the *ho thamma*. Villagers buy these palm-leaf sermons for specific, merit-making occasions to present to the temple, where they are kept for future use. Today, copies written into school notebooks with pen and ink are sometimes substituted for the palm-leaf variety that are increasingly difficult to secure. . . . (Kingshill 1991, 119)
>
> Buddhist literature within the village [of Ku Dæng in Chiang Mai province] was practically non-existent. The monthly magazine *Buddhist News*, published by the Buddhist Association of Chiang Mai, was regularly received by the temple for the monks and novices to read. Some villagers who came to the temple leafed through any issue that happened to be lying on the table. We failed to observe any determined or systematic reading on the part of lay persons in the village. (124)

As McDaniel has observed in the north today, most Pali manuscripts "sit locked up and dusty in monastic libraries and are more commonly read by local and foreign academics" (2003, 100). The conclusion cannot be avoided: while manuscripts did increase in importance throughout the nineteenth century, influenced by the years of Burmese suzerainty, increasing contact with Bangkok and the western world, and internal developments, their regular use as supports for the study of Pali texts remained restricted to certain more educated monks and enlightened rulers.

6 Overlooked or Looked Over?

The Meaning and Uses of Written Pali Texts

This chapter will delve more deeply into the attitudes and approaches towards the medium of writing and situate these within the constellation of beliefs and practices that make up Buddhism in Lan Na. It will therefore explore *how* manuscripts were being read or otherwise used, and *why* they were being made.

DONOR DESIRES

It is important to consider the words of those who actually made the manuscripts. Various reasons are given in the colophons for making the manuscripts, such as the desire to make merit, to support the religion, and to achieve *nibbāna* in a future life. These sentiments, broadly speaking, are not greatly different from those seen in colophons from Buddhist manuscripts in India and Nepal,[1] in donative inscriptions in India,[2] and in other donative contexts elsewhere in the Buddhist world.

A list from the colophons of the basic wishes and desires behind the making of manuscripts can help to highlight the key motivations underlying this process. Although they are sometimes expressed in slightly different language,[3] they can easily be divided into a few general categories. It should be noted that many colophons express several of these desires at once.

COMMON COLOPHON SUBJECTS

1. Whoever borrows this manuscript should really bring it back. If the borrower keeps it, that person will be reborn as a hungry ghost (*peta*) [or some other curse will be put on him or her]
2. It was very hard to make the manuscript, so take care of it
3. Take the manuscript to worship[4] (*prasong* or *pūjā*)

4. May the manuscript lead to *nibbāna*
5. May the donor be born in Metteyya's time [and reach *nibbāna* then]
6. May the manuscript support the Sāsanā [for 5,000 years]
7. Written in order to get merit
8. Do not try to alter the manuscript or add any writing
9. Please correct any mistakes
10. Please excuse the poor quality
11. May the manuscript lead to wisdom and knowledge [of the Dhamma/Tipiṭaka/Arahattamagga]

These colophons and the desires expressed in them are marked by many formulaic features. However, one should not let that completely overshadow an analysis of the sentiments expressed, for some became more (or less) common over time, reflecting changing attitudes towards the place of manuscripts in society. Since many of the colophons say little more than the title of the work or perhaps the date, it appears that lengthy, descriptive colophons need not have been written had the scribe not wished to do so for some particular reason. That is to say, he was not just filling space with empty words as required by convention. It is therefore important to attribute intentional agency to the authors of these colophons, just as one would to the authors of any other Thai texts. Colophons by the same scribe tend to express similar sentiments, again suggesting that they can be associated with genuine desires that differed from one person to another and that changed over time, even though they were expressed in a formulaic manner. If this were not the case, if instead there were a selection of standard acceptable utterances that were included at the end of these texts only to satisfy the demands of protocol, then one would expect to see a completely random distribution of sentiments.

That the sentiments in the colophons do reveal patterns is shown, for example, by the fact that the desire to be reborn during the time of Metteyya, the future buddha, is rarely seen in early manuscripts, but it becomes quite popular after about 1700 CE. This appears to reflect certain religious developments in the region, such as a possible rise in millenarianism spurred by deteriorating conditions under the Burmese. Furthermore, with very few exceptions the colophons to Pali texts are written in the vernacular. This suggests that the scribe was fully aware of what he was writing and that the words were intended to be understood by the reader. This fact also tells us a lot about the state of Pali knowledge at the time—namely, that even the literate community was not necessarily expected to be able to understand Pali.

Because of the conservatism inherent in all scriptural copying processes, which are designed to maintain the highest standards of fidelity and discourage innovation, the degree to which colophon sentiments changed over time is actually rather surprising. Because these changes represent a difference in the attitudes towards manuscripts and their place in the religious life of the people, they can be used to distill information salient to the history of writing in the region. The three wishes that seem evenly distributed over all periods are that the writing of the manuscript will lead to *nibbāna*; that it will lead to merit (*puñña*) either for the writer, his family, or other worthies;[5] and that the manuscript will support the religion for 5,000 years. The exhortation to "take good care of the manuscript because it was hard to make" can be found in manuscripts dated from 1527–1558 CE, with two more dated between then and 1650, but it does not occur in the more recent manuscripts that I have seen. This should not be surprising. At this early point, when the art of manuscript production was still in its primitive stages, manuscripts would have been rarer, and the skills required to prepare the leaves, the ink, and the stylus, as well as to execute the writing would have been less developed, underscoring the truth of the statement "it was hard to make." For related reasons the standard request found in manuscripts starting around 1780 CE for the user to excuse the poor quality of the writing is *not* found in the earlier colophons. This absence is consistent with a technique in its infancy; in the first century or two there would not have been a need to apologize because those people interested in such things would have been happy that the items existed at all. Potential critics would also not have had a long tradition of quality items with which to compare the manuscript at hand.

One would expect the early generation of manuscript producers also to have been particularly intent upon instilling in potential users the desire to return them promptly. Indeed, the colophons telling people who borrow the manuscript to bring it back or face the consequences are mostly from before 1559 CE. It is unfortunate that we are not given a better idea of what the manuscripts were used for when they were taken away. As I will discuss below, one of the possible uses was for worship, either as objects of devotion or as supports for the texts recited during the liturgy. Another possible use was for study. Many manuscripts were taken to be used as exemplars from which to make more copies at other monasteries; in fact it appears that someone who took an early copy of the JKM was not as careful as the colophons demand, because all known manuscripts of this text have a hiatus spanning several leaves. This error also indicates that all these copies descend from one earlier copy, suggesting that in the early period there were not many manuscripts of each text available. This would further emphasize the need to be careful with them.

There is a good indication of who was actually using these manuscripts in some of the older colophons. Many address potential users as *ton*, which, as Hundius points out, usually refers to members of the Saṅgha and therefore indicates that only they, and perhaps royalty, were expected to have access to the manuscripts.

MANUSCRIPTS AND THE TRANSMISSION OF KNOWLEDGE

The type of colophon that presents the most significant conceptual problems deals with the desire for the manuscript to lead to knowledge of some important Buddhist subject such as the Dhamma or Tipiṭaka (listed above as no. 11). These colophons are usually doing more than just soliciting a discursive usage of the manuscripts as transmitters of words that give the appropriate knowledge when read. They often assert that engaging the manuscript in some way, be it reading, writing, or even merely possessing it, can lead to penetrating knowledge of the whole corpus of Buddhist literature. A *Mahāvagga* (SRI 19-04-030-00) from CS 938 (1576 CE) serves to illustrate. The colophon to fascicle 19 of this Vinaya text reads:

> Fascicle 19 of the *Mahāvagga*. Mrs. Kæo Pha with Yut Chai who have pure faith and joy in the teachings of the Buddha were the supporters. They gave out monetary support and alms in order to be a support for the teachings of the Buddha lasting for five thousand years. May it give wisdom and knowledge of the *Dhamma* of the Buddha, ending in the three *Piṭaka*s (*hü mee prañya ru tham phra phuttha chao chop trai pidok*).

Let us consider carefully the question of whether the knowledge of the Dhamma in this case is supposed to be gained discursively through the mundane act of studying the text, or "karmically" through the merit gained from making or otherwise coming into contact with this manuscript. The wording suggests that the text itself is somehow able to confer knowledge of the entire collection of canonical texts, for the Dhamma that it transmits is explicitly equated with all three of the Piṭakas. This need not have been emphasized if the text embodied in this manuscript were believed to convey only the chapters from the monks' disciplinary texts that its title suggests. Something else must be going on here.

Some light can be shed on this issue by considering an episode from a Yuan text called *Banha Thera Chan*, which Penth believes was composed several hundred years ago (1974, 270). This text purports to relate certain queries undertaken by the monk who founded Wat Umong just outside of Chiang Mai. The monk, who was ordained in Chiang Mai about 1380 CE, went to Doi Suthep

> and for several days and nights recited holy texts, by which means he hoped to gain supernatural intelligence in order to learn and understand quickly the Buddhist Canon. While he was thus reciting, a beautiful goddess approached him, questioned him about what he was doing there and then asked if he would leave the monkhood once he had gained intelligence. When he replied in the negative, she handed him the desired intelligence as something small to eat. (Penth 1974, 271)

The monk apparently believed that reciting *some* texts could somehow help lead to knowledge of *other* texts through means other than conventional study, just as the *Mahāvagga* sponsors evidently believed.

A rare Pali language colophon from a *Malleyadīpanīṭīkā* (SRI 19-04-029.02) dated CS 981 (1619 CE) adds to the picture and seems again, based on the syntax, to suggest that knowledge of the Tipiṭaka can come not just through studying the texts in discursive engagement, but through the very act of copying them. The colophon on the cover of the first fascicle says:

> This compendium of the essence of the text was written by the monk Dhammakāma in the year 981, being the year of the goat, for my own benefit. The merit born from the act of writing this has been made by me. Through this merit, I have become one who knows the *Tipiṭaka* (*iminā katapuñena tepiṭako bhavāmihaṃ*).[6]

Here, the power of merit is explicitly put forward as the source of the knowledge attained by the monk. The colophon makes no mention of study or reading, but implies instead that the scribe's knowledge is engendered by the merit (*puña*)[7] itself, rather than by any reading that would have been a necessary part of the process of copying the text. Furthermore, the scribe is claiming more knowledge as a Tepiṭako than could have been gained from reading just one commentarial text, so there must be something more than reading as the root cause of his knowledge.

Another colophon in which the desire for knowledge is expressed is that of an Abhidhamma commentary called *Paramaṭṭhavibhūsanī* (HH-29) that was copied as part of the large project initiated by Anantaworaritthidet, the ruler of Nan in the 1860s. The scribe, a novice (*sāmaṇera*), gives voice to the hope that he will, through the merit acquired from writing this text, reach *nibbāna* and be endowed with the intelligence and wisdom to answer difficult problems and know the 84,000 *khandha*s (divisions) of the Buddha's teachings. Because the source of these felicities, which include attainment of *nibbāna*, is identified as the merit attendant upon writing the manuscript, I am tempted to agree with Hundius that they are hoped for in a future life. If this is the case, then here again the knowledge of the Buddha's teaching is not intended to be a direct result of actually *reading* the text in question, but rather is a karmic result of writing it.

It might be expected that making a manuscript leads to so much merit because the manuscript can be used to study and learn the words of the Buddha. However, if knowledge can be gained in this life or the next through the workings of karma, this seems to obviate the need to actually use a manuscript as a source of informational content. It becomes a token of the power of the Buddha's words. It is thus possible to imagine a cycle in which the merit from a manuscript would lead to a better birth or even enlightenment, but the manuscript would never actually be read. It is also possible that copying a manuscript was considered a form of meditation. There are, of course, some colophons that suggest that the manuscript itself should be studied and will lead to knowledge in that manner, but these are less common. None of the colophons that suggest that the very act of writing the manuscript itself leads to complete knowledge of the Dhamma are written by *araññavāsī* monks. Their scholastic leanings would have required the diligent study of many texts in order to acquire the benefits of their contents.

NIBBĀNA AS A RESULT OF GOOD KARMA

The hope that sponsoring the manuscript will lead to *nibbāna* helps us to discern the way ideas found in the Tipiṭaka have been understood by Buddhists in Southeast Asia. Spiro (1982) has famously and controversially divided Buddhism into three distinct modes, which he calls *kammatic*, *nibbanic*, and *apotropaic* Buddhism. He holds that the pursuit of good karma and of *nibbāna* should be considered separate paths, largely identified by, but not completely coterminous with, the practices of the laity and the monks respectively. Good karma (synonymous with *puñña*) and *nibbāna* are mutually exclusive because all karma is produced when one acts with worldly (*lokiya*) consequences in mind while under the influence in some way of the three faults (*dosa*s) of greed, hatred, and delusion. In contrast, *nibbāna* is attained only when one has rooted out these faults and destroyed not just one's bad, but *also* one's good karma. How, then, might the meritorious act of sponsoring a manuscript in a language that one does not understand help to further the aim of *nibbāna*, unless good karma and *nibbāna* are somehow intertwined? Regardless of the philosophical problems inherent in this process, the colophons leave little doubt that their authors perceived karma and *nibbāna* as lying on the same moral continuum. Manuscript colophons frequently express the hope that the making of the text will lead to the three kinds of happiness, with *nibbāna* at the pinnacle,[8] or simply that it will be a support for the attainment of *nibbāna* (*nibbāna paccayo hotu*).[9] We can find a similar sentiment inscribed on a manuscript box made by the king of Nan in 1795 CE that says that the box was made in order to protect the Tipiṭaka and thereby produce merit that will cause the makers to attain the three forms of happiness, with *nibbāna* at the top (CLNI, 5, 78).

These examples tell us a great deal about the way that actual practicing Buddhists have conceived of the relationship between these two central Buddhist concepts, much of which challenges the conventions often used in textbooks to describe Theravāda Buddhist belief. The persistent characterization in the colophons and inscriptions of karma and *nibbāna* as constituting part of the same path does suggest that we reconsider the nature of this path along the lines that Harvey Aronson has proposed. He has drawn our attention to the possibility that even in "canonical Buddhism," there is no impassable chasm separating the pursuit of good karma from that of *nibbāna*. Aronson writes that there is an

> intrinsic relationship between virtuous activity (karma) and the realization of nirvana. Although there are variations in emphasis that differentiate those seeking pleasurable rebirth and those seeking nirvana, the similarity of their ethical context cannot be overlooked. Physical, verbal and mental virtue is the bare minimum necessary to insure pleasurable rebirth. Concentration can be of use in securing even more pleasurable rebirth among the heavens. When these activities are coupled with the cultivation of insight they provide a context for liberation from rebirth altogether. The supramundane goal of freedom from rebirth is approached through mundane ethical activity. The mundane serves as the matrix for the transcendent. (1979, 34)

It is possible, on this understanding, that rather than simply causing one to "go to" *nibbāna*, the production of manuscripts was held by the more sophisticated believers to engender the good karma necessary for the achievement of the kind of position in this or a future life capable of supporting the real quest for enlightenment.

MANUSCRIPTS AS OBJECTS OF WORSHIP

It is clear from the colophons that some parties thought that making manuscripts was a highly meritorious act, capable of bringing great rewards to the sponsors and scribes through the fruition of the good karma derived thereby. In the Buddhist moral economy, most items whose production confers good karma can also be sources of merit when worshipped by the faithful. This is certainly the case with Buddha images and *stūpa*s, which are meritorious to make and also to worship, and this raises the question of whether this is true for manuscripts as well.

Determining the status of manuscripts within the devotional cultus must negotiate the difficult conceptual terrain surrounding the position of any religious artifact within the conceptual world of Theravāda Buddhism. Although the exact status of reliquary *stūpa*s raises some philosophical and doctrinal questions, these are compounded in the case of manuscripts by the fact that neither manuscripts nor writing were known when the canonical texts were formulated, so that time period offers no guidance on the topic. What little can be found in the Tipiṭaka about the place of worship in the religion is said with respect to the relics (*dhātu/sarīra*) of the Buddha and their accompanying *stūpa*s,[10] and this has served as the paradigm for cultic practice directed towards the other major objects of devotion, namely, Bodhi trees and Buddha images. These objects are considered by the fifth-century commentarial tradition to be *relics of use* and *relics of commemoration*, respectively, which occupy secondary and tertiary positions relative to the highest form of relic, the corporeal remains of the Buddha.[11] When this tripartite theory of cultic objects was developed, there was apparently no attempt to formulate a normative conception of written scriptures that would have placed them within one of these categories and clarified their cultic status.

The question of how the various classes of relics are to be seen in the context of normative Theravāda Buddhism revolves around the ambiguous role of devotion and ritual in the Tipiṭaka in general.[12] At the heart of the problem lies the Buddha's opposition to the use of ritual to cleanse oneself of wrongdoing,[13] coupled with his emphasis on the importance of ridding oneself of desire, ego, and ignorance through mental cultivation in order to reach the ultimate goal of *nibbāna*. It is easy to see how the worship of relics might not only be irrelevant to such an enterprise,[14] but could in fact hinder it, especially considering that the "ignorance" (*avijjā*) that must be overcome in this case is ignorance of the three characteristics of the world (*tilakkhaṇa*), foremost of which is impermanence (*anicca*), followed by soullessness (*anattā*) and suffering (*dukkha*). A relic is a part of the body of the Buddha that *remains* after the earthly death of the Teacher, and as such symbolically prolongs his presence in this world. This phenomenon is well-known in other religions, but the fact that seeing and accepting impermanence in all things is a central feature of the Buddha's teachings raises serious questions about the tactic of preserving parts of the Buddha after his life has ended. The *Mahāparinibbāna Sutta* records disapprovingly that some of the monks who had apparently not understood his message fell to the ground and wept upon hearing of the Buddha's attainment of *parinibbāna*, saying, "too soon has the Blessed One vanished" (DN, ii, 159). Furthermore, by associating relics with the power of the Buddha, the relics themselves become potential objects of desire: far from helping to quench attachment and passion, they may even encourage it. This danger is highlighted by the serious confrontation over the right to possess the relics of the Buddha that developed between his once tranquil followers immediately after his death (DN, ii,166); since then there have also been numerous occasions of relic theft, not just by lone thieves, but often by the leadership of various Buddhist communities (Trainor 1997, 120). It is not difficult to see how an understanding of Buddhist philosophy as found in the majority of early Pali canonical texts might lead one to believe that relic worship and other forms of ritual that do not have as their immediate aim the removal of the hindrances to the enlightened perception of impermanence are at best useless and at worst conducive to further entrenchment in the sorrowful world of sensual desire.

Two pioneers of western Buddhist textual scholarship, Hermann Oldenberg and T. W. Rhys Davids, drew a contrast, as Trainor succinctly puts it, "between the pure morality of the Buddha's original teaching and its subsequent decline into an externalized ritualism centered on the Buddha's physical remains" (1997, 20).

The discourse of a noble, intellectual religion decaying into popular superstition was routinely repeated by scholars until relatively recently, and this included the assumption that the veneration of relics was mainly an activity of the less-educated laity. Thus, whereas the tradition does not by and large seem to have perceived relic worship as a contradiction of the Buddha's teachings, it has been so regarded by many western scholars of the religion. As Schopen has meticulously argued,[15]

> the monastic community's status as principal heir of the Buddha's religious authority has depended not only on its possession of the Buddha's teachings; it has been supported, as well, by its physical proximity to the enshrined remains of the Buddha and its control over the distribution of the Buddha's relics. (1997, 20)

The apparent contradiction between some important canonical passages and the practices and beliefs of historical Buddhist practitioners is illustrated by an exchange between an early American publisher of Buddhist literature, Paul Carus, and a Sri Lankan monk. Carus wrote a letter in 1896 in response to an offer by the monk to send him a relic in appreciation for his efforts to spread knowledge of Buddhism in the West. The letter exemplifies the kind of attitude one might expect from someone acquainted with the teachings of the Buddha as distilled from the canonical literature:

> Words, thoughts, and ideas are not material things, they are ideal possessions, they are spiritual. It is true that they are transferred by material means in books and MSS, and by the vibrations of sounds, but it is not the book or the MS or the sound waves that are sacred, but the ideas which are conveyed by them. Thus, all the treasures which I regard as holy are of a spiritual kind, and not of a material kind. The worship of relics, be they bones, hair, teeth, or any other material of the body of a saint is a mistake. They do not possess any other value than the remains of ordinary mortals. The soul of Buddha is not in his bones, but in his words. . . . (quoted in Trainor 1997, 19)

Most practicing Buddhists in historical and contemporary Southeast Asia from both the laity and the Saṅgha, however, disagree strongly with this assessment. Instead, they regard worship of the relics as a fundamental duty of every devout Buddhist. It is in fact over the importance of relic worship that the Sinhalese modernist and reformer Anagārika Dharmapāla parted company with the scientifically oriented Colonel Henry Olcott, who had written in his widely distributed *Buddhist Catechism* that the Buddha rejected veneration of religious objects.

One of the classic formulations of the argument that it is important to honor the relics is found in the *Milindapañha*, where Nāgasena says that obeisance bears fruit not because of any power of the Buddha, who indeed is no longer present in *saṃsāra*, but rather because in making an offering, the devotee is directing the mind towards pure thoughts and striving for a righteous goal (Rhys Davids 1890, 144–147). The monk in dialog with Paul

Carus displays some similar considerations two millennia later when he says that relics ought to be worshipped

> as a mark of gratitude to Him who showed us the way to salvation and as a token of remembrance of the many personal virtues which His life illustrated. . . . We do not believe that by "worshipping" relics we attain Nirvāṇa, obtain any remission of our sins, or gain even merely any worldly benefit." (quoted in Trainor 1997, 21–22)

Neither Carus's interlocutor nor Nāgasena suggests that worship of relics can lead directly to *nibbāna*. This would indeed conflict with numerous passages attributed to the Buddha that state that only by purifying oneself of defilements such as ignorance and desire can one reach this goal. Rather, in their conception, worship can lead to good karma and hence a better rebirth. Since karma operates independently, the Buddha himself need not exercise any instrumental power of his own to help this process along. In other words, his being dead does not affect the proceedings.

This reasoned traditional Buddhist position does raise a very serious point, however: if the efficacy of ritual resides in the alteration of karmic formations in the mind of the performer, and not in any power inherent in the object of veneration itself, why should the object have to be genuine as long as the devotee *thinks* that it is? Furthermore, since the vast majority of relics are buried deep within a *stūpa* and are never seen, why should the relic have to exist at all? If we now bring manuscripts under the rubric of relics, a similar argument can be put forward for them as well: if a manuscript is to be honored in order to purify the mind of the devotee, does it really matter what it actually says or if there are any mistakes in it? There is no Buddha left to be perturbed by a misquote, and the *idea* that his words are present in the manuscript would still be effective for the devotee.

The traditional answer is that it *does* matter. The monk who offered the relic to Carus writes back to him that he is mistaken if he considers relics to be the same as the bones of any other person. Rather, he says, they are "lasting monuments" of the Buddha's virtuous teaching (Trainor 1997, 21). The importance of authenticity is also demonstrated by the fact that there are so many Pali and vernacular chronicles tracing the career of important relics whose very purpose is largely to attest to the authenticity of these sacred items.[16] The same quandary applies to images, which, like relics, ought in theory to imbue in the devotee a sense of the "felt presence" of the Buddha. They, too, are required to have some genuine connection to the Buddha;

they cannot be statues of just anybody masquerading as the Buddha. "It is held that in order to inherit some fraction of the infinite virtue and power the Buddha possessed, an image *must* trace its lineage back to one made in the 'authentic' likeness of the Master himself" (Tambiah 1984, 231).

An example of this phenomenon is the story of the Phra Buddha Singh image, which holds that the origins of the image lie seven centuries after the death of the Buddha, when a Sri Lankan king wished to see a likeness of the great Teacher. Through the virtues of several enlightened monks, a serpent deity (*nāga*) appeared and fashioned an exact image of the Buddha that was then copied by the best artisans and cast with an alloy of precious metals. This image became a resplendent statue of the Buddha that was immediately venerated. When word of its wondrous power reached the great Thai king Ramkhamhæng, he brought it to Sukhodaya by way of Nagara Śrī Dharmarāja after some trials and tribulations. Over the years various kings desired to possess it, and the image made its way through a number of important cities in Thailand, being copied several times along the way.[17] We can assume that the power of the image was transferred to its copies through the same elaborate rituals that are still performed today, which usually involve the use of a sacred cord that connects the copy to the original image.

Just as an image is supposed to present an authentic likeness of the Buddha, a manuscript must contain his authentic words. While every relic is actually a part of the Buddha, both images and manuscripts, being merely indexical, can multiply without limit. "The ease of reproducing images allows for their proliferation outside monastic control to an extent that distinguishes them from relics, which are usually confined within the ritually defined boundaries of monastic complexes" (Trainor 1997, 30–31).

This problem is addressed by the fact that images are formally consecrated, often by transferring power from one to another with a cord, as mentioned above. This transference confers upon them the mantle of the Buddha in much the same way as ordination operates upon the monks. Manuscripts sometimes undergo this process, but there are no references to it in any of the colophons or related literature that I have seen. Often no power was transmitted to the new manuscript other than the denotative power of the words inscribed therein, and no formal or ritual connection is made between a manuscript and its forebears.

Where the notion of an unbroken lineage *does* adhere in the textual realm is in the oral tradition. As we have seen, there are numerous references in Theravāda literature to the idea that the texts were heard directly from the mouth of the Buddha or his early disciples and from there passed on directly by way of the "oral portal" down through the generations. Looking back to the CDV, we find that in chapter fifteen, King Ādittarāja has the opportunity to hear the long-lived king of the crows, who had in fact been taught by the Buddha himself, preach the Dhamma. Ādittarāja then comments on the quality of the crow's preaching and says that because he heard the Dhamma directly from the mouth of the Buddha, it is as if the Buddha himself were delivering these teachings. Oral authority is a crucial element in the Vedic tradition,[18] and this ethos was imbibed by Buddhists in Thailand and other localities, as is evident by the Vedic term used to refer to the canonical selections that are chanted daily by the Buddhist monks: *mantra*. The oral tradition must be unbroken because if there is a break in the transmission of the texts, the transmission ceases to exist. The written word, on the other hand, can be lost and then found generations later and read, thus denying a direct link with the teacher. This fact doubtless played a role in the lesser importance of writing as a conveyor of religious power in comparison with oral tradition.

In sum, authentic relics and images were and are conceived as effective fields of merit for the Buddhist faithful. Venerating them leads to an increase in good karma, which seems sometimes in inscriptions to bleed into the actual achievement of *nibbāna*. There is some canonical support for this behavior in the admonition to worship at *stūpa*s found in the *Mahāparinibbāna Sutta*. Both monks and laypeople commonly venerate the objects in *stūpa*s, although fetishization of this practice, its elevation above study of the Dhamma and meditation, and its possible role in the attainment of *nibbāna* are at least problematic in light of other key ideas found in the scriptures.

How might written texts fit into this melange of practices and beliefs? Clearly, written scriptures evince features of both relics and images. Written scriptures can serve to direct the minds of the faithful towards the venerable author of these words, namely, the Buddha. Already in the canon can be found the Buddha's statement that "whoever sees the Dhamma sees me" (SN, iii,120), and surely what could be closer to "seeing" the Dhamma than looking upon a copy of a canonical text? The manuscript would then perform a role similar to that of a Buddha image, "representing the story, wisdom, and power of the person of the Buddha," as Swearer has said (1995, 51). It seems from this that there should be ample basis in the tradition for a full-blown cult of the book to arise in Theravāda lands, where *stūpa*s and images already function as key axes around which devotional activities occur. Indeed, there is at least one later text that explicitly relates manuscripts to the third category of relics, relics of commemoration, the category usually occupied by Buddha images. The *Saddhammasaṅgaha* (Law 1963), a chronicle that was likely written in the late fourteenth century by a central Thai monk who had lived and been ordained in Sri Lanka,[19] relates in chapter ten that the Buddha said each *akkhara* (letter) in the Tipiṭaka should be considered as one Buddha image and therefore should be written down. Whoever writes down canonical texts fulfils their obligations for right conduct. Thus writing was clearly thought to be a merit-making exercise by the time of this work, although even here, Penth rightly points out that "acquiring merit by writing down the holy texts must have been something rather new or less well known, otherwise the author would not have had to emphasize that one single letter of the texts brings as much merit as an entire image of the Buddha" (1977, 275).

Unlike the chronicles from northern Thailand, which were at pains to avoid egregious anachronisms, this text is not bothered by such considerations; it is the Buddha himself who proclaims the importance of writing, even though during his time there were neither written scriptures nor Buddha images. The *Saddhammasaṅgaha* did not have very much influence in Lan Na, for there are no references to it in the literature, nor are there copies of it written in Dhamma script. In Burma, however, as has been suggested, the kind of approach to writing advocated in the *Saddhammasaṅgaha* was more prevalent. It is very common to see colophons that equate the words in the manuscript to Buddha images using the following formula:

> *Akkharā ekamekañ ca Buddharūpaṃ samaṃ siyā tasmā hi paṇḍito poso likkheyya piṭakattayaṃ.*
>
> Each letter should be considered as a Buddha image, therefore the wise should write the *Tipiṭaka*.[20]

Looking at places like Burma, central Thailand, Sri Lanka, and, as we shall see, Cambodia, where there is evidence that writing had a markedly hieratic function, it becomes apparent that this ethos is in some way a vestige of Mahāyāna influence. We can identify in certain Mahāyāna ideas the philosophical foundations for the practice of worshipping books. Paranavitane, one of the earliest scholars to broach the subject of Mahāyāna influence in Sri Lanka, advanced some very plausible reasons for the veneration of written texts among "Mahāyāna" Buddhists:

> Small and disconnected fragments [of text] would bear the same relation to the whole body of the Dhamma as a small relic of the Buddha's body does

> to his corporeal frame. . . . the Mahāyānists held that the Buddha had three bodies of which the Dharmmakāya or body of the law was the most important; and the earthly body, the Nirmāṇakāya, to which belonged the relics enshrined in the early *stūpas*, was the least. To the mind of the average man the Dharmmakāya must have been represented by the written words of the Buddha . . . and enshrined in *stūpas* instead of bodily relics. (1928, 44)

A natural evolution of the identification in Mahāyāna literature of the Dharma with the body of the Buddha was the worship of the Dharma in the form of written scriptures in the place of the Buddha or his relics. Commenting on the genesis of this phenomenon, and the preponderance of inscriptions that can be found inside *stūpa*s encapsulating the core of the Buddha's teaching as expressed through the chain of dependent origination, Dan Boucher has noted:

> The cult of the book in early Mahāyāna consolidated the identification of the Buddha and the *Dharma* by linking the locus of their written *sūtras* to the well established and popular pilgrimage center at Bodh-Gayā, where the Buddha was thought to be in some sense still present. The reliquary inscriptions of the *pratītyasamutpāda* indicate a parallel attempt to appropriate the enlightenment experience of the Buddha—his cognizance of the chain of causation—into the *stūpa* cult that venerated his corporeal remains. (1991, 5)

The first direct reference to this kind of reverential treatment of writing in Pali literature comes from the twelfth-century Vinayaṭīkā (*Sāratthadīpanī-ṭīkā* 1: 172), written shortly after the period of greatest Mahāyāna influence in Sri Lanka. Here it is said that there are three types of *cetiyas: paribhogacetiya, dhātucetiya*, and *dhammacetiya.* The first type houses articles used by the Buddha, the second houses his relics, and into the third are to be deposited books inscribed with the dependent-origination formulation and other texts (*paṭiccasamuppādādi-likhita-potthakaṃ*). This passage is also found in a more accessible early fourteenth-century compendium of Buddhist doctrine called the *Sārasaṅgaha*, composed in Sri Lanka by Siddhattha Thera (Sasaki 1992). It is noteworthy that this text was composed by a monk in the very *araññavāsī* lineage that was shortly thereafter to foment a scholarly nascence in Lan Na (Sasaki 1992, ix). I have found only a single line suggesting that these ideas might have been known and accepted in Lan Na. An undated vernacular text called *Tamra Kan Kosang Phraphuttharup*, which may be several centuries old, gives instructions for making Buddha images and *cetiya*s; it says that relics (*dhātu*), including "abbreviated stanzas of the 84,000 teachings of the Buddha," may be enshrined in the heart of a *cetiya* (Swearer 2004, 52). At any rate this makes it clear that the idea that manuscripts and writing could be open to the kinds of cultic use enjoyed by relics and images was not anathema to authoritative Theravāda thinkers or at least to a few anonymous monks from Lan Na, which forces us to consider whether they may have been commonly worshipped in Lan Na.

THE CULT OF THE BOOK

Before focussing on the possibility of a cult of the book in Lan Na, we need to look elsewhere in the Buddhist world for what this kind of practice might entail. We have to know what we are looking for before embarking on the search. Turning to China, it is not difficult to find evidence of a strong cult of the book, especially in connection with the *Lotus Sūtra*. A popular eighth-century Tang dynasty text called *Hongzan fahua zhuan* (*Accounts in dissemination and praise of the Lotus*)[21] includes many examples of worship of the *Lotus Sūtra*. As the *Hongzan fahua zhuan*, which was based upon local traditions, was a source of stories enjoyed and endorsed by clergy and laity alike, this example serves as a strong testament to the sanctity of *Lotus Sūtra* manuscripts across a wide swath of Chinese society and represents the attitudes towards this kind of religious item that would have been current in the region. In one vignette about a novice who could recite the *Lotus* with great fluency, but who would inevitably forget two words, we find that his master has had a dream about the situation and is told to go to a certain house. He does so and

> after introducing himself he said to the head of the family, "Do you have a special place for making offerings?" The man replied, "We do." "What scriptures do you keep there?" he asked. To which the man replied, "We have a single copy of the *Lotus Sūtra.*" (Stevenson 1995, 438)

It turns out that the novice was living in this household in a previous life and studied from this text. It is, of course, missing the two words he keeps forgetting. But the key point here is that the master immediately assumes that scriptures of some kind will be a central component of the most sacred place in the house and hence a focal point of the family's devotion. In another story a governor hears that a devout nun "has made a personal copy of the *Lotus Sūtra*, which she keeps devotedly and to which she makes regular offerings, all according to proper ritual procedure" (Stevenson 1995, 449).

She has, moreover, made this copy out of a staggeringly large amount of silk, engendering in the governor a desire to see this expensive book. The nun does not wish to let the governor see it because he is not pure enough, but she finally gives it to his envoy after he has purified himself with perfumed water and donned clean new clothes. When the envoy brings the text to the governor, the governor opens it but sees only blank pages. Enraged, he summons the nun, and when she enters the hall, the letters, shining with a golden hue, surround her in the air. At this the governor vows to make 1,000 copies and circulate them as a votive offering. He therefore asks the nun how a copy of the text should be made. She replies that it is essential to find a copyist of good character who can keep ritually pure. Then she says:

> For the copy room, once again I mixed perfumed water with mud and went about constructing the room with the greatest purity. When the chamber was finished the copyist changed into a new and purified robe. But, before beginning the task of copying out the text, he maintained a purificatory fast for a period of forty-nine days. After that he began to write. Whenever he passed in and out of the copy room he was required to change his clothing. Only when he had bathed himself did he start to copy. As he wrote, I would kneel before the sūtra in the foreign posture [of adoration]—right knee to the ground—and make offerings with incense censer in hand. When the copyist stopped, I also would stop. And whenever the copyist went to sleep at night, I would arise alone to burn incense and ritually circumambulate the sūtra. This routine I kept up without the slightest lapse. When the sūtra was finished, I made splendid accoutrements for it. . . .
>
> Because of this the governor himself took refuge in the faith, after which people everywhere turned to the *Lotus Sūtra* as their principal form of religious practice. (Stevenson 1995, 450)

Here we have some powerful indications of what veneration of a book in a Buddhist milieu might look like. But turning to northern Thailand, we find that this kind of profound reverence for the written word is completely lacking in sources from the region. However, an early central Thai source describes the worship of a text as *pūjā*, which is the term most commonly used in Buddhist countries to denote the devotional practices such as lighting incense, offering flowers or fruit, and bowing with hands folded together in the *añjali* (called *wai* in Thai) that come under the rubric of "worship." This early source is a 1536 CE inscription from Wat Khema in Sukhodaya that says that merit-makers or *nak pun* presented silk for the lectern to support the sacred books and one piece of cloth with embroidered borders to place under the *Mahāvessantara*. It also says that Amdæn Sen worshipped (*pūjā*) the *Vessantara* by having a copy of the text made (EHS, 651–652). Even this, however, does not necessarily mean that the manuscript itself was worshipped, but rather may indicate that the act of writing out a copy of the text was a way of paying obeisance towards the *content* of the text being copied. Whatever the exact sentiments, similar inscriptions from Lan Na have not yet come to light, nor do the literary sources describe in any detail processions of manuscripts during which the faithful would salute or otherwise honor the items as they passed by, save for the single phrase "a festival was held" for the golden Piṭaka mentioned in the JKM.

Sources from elsewhere in Thailand, in the central and southern regions, also exhibit features of this cult, again highlighting the lack of attention given to it in Lan Na. An informative inscription (PSC, 6: item 186) is located on the inner wall of the *uposatha* hall at Wat Nivesa Dharma in Ayudhyā province and adds greatly to our image of book veneration in the Thai world. Dated CS 1239 (1877 CE), the inscription says that the king ordered his officials to make the Tipiṭaka by splitting up the work among different people. The king hoped that from these manuscripts the monks and novices will be able to study, recite, and learn the Vinaya, Sutta, and Abhidhamma Piṭakas, which totaled 119 texts in all. We are told that leather boxes with the royal seal were sewn together in order to contain the separate volumes and were to be stationed throughout the kingdom. Upon completion, the king held a great festival in honor of the Tipiṭaka and a Buddha image. The king then invited images of the Buddha and some important followers, along with the Tipiṭaka, to be put onto a steamship from Bangkok and brought to stay at Wat Choeng Len across from Bang Sai. There was then a great parade from the *wat*, and the Tipiṭaka was tied to the roof of a boat, while the monks got in another boat, and they all followed the course of the river in procession to the island Bang Pa. When everyone reached the shore, there was a regal procession of the items onto the land, after which they were brought to the *uposatha* hall. The images were placed in a case against the wall, and the texts were arranged for worship on either side of the main image.

The display of manuscripts in such close proximity to images is a sure sign of their sanctity, a situation seldom encountered in Lan Na. Their location guaranteed that they would partake, as representatives of the Dhamma, of the veneration accorded to the Three Jewels[22] by the Buddhist faithful.

Lorraine Gesick (1995) has written an important work on the historiography of southern Thailand, in which she describes the attitudes of the local population towards manuscripts relating the history of Phatthalung, a town just south of Nagara Śrī Dharmarāja. She cites the childhood recollections of two older sisters about the manuscripts, which were in this case not written on palm leaf but on paper made from mulberry bark (called *phlao* or *samut khoi*):

> Reading the manuscripts, they said, was extremely dangerous and was rarely if ever done, and then only with ceremonial precautions. The manuscripts, they agreed, could only be read—the clear implication is "read aloud"—from the back of a white elephant. Otherwise, whoever attempted to read the manuscripts would cough blood from the larynx and die. (Gesick 1995, 20)

Gesick also cites a description, given by a monk in 1899, of the ceremony with which the manuscripts were brought for him to see:

> When they brought the manuscripts [*tamra*] for me to look at, the custodians had to light candles and pay homage to them. Then they invited the manuscripts to be carried on a tray on the head, while an attendant held a [ceremonial] umbrella over it. Before opening the box [which held the manuscripts] they again made obeisance to it. (1995, 20–21 [brackets in original])

Further evidence from Southeast Asia attesting to the ritual importance of written texts originates from Cambodia, where hieratic functions of writing have long been appreciated among the Khmer. Catherine Becchetti has written about the sanctity of religious texts in Cambodia, citing the "mystical" significance of the letters and the "quasi-magical" power of the texts as elements contributing to the sanctity of written scriptures (1994, 48). While her transposition of the sacred power of vocalized phonemes, a power well known in Indic cultures, onto written instances of these phonemes does not sufficiently take into consideration the significant conceptual differences separating these two media, it is nevertheless clear that writing did have an important cultic role in Cambodia. Manuscripts were and are frequently burned as offerings or interred inside *stūpa*s, and they are held in such high esteem that Bizot is able to cite an instance in which an abbot was struck down with illness because he allowed a manuscript to be taken off the monastery's premises (1994, 119). Judging by the almost completely arbitrary relation between the provenance of manuscripts in northern Thailand and their current repositories, a reluctance to lend them does not seem to have characterized many abbots in Lan Na. Bizot and François Lagirarde also tell of Buddha images that are made by adding a resin to the powder produced by erasing sacred words written on slate, which represents a sort of desiccated essence of the Dhamma (1996, 51).

In Cambodia copyists take care to maintain proper ritual behavior and proffer regular offerings while making a manuscript, which, when it is completed, is formally consecrated in a manner similar to a Buddha image, for it is regarded as the sacred Dhamma body of the Buddha (Becchetti 1994, 54). In a Khmer text called the *Dhammaviṅsuṅ* cited by Becchetti, it is said that the world and the Dhamma were essentially coeval, the very letters of the Dhamma allowing for the actualization of the multiform sensate world. Therefore the act of copying out a text is a symbolic reenactment of the creation of the world, requiring the greatest care and accompanied by ritualized gestures. The aspirant may also attempt the assimilation of his own psychophysical constituents to the "body" of the Dhamma (as represented by the text) in a series of ritual actions similar to *nyāsa* in Tantric Buddhism, which was known in Cambodia since the Angkorian period. The physical text itself is often compared with the human embryo, with the words, leaves, cords, and coverings homologized with the organs, bones, sinew, and skin of the human being, who is in this way born anew from the matrix of language (Becchetti 1994, 55). The beauty and regularity of the writing is also regarded as a sign of devotion to the Buddha. With all of this in mind, it is easy to see why the Khmer-script Pali manuscripts produced in Thailand are so beautifully written and ornate. This sense of the sanctity of writing must have been deeply linked with the vestiges of Khmer culture and hence with their script.

Can the veneration accorded manuscripts in the arenas discussed above be found in Lan Na? Looking at manuscripts from the Golden Age and shortly thereafter, we find that a significant number bear colophons that may state that people should take them for worship.[23] The following is Hundius's translation of a representative colophon from a 1550 CE *Jātaka Paṇṇāsanipāta* (HH-05) whose provenance is Tha Søi:

> [this manuscript was] made at the behest of the Venerable Mahāsaṅgharāja in the Year of the Dog, CS 912—Whoever [among you] takes [this manuscript out for] worship (*prasong*), [if you do] not clearly know the meaning and the wording, do not add any writing on [it]: do not [try to] make any

corrections; if [you do] not follow [my advice], [you will] be [reborn as] a *peta*. After worship, see to it that it is brought back again quickly, [for] hard work it was, indeed, to make it, so do take good care!

Because the exact meaning of the term *"prasong"* is unclear, however, it is difficult to be sure that actual worship of the texts is documented in these colophons. *Prasong* is derived from the Sanskrit *praśaṃsa*, meaning "to praise," and has thus been translated by Hundius as "worship," but in the Tai languages *prasong* usually means "to desire," leaving us with no definitive statement about the worship of these manuscripts. Even if *prasong* does mean "worship" in these colophons, it may not refer to worship of the manuscript itself but to worship of another cultic item, such as a Buddha image, by means of the chanting of text on the manuscript. If this is the case, the manuscript would be a textual support for the appropriate chants and not the object of worship. This scenario would also account for the admonition not to make corrections if some anomalies are discovered during said worship: although ritual adoration and critical reading of a manuscript are not necessarily mutually exclusive, it would be uncomfortable and embarrassing to correct the text after having just honored it as a perfect embodiment of the Buddha's words.

So far, I have seen the term *prasong* used only in manuscripts from the Tha Søi region. It is quite possible that written manuscripts were more highly valued in Tha Søi than in other places and thus played a more central role there in the day-to-day practice of Buddhism. It may even be that they were indeed worshipped there. This conjecture is bolstered by the observations made in Chapter Three that Tha Søi was probably a major center of *araññavāsī* monks, whose attitudes would have been affected by the treatment of manuscripts in Sri Lanka. Pali manuscripts were worshipped in public festivals in Sri Lanka in much the same way as were relics such as the Buddha's Tooth, and the monks ordained into the Sinhalese *araññavāsī* order would have brought these attitudes with them to Lan Na. Scholarly *araññavāsī*s were more inclined to see the value of the written word for communicating and preserving Buddhist texts than were other contemporary groups. If this is in fact the reason behind the conspicuous use of the term *prasong* in these manuscripts, and if the term does refer to worship of the manuscripts themselves, then this also tells us something about the relationship between cultic and discursive uses of manuscripts. It suggests that they arise in tandem and that the worship of the item is ultimately tied to its utility in the discursive realm. This conclusion accords with Gombrich's controversial argument (1990) that the written word was conspicuously worshipped in Mahāyāna contexts because it was particularly central to the existence of these new Mahāyāna texts that operated outside the bounds of the established oral lines of descent.

Whatever the *araññavāsī* approach to written texts may have been, they were a small section of society, and the colophons that they wrote do not tell us about the general position of manuscripts in premodern Lan Na. A more profitable source for information on common attitudes towards manuscripts is the story of the monk Māleyya (Thai: Phra Malai), a popular tale in Thailand that exists in a number of Pali and vernacular versions, all of which tell a story that Bonnie Brereton has called "one of the most important and pervasive themes in Thai Buddhism" (1995, 183). The various Māleyya texts are often read in association with the *Vessantara Jātaka* because the Māleyya texts enjoin the faithful to listen to Gotama Buddha's penultimate birth story if they wish to arrive in heaven. In this sense they actually encourage the aural consumption of texts. In addition, they suggest that manuscripts were not worshipped in any significant way, as will be shown below.

While it is unclear exactly when the core Māleyya story was composed, it is generally agreed that the Pali *Māleyyadevatheravatthu* examined here originated in Lan Na in the late fifteenth century.[24] It is yet another window onto the religious world of Golden Age Lan Na and can be used to identify elements of daily life that have worked their way into the story. The story itself is said to take place during an undisclosed period in the past, but we must distinguish this legendary past from the historical past of the chronicles, in which historical accuracy is an important aim. In the Māleyya texts, as in works of literature generally, the world of the authors is reflected in their telling of the tale, the more so because it is intended to localize certain Buddhist principles and therefore must portray a world recognizable to the listener. We can thus read the following climactic passage as telling us about the state of the religion in the author's Lan Na. In this passage, Māleyya has gone to heaven and has finally met the future buddha Metteyya, who asks him how human beings make merit, to which the monk replies:

> Great king, some human beings in Rose-Apple Island give alms, some preserve morality, (or) give the gift of the Truth, keep the Uposatha day(s), make images of the Buddha, build monasteries or residences (for the Order), give rains-residences, robes, almsfood (or) medicine, tend the Bodhi-tree, build *stūpas*, shrines, parks (for the Order), causeways (or) walkways (for meditation), dig wells (or) canals, give (the monastic) requisites (or) the ten-

> fold gift, look after their mother and father, offer sacrifice for the sake of dead relatives, worship the Three Jewels, have their son enter the Monastic Order (as a novice), or worship the Buddha-image. (Collins 1993, 84)

It is not mentioned here that worshipping manuscripts plays a role in the merit-making activities of humans. No more appropriate place could be imagined in which to proclaim the benefits of making and worshipping manuscripts, if this had been generally regarded as an important religious activity at the time.[25] It should not be surprising, in view of the picture that has emerged of the Lan Na cultural world, that in the vernacular versions there are also no allusions that could be interpreted as referring specifically to the worship or donation of manuscripts.

A further source that needs to be taken into consideration is the *Paññāsa Jātaka* (Jaini 1983), an apocryphal collection of fifty stories[26] about the previous lives of the Buddha and his chief disciples produced by anonymous authors during the fifteenth or sixteenth century.[27] While there is no indication within the stories about their provenance, most of them were likely composed in Chiang Mai and constituted a body of more popular literature among the corpus of works produced during the Golden Age.[28] These tales naturally reveal much about life during this period and highlight the cares and concerns of the Buddhist faithful of Lan Na. Six of them speak of the importance of giving to the Saṅgha, and four of them deal with the construction or repair of Buddha images. Stylistically, they endorse this behavior in a manner much less like a canonical Jātaka and rather more like an Ānisaṃsa text. The texts are not the most sophisticated contributions to Pali literature and are marked by heavily stereotypical language and even more repetition than is usual in Pali texts. There are also fewer complex, descriptive passages when compared with similar stories in other collections, such as the *Divyāvadāna*, suggesting that they were intended to be recited orally (Fickle 1978, 257).

One tale found in the Thai, Cambodian, and Burmese recensions (but which is absent from the Laotian) centers on the copying of the Tipiṭaka and the benefits accruing to those who do so. It is certainly possible that this was composed by a monk or even a novice or former monk from Lan Na during the sixteenth century as an expression of what he felt to be the importance of making manuscripts. However, there are some strong reasons to doubt its provenance, as will become clear presently. The Jātaka in question, which is usually number twenty-one in the Thai recensions, is known there as the *Porānakapilapuranarinda Jātaka* because of the role in the story of a king called Kapila, from a previous eon. The text starts out with Sāriputta asking the Buddha what kinds of happiness can be expected by those who write or cause to be written the Tipiṭaka, which are the words of the Buddha (*Buddha-vacanam*). The Buddha replies that the rewards for such an act are boundless and he relates a birth story that took place in the distant past, in a former eon when there was another Gotama Buddha who taught the Dhamma. The Gotama Buddha of our eon was at that time born as a minister to King Suddhodana, the father of the former Gotama Buddha, and he desired to preserve the Dhamma for 5,000 years by writing it down, which he did. He then convinced others to copy out the Tipiṭaka and told them they should always worship it with the various articles of worship (*taṃ pūjeyya pūjābhaṇḍena sab-badā*). When the former buddha heard of this, he praised them, saying that they would live long, be happy, and be born only as gods or humans from now on. As a result of his deeds, the minister is reborn in the Tāvatiṃsa heaven, and after enjoying its fruits, he is reborn in the womb of the queen of Kapila, later ruling the kingdom with wisdom and justice. The Jātaka contains a bewildering variety of benefits bestowed upon those who make and honor the Tipiṭaka. These include wealth, happiness, high rebirth, pleasant voice, good reputation, and other such felicities, which are equivalent to those acquired through the construction and worship of Buddha images.

One of the most striking features of this story is its complete opposition to the Theravādin tradition about committing the scriptures to writing and even the composition of the scriptures themselves. Serious histories produced from within the Theravāda tradition hold that the teachings were passed on orally for four centuries and were written down only in the first century BCE. Modern scholarship, too, has generally held this to be the most likely scenario. Leaving aside the glaring point that even an oral corpus known as the Tipiṭaka did not exist at the time of the Buddha but rather came into being sometime after his death, the idea of the Buddha suggesting that people write down the scriptures is foreign to the tradition and entirely anachronistic.[29]

The historical inaccuracies staining the text do not tell us too much except that the author was far less meticulous than the author of the roughly contemporaneous JKM. However, the suspicion that this tale does not quite fit in with many of the others in the *Paññāsa Jātaka* is raised by the title of the work. In the Burmese version, where the Jātaka is listed as number forty-three, it is called the *Akkharalikhita Jātaka*, which means "the written letters." This refers to the fact that the story focuses on the writing of scripture. This Burmese title is virtually the only one in the *Paññāsa Jātaka* that is based not on a main character, but on a theme of the story. This is also the only Jātaka for which the Burmese title is completely unrelated to its title in the Thai collection, although this may simply reflect the different concerns of the compilers. Furthermore, the denouement (*samodhāna*), in which the characters in the story are identified as past incarnations of the Buddha and his associates, links Sakka, the king of the gods, with the monk Moggallāna. While this is unremarkable in itself, the fact that Sakka is identified with the monk Anuruddha in the other thirty-four Jātakas from this collection in which he appears forces us again to consider that there is something unusual afoot: perhaps this story was not composed by the Lan Na monks who composed the bulk of the other tales. Based upon what appear to be Burmese attitudes towards books, we can see that the story reflects a Burmese sensibility about the sanctity of writing and may very well have been composed there. Whatever its provenance, this Jātaka does not seem to have ever become very popular in Thailand.[30]

When we add to these literary sources the silence of the early chronicles and inscriptions on the topic of manuscript veneration, it becomes clear that none of the sources from Golden Age Lan Na give anything but the barest suggestion that some books might have been worshipped in some sectors.

If manuscripts were rarely worshipped around the Golden Age, they came to be viewed as items somewhat more worthy of formalized reverence after the two centuries of Burmese hegemony. One of the few unambiguous exhortations to worship a manuscript in the northern Thai colophons can be found in a *Cakkavāḷadīpanī* (HH-16) that was part of the massive project in Nan executed under the leadership of King Ananta in 1869 CE. In this work the scribe says that the manuscript was made in order for people to be able to worship it, and the term used here is, unlike *prasong,* the usual one for worship, *pūjā*:

> [He] received the Royal invitation of His Majesty the Great Ruler to join in making a manuscript of the Pali work named *Cakkavāladīpanī*, in order to enable people to pay their worship to it and enhance the Teachings of the Lord Gotama throughout the 5,000 years. . . . (Hundius 1990, 97)

In this colophon there are a number of roughly synonymous terms such as *sakkara* and *pūjā* that Hundius translates as "worship" and which clearly indicate that the manuscript itself is intended as an object to be revered. The term *pūjā* is commonly used to describe the type of cultic activities done on behalf of a religious image, such as lighting incense and leaving offerings of flowers or fruit.

The clearest indication of a strongly reverential attitude towards writing is an Anisong (Pali: Ānisaṃsa) text called *Anisong Sang Tham* (MF 84.135.01I.039) that tells of the benefits of writing the Dhamma. The beginnings of the Anisong genre are unclear, but whereas most vernacular genres are represented by some copies dated from before the eighteenth century in the Social Research Institute's catalog of several thousand titles (Premchit 1986), this one is not. The Red Cliff Cave collection found recently in Mæ Sariang at the western edge of Lan Na includes eight Anisong texts with the earliest dating from CS 1088 (1726 CE) and the latest from CS 1137 (1775 CE). They deal with such topics as the benefits of entering the monkhood, presenting robes to the monks, and listening to the *Vessantara Jātaka*, but none speak of the importance of copying manuscripts. The earliest attestation of an Anisong praising the making of manuscripts is to be found in the collection of Thai manuscripts kept at the Royal Library in Copenhagen, dated to CS 1160 (1798 CE) and cataloged as Laos 71 (Coedès 1966). A number of similar Anisong texts are found in the Danish collection dating from the height of the reconstruction efforts under Kawila and his successors.[31] It is possible, then, that the *Anisong Sang Tham* texts did not blossom until the nineteenth century, when the need to reconstitute the textual tradition that had been damaged during the previous centuries was most acutely felt. Anisong texts encouraging the production of manuscripts would have had a motivating effect in this regard. Like the *Porānakapila Jātaka*, the *Anisong Sang Tham* text begins with a dialog between the Buddha and Sāriputta about the benefits of writing down the Dhamma. Most of the text tells in rather tedious detail of the many different types of rebirth in pleasant realms that will occur if one contributes in any way to the making of a manuscript, from the cutting of the palm leaves to the wrapping of the finished text in cloth. Some select passages from *Anisong Sang Tham* (MF 84.135.01I.039) follow:

> There are an infinite number of immeasurable benefits which accrue to all those who make written copies of the Dhamma. All those people will surely be great, wheel-turning monarchs for many existences; they will be kings of kings or even rule over the gods for a thousand lifetimes; they will become (*brahma* or a brahman) for a thousand lifetimes. (recto, leaf 2)
>
> Anybody who takes a cloth in order to wrap the Dhamma book in order for it not to be damaged or broken, when they are reborn in another existence they will not experience either hot or cold. There will be no danger (for them) and there will be a wishing tree and much clothing and they can partake as their heart desires. (recto, leaf 11)

> Any person who makes a leg-cushion for putting the distinguished Dhamma book on so as to elevate it, he will be reborn as a ruler who is greater than all the other noble rulers, with a palace adorned with seven different kinds of jewels, etc. . . . (verso, leaf 11)
>
> When he is searching for palm leaves with determination, he takes pleasure in that. (recto, leaf 12)
>
> Whoever makes a box for keeping the three Piṭakas inside will have immeasurable benefits. It is thus said by them. If it is not found, I request all of you to finish this fascicle of the Dhamma. . . . This is the last page about the Anisong for making boxes. (recto, leaf 23)

In the north of Thailand today, manuscripts are still not generally objects of worship per se, although they are strongly associated with merit-making practices. For example, it is not uncommon for manuscripts to be burned in order to make merit. Some people may also crush the palm leaves into a powder that is mixed with a resin to make protective amulets. These are sure signs of a growth in prestige accorded to writing, prestige that is not matched in premodern sources.

A final word on this topic: there is no need to posit an absolute distinction between those who worship the scriptures and those who do not. Charles Hallisey (1988) has proposed a useful spectrum to help define the different approaches to *pūjā*, ranging from the rote imitation of gestures within a ritual context, to the heartfelt outpouring of devotion that might occur on the part of one who is fully aware of the teachings of the Buddha and realizes that the worship itself will not banish ignorance from the mind. In the case of the manuscripts, some who might have worshipped them might have done so after having carefully read them and ruminated on their contents, whereas others might simply have believed that paying obeisance to the manuscripts would bring good things in the future if done properly, based on the powers inherent in the texts.

PALI INSCRIPTIONS AND THE POWER OF THE WRITTEN WORD

The Pali reading practices that were followed in Lan Na, as well as the role of the written word in producing merit, can be further understood by looking at the other extant evidence of written Pali texts—inscriptions. As it happens, there are very few Lan Na inscriptions with Pali passages from the Tipiṭaka, and most of these are inscribed on the bases of Buddha images, rather than on monumental stone faces such as the Tipiṭaka of King Mindon in Burma[32] or the Paritta inscriptions from Śrī Kṣetra (Skilling 1997b, 152–157). This suggests from the outset that the desire to produce canonical texts in order to disseminate the teachings of the Buddha to the public and to preserve them far into the future was not at the forefront of the minds of the guardians of literate culture in Lan Na.

One group of early Pali texts is inscribed in Lan Na Dhamma script on the pedestal of an unusual late-fifteenth-century Buddha footprint, on which in turn a statue of a full Buddha stands (LNI, Chiang Rai 15). The fairly substantial Pali portion consists of a well-known description of the Buddha and a canonical pericope enumerating the twelve links of the causal nexus known as *paṭiccasamuppāda*.

> *Iti pi so bhagavā arahaṃ sammāsambuddho vijjācaraṇasampanno sugato lokavidū anuttaro purisadammasārathi satthā devamanussānaṃ buddho bhagavāti.* (DN, i, 62)
>
> *Avijjāpaccayāsaṅkhārāsaṅkhārapaccayāviññāṇaṃ viññāṇapaccayā nāmarūpaṃ nāmarūpapaccayā saḷāyatanaṃ saḷāyatanapaccayā phasso phassapaccayā vedanā vedanapaccayā taṇhā tanhāpaccayā upādānaṃ upādānapaccayā bhavo bhavapaccayā jāti jātipaccayā jarāmaraṇasokaparideva dukkhadomanasupāyāsāsambhavanti evametassa kevalassa dukkhandhassasamudayo hoti* (SN, ii,1 [*Nidānavagga*]).

> Thus is this Bhagavā: he is the deserving, perfectly enlightened one who is endowed with knowledge and proper behavior, the well-gone one, who knows the world, who is an unexcelled tamer of men who are to be tamed, who is a teacher of men and gods, an awakened one, the Lord.
>
> Mental formations arise from the condition of ignorance, consciousness arises from the condition of mental formations, the mind and body arise from the condition of consciousness, the six sense-spheres arise from the condition of the mind and body, contact arises from the condition of the six sense-spheres, feeling arises from the condition of contact, craving arises from the condition of feeling, grasping arises from the condition of craving, existence arises from the condition of grasping, birth arises from the condition of existence, and old age, death, grief, suffering, sadness, and distress arise from the condition of birth. Thus there is the arising of this whole dark mass of suffering.

These are central texts that were then, as now, known by heart by most people who had ever spent time at a monastery; they have often been regarded as encapsulating the teachings of the Buddha.

Another slightly later inscription is on the pedestal of the Buddha image of Wat Phra Koet Khongkharam and contains text from the *Buddha Udāna Gāthā* in Pali (LNI, Chiang Rai 62, dated CS 876 [1514 CE]). The inscription consists of the first three *gāthās* (verses) of the collection, exactly as they are found in the *Chaṭṭha Saṅgāyana* version. These words, like those of the previous example, encapsulate the essence of the Buddha's enlightenment and his understanding of conditioned origination. The similarity between the *Udāna Gāthās* as found in this inscription and in modern, edited versions is in marked contrast to the numerous variations found among the short heart-letter verses discussed in Chapter Four. This discrepancy may be attributed to the different methods of transmitting the two texts. The inscriber in the present case probably had access to written versions of the *Udāna*, whereas the heart-letter verses were clearly transmitted orally, as their very form is molded to fit well into such a system of transmission.

What was the purpose of inscribing these texts? If we look at the dedicatory sections of these inscriptions, the vernacular portion of Chiang Rai 15 in Fak Kham script says that in CS 943 (1481 CE) the image was installed on the pedestal by Chao Wichian Panyo, in hopes that he would become a future buddha through the merit attained from this deed. After the three *Udāna* verses in Chiang Rai 62 comes a further dedication in somewhat corrupt Pali requesting that the merit born of making the bronze Buddha, and of giving gifts and acting morally, cause rebirth in the assembly of the gods. In neither of the dedicatory sections is there any reference to merit being made through the inscribing of these seminal Pali passages; instead, the image itself and the act of consecrating it are highlighted as the causes of the merit. Even when other worthy deeds are listed, such as gift-giving and moral behavior, the publication for thousands of years of the words of the Buddha is, apparently, not deemed worthy of specific mention.

It is also important to note that in both cases the images were made under the aegis of laymen, at least one of whom was a person of royal descent (*chao*). Although one might expect the few images that do have Pali texts inscribed upon them to be the results of some monastic stimulus—and there are many images that were sponsored by monks[33]—I have already suggested that the monks may in fact have been less amenable to the writing down of texts from the Tipiṭaka than those with political power. These examples help to further this thesis.

A deeper understanding of the role that writing played in the formation of the power of an image can be gained by looking at a representative from the genre of consecration texts. These texts have been recited for centuries at the consecration ceremonies of Buddha images and provide a window onto the functions that the images were believed to have had. Swearer says that the text

> provides an abbreviated summary of the life of the Buddha derived from Pali canonical and commentarial texts; it links the life of Prince Siddhārtha with the lineage of previous buddhas recounted in the *Buddhavaṃsa* and *Cariyapiṭaka*, and the moral perfection attained through previous bodhisattva rebirths, such as Prince Vessantara. Perhaps most importantly, the ritual infuses these elements into the Buddha image, a material object representing the story, wisdom and power of the person of the Buddha. (1995, 51)

Swearer then translates a printed version of such a text in Yuan, which is similar in its essential features to a manuscript version of another text copied in 1576 CE. After relating the life of the Buddha, Swearer's text says:

> May all his qualities be invested in this Buddha image. May the Buddha's boundless omniscience be invested in this image until the religion ceases to exist. . . . May the supermundane reality discovered by the Buddha during his enlightenment under the bodhi tree be invested in this image for the five thousand years of the religion. . . . May the knowledge contained in the seven books of the *Abhidharma* perceived by the Buddha in the seven weeks after his enlightenment be consecrated in this image for the rest of the lifetime of the religion. . . . (1995, 57)

There are some rather interesting vectors among these desiderata, especially when considering them in light of the attitudes in this world towards written canonical texts. Here, the image itself is viewed as a receptacle not only of the qualities of the Buddha—what may be considered the *rūpakāya*—but also of the knowledge of his teachings—the *dhammakāya*.[34] Thus the knowledge of Buddhist doctrines and philosophy is not simply overlooked in this text in favor of the cultic power of the image; rather, such knowledge is subsumed within the image and is part of what gives the image its power. Conversely, the inscriptions presented above that actually consist of Dhamma texts do not mention their possible use as bearers of knowledge about the Buddha's teachings. One is not instructed to read them and thereby learn important truths that the Buddha taught, nor are there any gestures towards the idea that the inscription increases the cultic value of the image. The impression of the dedicatory epigraphs on images themselves and from the consecration text is that the images were felt to embody the very teachings of the Buddha more effectively than written texts documenting these teachings in language. The visible writing of canonical passages on an image, then, seems to make little appreciable difference to the salutary power of the artifact, to its role as a representative of the Buddha, or even to its role as a representative of his teachings.

I turn now to recent work by Swearer (2004) that suggests that *unseen* or *unreadable* written words can, in fact, add power to Buddha images and *cetiyas*. The practice of putting written verses into icons in order to increase their power has historically been quite common in many of the areas surrounding Lan Na, such as China and Burma, as well as in Japan and other Buddhist countries,[35] and we would expect this practice to be known in northern Thailand as well. Swearer cites an example of an undated vernacular consecration text, *Tamra Kan Kosang Phraphuttharup*, that he believes may have had its origins in the Golden Age. This text tells of the importance of inscribing *yantras*, which are geometric diagrams containing Pali verses, onto clay tiles and then placing these at various positions inside a *cetiya* or image (Swearer 2004, 51–53). When speaking of how to make a wooden Buddha image, the text says:

> Afterward, carve out the Buddha image and inscribe the horoscope of the sponsor on a silver plate. Then install into the image the *gāthā* which represents the Buddha by chanting three times, "*Buddho bodheyya mutto moceyyaṃ tiṇṇo tāreyyaṃ*" [Having attained Buddhahood, I shall enable others to attain it; having myself gained release, I shall enable others to attain release; having crossed over, I shall enable others to cross over]. . . . Finally, inscribe around the horoscope the following *gāthā*, which will make the mind firm and stable, "*Satimā satinimittaṃ anubanditvā satimā minanaṃ daḷhaṃ yatha thambhe daḷhaṃ cittaṃ mama*" [With mindfulness follow the object of the mind; with mindfulness measure firmly; like a stable post let my mind be fixed], and repeat this three times. Having done this, put the dried fruit of the *dua pong* tree on the seat of the image; roll up the silver plate on which the horoscope has been inscribed and put it inside the chest of the image. (2004, 56–57)

We can see that writing is in these cases viewed as integral to the full development of the object as an item imbued with the power and wisdom of the Buddha and worthy of cultic veneration, although it must be added that the installation of the written word is always accompanied by recitation of appropriate verses and seems never to be efficacious on its own. In these cases the writing is not intended to be seen by the devotees and is not used to instruct them in any discursive way about the teachings of Buddhism; rather, the writing has the power to "instruct" the cultic artifact itself.

Yet another point further problematizes the idea that these instances illustrate the power of the written *word*. In most cases the Pali verses were not written continuously, but rather, as I have said, were placed within *yantra*s. These *yantra*s, however, are figures in which the geometric forms seem to be more important than the meaning of the words themselves, because the syllables of the words are placed out of order in separate squares in such a way as to make reading them very difficult.[36] Here the denotative power of the written word is obviously secondary to the magical power believed to inhere in the esoteric significance behind the forms themselves, and indeed perfectly functional *yantra*s are found all over the Indianized world that consist only of geometric shapes and bear no written syllables.

*Yantra*s are most closely associated with Hindu and Tantric practice, and their use suggests that these traditions have influenced Thai Buddhism more than is generally acknowledged. In fact, while examples of writing being installed in images are not common in the historiographical literature from Lan Na, the only example that I have found does explicitly connect this practice to Hinduism rather than Buddhism. Camille Notton's French version of the vernacular chronicle *Phongsawadan Yonok* (1926) is a compilation of shorter texts made by Phraya Prachakitkorajak at the end of the nineteenth century. The section entitled *Chronique du Mahāthera Fa Bot* is a text of uncertain date but may be quite old. It narrates the construction of the Chedi Luang in Chiang Mai by King Tilaka and includes some additional information not found in other texts that discuss this event. It says that two elephant and two Rājasī statues were constructed to the north to guard the edifice and in their hearts were placed *Vedic* formulae (Notton 1926, 51). Presumably in this case the written *mantra*s were perceived to have some apotropaic powers and were expected to be able to ward off misfortune, but the texts are here called "Vedic" and not Buddhist. Since there are consecration texts, such as the ones presented by Swearer, that instruct the faithful to place Pali verses in one form or another inside Buddha images, and a practice similar to this is acknowledged in a chronicle, why are there not other accounts in other chronicles in which verses are placed into Buddha images?

An examination of more salient evidence shows that this practice was simply not as common in Lan Na as in other parts of the Buddhist world. First of all, Swearer mentions that "[i]n contemporary northern Thailand, the ritualization of image construction has been largely appropriated by the eye-opening ceremony of image consecration held within the precincts of a *wat*" (2004, 69). In other words, the specific steps outlined in the image construction text are not generally followed today, and of course it is difficult to know the extent to which this text was ever descriptive of actual practices commonly carried out in historical Lan Na. One way of accessing this knowledge would be to systematically examine the historical remains, which is impossible because the texts and *yantra*s that we are interested in would be embedded within valuable cultural artifacts such as images and *cetiya*s that should not be opened. In the absence of this possibility, we can get at least some idea of the popularity of the use of writing to represent or add to the power of the Buddha by examining writing that *is* visible either because it is on the outside of the items or because the objects have collapsed of their own accord over time. Boucher (1991) has convincingly argued that the popular Buddhist formula *ye dhammā hetuppabhavā tesaṃ hetuṃ tathāgato āha, tesañca yo nirodho ca evaṃ vādī mahāsamaṇoti*[37] was used early on to represent the Dhamma in general, as well as the Buddha himself, on the strength of verses such as "he who sees the Dhamma, Vakkali, sees me" (SN, iii,120), and others that equate *paṭiccasamuppāda* with the essence of the Dhamma. Scores of *stūpa*s have been found, primarily in India and Central Asia, containing many four- or five-inch miniature *stūpa*s in which the Sanskrit version of the *ye dhammā* verse has been placed (Boucher 1991, 8). However, among the dozens of inscriptions from Thailand with the *ye dhammā* formula, there are virtually none that come from the North or that are written in the Lan Na Dhamma script.[38] There is one known example in Lan Na of this verse, which is written in Sanskrit in a north Indian Pāla period script on a small stone Buddha image kept at Wat Chiang Man in Chiang Mai.[39] Other than this exception, which, since it is originally from India, appears to prove the rule, inscriptions bearing this verse in Thailand are by and large found in the Mon and Khmer heartland, namely, around Nakhøn Pathom and Lopburi. While this brief study is suggestive, future archaeology will be required to better determine the extent to which the idea that written verses could stand in for the Buddha actually resonated in Lan Na.

This investigation would not be complete without discussing a case in which writing is commonly given some degree of power, generally apotropaic in nature—the ubiquitous tattoos on the arms and legs of people in northern as well as the rest of Thailand. These markings may be purely geometric *yantra*s or may include short texts, often but not always in Pali. Powerful "holy men" who are not necessarily monks will write *yantra*s onto the palms or foreheads of people who are in need of them (Tambiah 1984, 295), but when they are made by monks, the meritorious monkish power is retained by the markings, thus giving the tattoos more efficacy than those written by lay ritual specialists (whose draftsmanship may be of a better quality) (Terwiel 1975, 84–85). The markings are believed to have the ability to keep malevolent spirits at bay and ward off misfortune, which tells us that written symbols or words *could* have been viewed as effective bearers of certain types of numinous or magical power. Yet it seems that when the subject matter goes from being short texts arranged in an unreadable geometric formation, to substantial, continuously written canonical Pali passages, they actually seem to *lose* much of their power in the eyes of most pre-twentieth-century Lan Na inhabitants.

MANUSCRIPTS AS SUPPORTS FOR READING AND STUDYING

It is striking that colophons rarely express an unequivocal desire for the manuscript to be used for study (*rian*). The manuscripts were not generally conceived as physical locations in which word, meaning, and interpretation converged. The only reference to studying that I found in a Golden Age manuscript is from a commentary to the *Petavatthu* written in CS 876 (1514 CE) (SRI 04–029). It specifies the various uses for which one might take the manuscript away: "It is good, if you take it away to study it (*rian*), good to write it (*khian*), good to read it (*lao*),[40] good to take it away as you like, for this is the merit for me, the person who made {this manuscript}" (von Hinüber 1990, 62).

A frequent trope found only in colophons from 1527–1558 from Tha Søi is not to attempt to alter the text in any way if one does not know the meaning or the proper words. Many of the manuscripts say: "{if you do} not clearly know the meaning and the wording, do not {try to} make any corrections. . . ." This colophon and its variants suggest an interactive reading process in which the reader will make a correction if he feels that there is a mistake in the manuscript. As pointed out in Chapter Four, one does indeed see corrections of two main types: either inscribed with a stylus like the main text or written in ink or lacquer over the text. Clearly this process was going on already in the sixteenth century, which suggests that there was at least an expectation that the prospective reader might not merely recite the Pali text but actually try to understand it. Furthermore, it is even considered a possibility that he might brazenly try to correct the text according to his own understanding. But then we should recall that the metatextual markings encountered in extant manuscripts are always limited to a few letters that were left out or mixed up and only rarely is an omitted phrase or two put back in. A vigorous literate Pali culture Lan Na may well have had, but it was not one in which debates about the philosophical, grammatical, or other meanings of the words were expressed in the margins or interlinearly, as was the case in Europe at the time. As mentioned in Chapter Four, these subjects were, however, sometimes taken up in the Nissayas.

Just because colophons do not highlight the practices, it does not mean that readers in the Golden Age did not use manuscripts for reading and study. There seems to be little doubt that many monks knew numerous texts by heart and recited and studied them in this manner, and other monks certainly used manuscripts both as memory aids placed on their lap or on a stand, and as direct sources for the public recitation of texts, as well as for private study—hence the corrections. While the broad tendencies of different monastic groups towards writing have been outlined already, it is also important to realize that any individual monk, regardless of his order, may have been more or less inclined to read and study manuscripts. It is unclear, for example, whether two of the most prolific producers of Pali commentarial texts from this period, Sirimaṅgala and Ñāṇakitti,[41] belonged to the *araññavāsī* lineage. Nevertheless, they must have had access to and studied numerous written texts in order to produce their works.

In later manuscripts, written after the Burmese conquest, we begin to see more references to reading and studying, such as that in a colophon from a *Maṇipadīpa* (HH-23) copied in 1833 CE as part of the project initiated by Mahāthera Kañcana Araññavāsī. Fascicle 5 bears the following colophon:

> Written by Bhikkhu Jeeyyanaam while he stayed spreading Loving-kindness at Waḍ Paan Düün, in a village that is part of remote Müüaṅ Jlääṅ, far away. Because it was not an easy task at all to read the script [of the original], I only wrote four of the phuuk (fascicles). Therefore, [respected reader], do read with careful consideration. Whoever among you, dear Monk-Brothers, uses this manuscript for his studies or as his reading (*dai rian dai an*) please do use thorough consideration, because the handwriting has turned out extremely uneven. (Hundius 1990, 125)

The scribe of the fifth fascicle of a *Cakkavāḷadīpanī* (HH-16) also expects the text to be read and feels compelled to point out that he did the writing by himself, but is worried that he was not very well suited to the job:

> My writing does not look beautiful at all. Senior people are worried that it will be very difficult to read (*yak cha an*); oh yes, there is no doubt about that. CS 1231—Year of the Snake; I was not keen on writing at all! (Hundius 1990, 98)

A Thai-Lao text of unknown date[42] called the *Saddavimala* (Bizot and Lagirarde 1996) has been found in monasteries in northern Thailand and Laos, although it seems to have fallen out of use in the former areas. Similar to the Khmer *Dhammavinsuṅ*, this little-studied text outlines a series of practices that allow aspirants to purify themselves and transform the microcosm of the body into an active participant in the greater cosmos through the power of Dhammic syllables. While most of this text deals with vocalized syllables, chapter twelve recalls a story in which the Buddha and some of his disciples discuss grammar and the power of words. At 12.5, the Buddha (anachronistically) lays out the responsibilities of the *ganthadhura*s, those monks charged with maintaining the texts, which include the study (*rian*), writing (*khian*), and reading (*an*) of the texts.

Of course, the act of "reading" a manuscript, as should be clear by now, may have many different permutations. The anthropologist Richard Davis relates a use of manuscripts as supports for reading by the Yuan that is remarkably different from what one might think. Towards the end of the eleventh month, there is a ceremony to cleanse the rice fields of any pestilence that might affect the crop. A highlight of this ceremony is the chanting of two vernacular Jātaka stories from manuscripts that have been untied and distributed among the monks and then read *simultaneously*. As Davis remarks, "It is of course impossible to follow the thread of either story through the resulting cacophony, nor is the congregation expected to listen. The very fact of being unintelligible transforms the sermons into a magic spell" (1984, 187). A little thought reveals that this kind of rite would be very difficult without the aid of manuscripts. If the verses had been memorized instead, the monks would likely have lost their concentration because of the din.

MONASTIC EDUCATION

Having looked at the evidence for the use of manuscripts as bases for the study of Buddhism in northern Thailand in the past, it is appropriate to discuss the nature of religious education in general in order to get a better perspective on the kind of world within which these manuscripts would have been used. It is unfortunately difficult to get a good picture of what the educational system was like in the premodern period of Thailand, but we can come to some basic conclusions based on what information is available. The monasteries in Sukhodaya, Ayudhyā, and Lan Na were the educational centers to which young boys would come to learn not just Buddhist doctrine, but grammar, arts, law, medicine, arithmetic, astronomy, and the other branches of knowledge found in regions influenced by Indic culture. Reading and writing, however, were not two of the classical ten arts taught in the Brahmanical system of India. The actual process of education in historical Lan Na is being studied in detail by Justin McDaniel, whose forthcoming work will add greatly to our understanding of pedagogy in the region. For the present we will have to settle for what was said about the subject by travelers to the Siamese capital of Ayudhyā in the seventeenth century. Before turning to this, however, I should note that even at the turn of the twentieth century, monastic education still focussed on memorizing Pali texts and grammatical rules. Jane Bunnag states that in a year of observing monks in modern-day Ayudhyā, she witnessed only one occasion when the monks were required to recite a text that they had not memorized. In this case they "kept hand-written copies of the chant semi-concealed on their laps" (Bunnag 1973, 63).

As for the general state of education in central Thailand in the seventeenth century, Joost Schouten, a Dutchman who visited Siam in the 1630s records:

> Till their fifth year the children are allowed to run about the house; then they are sent to the priests to learn to write and read and to acquire other useful arts . . . when they can read and write properly they are sent to learn a trade or to take up some other employment. Frequently, however, the cleverest of them are allowed to pursue their studies, on account of the greater talent which they display. Instruction secular as well as religious is given solely by the priests, till they are qualified to fill public positions and offices. Then they discard their yellow robes, but many intelligent and talented pupils remain in the monasteries, in order to become Heads of temples and schools, or Priests. (quoted in Wyatt 1969, 10)

The monasteries functioned as the schools, and young boys were under the tutelage of one or a small group of monks. As the boys got older, some would formally enter the novitiate, and others would go back to helping their families in the fields or with the family business. Because it was (and still is) both easy and common to leave the robes when one felt that one had benefited as much as one could from the experience, the higher ordinations functioned almost like a higher education, allowing one to pursue in-depth study of Pali and other subjects that were available at the monastery where one resided.[43]

Educational efforts were not always successful, for French visitor Nicolas Gervaise writes in 1688:

> After the meal the wisest monks devote the rest of the day to the study of Pali, which is greatly esteemed in this kingdom and absolutely essential for the monks. In order to become *badloüang*[44] they must at least be able to read and expound a little. This rule had been so neglected for many years that most monks could not even read the script until four years ago, when the king found a remedy for this neglect. As he was in need of additional labour for his building works, he sent a certain Pali book to all the pagodas in the kingdom, with the command that everyone who was unable to read it should be expelled. This command was promptly executed and a few days after thousands of men still wearing their monk's robes could be seen working on the land, carrying bricks and suffering punishment for their ignorance.
>
> In every pagoda there is a learned monk in charge of instructing the *ocnenes.* He conducts his classes in the afternoon and all the young novices attend them very punctually. He teaches them to read and write Thai, the history and customs of the country, and Pali script and grammar. The Pali language is very different from Thai and has many resemblances to European languages, it being the only oriental language that has declensions, conjugations, and tenses.[45] Few monks can teach it correctly and scarcely any can speak it. (Gervaise 1989, 130)

Also, in 1688, Simon de la Loubère writes that the *sāmaṇera*s are taught mainly to read and to write, along with some mathematics and, of course, Pali and the principles of Buddhism (Loubère 1693, 59). He adds that few students make much progress in their knowledge and understanding of Pali, because it is only useful in limited spheres. Bunnag echoes these sentiments in her study of monastic life in Ayudhyā three centuries later: "In Ayutthaya, most of the younger monks seemed to study fairly regularly though not necessarily to any great effect; the fact of studying appeared to be more important than its fruits for many *bhikkhus*" (1973, 58). Note here the similar attitude not just towards study itself, but toward the possibility that an action, in this case studying, but it can easily be projected onto the act of copying, is meritorious in itself, regardless of the discursive knowledge transmitted through this process.

It is reasonable to assume that the state of education in Lan Na was not dissimilar to this picture from Siam. Many young boys would have learned basic reading and writing skills, but fewer would have been able to understand the texts that they encountered. Memorization was, of course, the most important mode of engaging with the texts. This situation dovetails well with the impression that colophons give of how manuscripts fit into the daily practice of northern Thai Buddhists.

CONCLUSION

The motivations behind making Pali Buddhist manuscripts were quite varied, but one is left with the impression that the desire to gain merit was at least as much a factor as the desire to provide textual support for study of Buddhist doctrine. The user is seldom specifically directed to read the manuscripts, and only rarely does one encounter the admonition to learn something from a discursive engagement with these texts. The merit that ensues from manuscript production, however, is highlighted in colophons, inscriptions, and texts such as the *Anisong Sang Tham*. If the making of manuscripts sometimes eclipsed the importance of their use, then it is easier to see why the way that manuscripts were stored in old libraries—covered with often untitled pieces of wood and piled deep inside boxes—would have been an acceptable arrangement.

No doubt a few of the most popular manuscripts would have been kept in a more accessible place, and the study of these manuscripts did leave its mark in the form of corrections that were written or inscribed into the palm leaves. What are noticeably absent from these texts, however, are marginal comments about the contents of the text such as can be seen in manuscripts from the western world. If the reader had any comments, these were probably made orally to the other monks participating in the study, or they may have found their way into Nissayas or even a separate commentarial text if the monk was so inclined, as were monks like Sirimaṅgala and Ñāṇakitti.

The important question of whether manuscripts were worshipped as cultic items is difficult to answer. I have shown that the colophon to a later manuscript employs the word *pūjā*, which is the common term for the worship of an item with offerings, incense, and the like. However, in Golden

Age manuscripts, we instead see the term *prasong*, the meaning of which is much less clear. We do know that most colophons of old manuscripts employing this term also touch upon the making of corrections to the text, which suggests that the manuscripts were intended to be used discursively as well. In this case, at any rate, it is possible that a reverential attitude towards the texts was tied to the utility of the manuscripts in other arenas, just as Gombrich has argued that the Mahāyāna veneration of books emerged out of a realization of the importance of writing to the Mahāyāna religious project. On the other hand, unlike elsewhere in Thailand and Southeast Asia, inscriptions in Lan Na are entirely silent about ceremonies in which manuscripts were worshipped, and the only allusion to such an event in any chronicle consists of a few words in the JKM regarding a golden text about which we hear nothing more.

Palm-leaf manuscripts themselves, while bringing good karma to their makers, seem not to have been viewed thereafter as embodying the same degree of numinous power possessed by other meritorious items associated with the Buddha's presence, such as relics and images. However, written Pali texts in another form—inscribed onto *yantra*s—were indeed used to consecrate images and reliquaries, essentially animating these items with the power of the *dhammakāya*. Again, as we have seen throughout this chapter, because the words themselves are difficult or impossible to read, the question arises as to whether this power proceeds simply from the denotative power of writing or from some other, more mysterious element of the written word.

Conclusion

Scribes, manuscripts, writing, and memorization have occupied different positions in the various civilizations of the world. A full understanding of the impact of the texts central to these civilizations cannot be reached until the nature of these positions has been at least broadly understood. However, this information, being so fundamental to the actual creation and transmission of the historical record itself, is often buried within it. In this book I have attempted to allow us to "see the strings"—to see the mechanism by which much of the literary wealth of Buddhism in northern Thailand has been created, sustained, and passed down. The difficulty of this task with relation to literate culture has been compounded precisely because of the ambiguous standing of literacy and written materials in Lan Na. The importance of the scribe in ancient Egypt, in contrast, "led to the creation of a special iconography in reliefs and statuary: the seated scribe, the only trade to be marked out as noble in this way" (Donadoni 1997, 68). Such a clear demonstration of the status of scribes did not occur in northern Thailand, making it rather more difficult to discern their position and that of the fruits of their labor—manuscripts. This project has been an attempt to initiate the inquiry into this topic in Lan Na. I view this book as comprising the first tentative steps into a new but important field that is fundamental to our understanding of the Buddhist world. I have asked the reader to put aside any preconceptions born from the graphocentric, highly literate world that we now occupy and to let the sources speak for themselves.

Establishing the existence of Pali manuscripts and inscriptions during the period under study has only been the first part of the journey. I have not assumed that just because these existed, they were read in the same way that scholars today might read them. Circumstances have led me to ask whether, in some cases, these manuscripts were read at all or were made just for merit, destined to be kept between their protective covering-boards. I have tried to open up the question of whether the merit gained from writing these texts was the primary aim of the sponsors and scribes, with the possible use of such manuscripts as sources for discursive knowledge of their contents being only of secondary importance.

Besides the wide variety of uses to which manuscripts were put, attitudes towards this medium that stretch from one end of the spectrum to the other have also been evident in Lan Na. Perhaps some of the notions underlying the often ambiguous attitudes towards writing were similar to those attributed to the king of Egypt in section XXV of Plato's *Phaedrus*. When the god Thoth proudly shows the king the art of writing, the king says that if people learn it,

> it will implant forgetfulness on their souls; they will cease to exercise memory because they will rely only on that which is written, calling things to remembrance no longer from within themselves, but by means of external marks. What you have discovered is a recipe not for memory, but for reminder. And it is no true wisdom that you offer your disciples, but only its semblance, for by telling them of many things without teaching them, you will make them seem to know much, while for the most part they will know nothing. And as men filled not with wisdom but the conceit of wisdom, they will be a burden to their fellows. (Hackforth 1953, 157)

By and large, people of means in Lan Na felt that their money was better spent on meritorious acts such as making Buddha images, image houses, and *cetiya*s. However, there were certain circles that attempted to stimulate appreciation in the general population for manuscripts. Their efforts did eventually bear fruit as is evinced through the post-reconstruction Ānisaṃsa texts that tell of the importance of making manuscripts and the great riches and felicities that will rain upon those who help to make them. The question is, can the different attitudes be ascribed to specific sectors or subgroups within society, thereby providing a powerful analytic tool for understanding some of the manners and beliefs of these groups, or must we throw up our hands in the face of the historical gap and say that we cannot know?

The information presented in this book has suggested that different groups approached the written word differently and that this in turn deeply affected, and was affected by, their social and religious roles, as media theorists have often claimed. The literary products of these different groups themselves exhibit features that probably are not unconnected with the degree to which writing had permeated the world of their authors. Swearer comments that "on general stylistic grounds there appears to be an evolution from the loose, narrative expositions of the CdW [*Cāmadevīvaṃsa*] to the more descriptive style of the MS [*Mūlasāsanā*] to the comparatively terse directness of the JKM" (1974, 69). I believe that this is in fact a consequence of the incremental permeation of writing and literate culture in the region, along with its accompanying mentality, as well as the institutional affiliation of those who produced the works Swearer mentions. In the chapters concentrating on the CDV, JKM, TPD, and MS, I suggested that the CDV was produced by a monk from an order that engaged texts primarily orally, and at a time when the first stirrings of literate culture were being felt in the region, and this accounts for its more florid style. The MS, although begun at this time, was completed later on and was the product of an order that was related to the stricter forest-dwellers of Sri Lanka. Thus its style and subject matter are characterized by both oral and literate aspects. The JKM was composed by a monk who had the closest and most recent relationship to the forest-dwellers. He also resided at a monastery that had two libraries and presumably therefore relied more on written texts. This text, not surprisingly, contains what is probably the most accurate historical information and is written in the most direct and lucid style. The TPD was also written by monks from this order, and as such it contains numerous references to written texts and even an incident in which the written word is endowed with magical power.

It was not common in either monastic or lay circles in northern Thailand, especially in the sixteenth century and earlier, to extol the virtues and importance of manuscripts. There is little direct evidence that manuscripts were frequently placed inside *cetiya*s or made of precious metals that might have served to increase their longevity, as was done elsewhere in the Buddhist world. Nor were manuscripts often placed inside Buddha images as they were, for example, in Burma and China, although *yantra*s bearing (often scrambled) Pali phrases were held in consecration texts to be essential ingredients for infusing the power of the *Dhammakāya* into an image. Some of the ambivalent attitudes may have had to do with a deep understanding of and connection to the rich world of oral texts that eclipsed the written word in most people's minds. The sensuous envelope of rhythmic chanting, sonorous voices, and personal contact may have simply had too much of a pull on most people to allow them to be overly interested in static, written texts. For enduring monuments to the religion that were beyond the contingencies of human life, they chose instead to make Buddha images and *cetiya*s, which were also more pleasing to the eye and more tangible than manuscripts. There is some evidence that manuscripts were treated by a select few, particularly the forest-dwelling *araññavāsī*s, as objects worthy of worship, but this appears not to have been the general practice, and a cult of the book cannot be said to have flourished in Lan Na.

The literacy rates in historical Lan Na are difficult to ascertain because the data simply are not available. As in all Theravāda countries, the monasteries were the main sites for male education, and reading must have played a part in the curriculum from at least the early fifteenth century, when the copying of Pali texts began in earnest. However, how seriously literacy was taken and how widespread it became is unclear. While I am unable to provide figures that would represent the literacy rate at different periods, Reid cites the accounts of nineteenth-century French missionaries, who claim that the literacy rate in central Thailand was then about 20 percent among the males (1988, 223). In contrast, an early nineteenth-century report on Burma says that most peasants were able to read somewhat, and the census of 1901 showed that 60.3 percent of Burmese males over the age of twenty were literate (Reid 1988, 222). These numbers seem to corroborate the place of literacy in the Thai and Burmese worlds that I have offered in these pages using entirely different methods.

To put the uses of manuscripts and the attitudes that were held towards them into perspective, let me highlight what I believe are the most important and compelling points.

In the early fifteenth century, vernacular texts were not yet being written. The evidence from one of the only extant Pali texts composed in Lan Na at this time, Bodhiraṃsi's CDV, suggests that it was based on tales largely in the vernacular that were orally transmitted (*bhāsamāna*). I have discussed the fact that there is not a single extant manuscript of a text in a northern Thai vernacular dialect from before Bodhiraṃsi's time. The oldest epigraphic evidence of the Dhamma script in Lan Na is from a Buddha image dated to 1465 CE, making it very unlikely that vernacular texts were written before 1410. The evidence suggests that Pali manuscripts were in use prior to vernacular ones and that the transition period was likely marked by the production of Nissayas, as occurred in other parts of South and Southeast Asia during the nascence of vernacular literature. The admirable state of many Pali manuscripts from the oldest strata suffices to suggest that there is no physical reason for manuscripts of even greater age not to have survived if they ever existed in any great numbers. The best way to explain the sudden appearance of manuscripts in good condition from the latter part of the fifteenth century is simply to allow that they were not produced in any significant manner until just before that time. I therefore conclude, along with other scholars in the field, that the oldest manuscripts that we have today probably coincide closely with the beginnings of the tradition itself. This suggests that the tradition of writing Pali manuscripts in the Lan Na script only started in the fifteenth century. Again, this coincides with the delegation of monks that went to Sri Lanka in the 1420s and, according to the JKM, studied Pali, and possibly even writing while there.

While the effect of this group of monks upon written Pali manuscripts must have been profound, the effects of earlier, Mon monks is unfortunately difficult to ascertain because they have faded into the deep recesses of time. We do know from inscriptions that the Mon produced written Pali texts, and legends hold that they had complete sets of the Tipiṭaka from even before the eleventh century. It is also clear that words, customs, religious ideas, and practices were adopted from the Mon by the Tai as they settled in the southern regions of what became Lan Na. However, the place of written Pali literature does not seem to have been one of the elements that was transferred from the one civilization to the other. Although it is at this point impossible to explain exactly why this was so, there is no doubt that Mon civilization was host to different levels of literacy just as this book has shown to be true for Lan Na. Perhaps, then, it was nonliterate Mon who flowed into the Tai culture, or perhaps writing simply didn't resonate with the Tai at this point, just as in Europe it did not with many of the groups that became heirs to Roman civilization.

Once manuscript production did emerge in earnest during what is known as the Golden Age of Lan Na, manuscripts appear to have been used for a very wide range of purposes. They were used discursively in order to compose works, because Bodhiraṃsi tells us that the CDV was well written (*sulikkhita*) by him. There is firsthand evidence of their use to display texts, as seen by the corrections found on manuscripts indicating that they have been read, as well as secondary evidence such as accounts of monks bringing texts with them to a debate. Finally, the common wish seen in colophons that the manuscript will support the teachings of the Buddha for 5,000 years emphasizes their participation in a third mode of discursive usage, the storage of textual contents.

I have also presented what little evidence there is of the cultic usage of texts. Some of the colophons could be saying that the text should be worshipped (*prasong*); the JKM states that Bilakapanattu made a golden Pali text and held a great festival in honor of it, although unfortunately no details about the festival are provided; in addition, geometric *yantra* designs with Pali phrases inscribed within them were used to consecrate Buddha images. It must be emphasized, however, that such instances pale in comparison with the cultic uses of books, manuscripts, and other forms of writing that are found in the other major Theravāda centers of Sri Lanka and Burma, to say nothing of Mahāyāna countries such as China and Japan.

Having said all this, we must not forget that the oral tradition was alive and well at this point, too. The heart-letter verses that were commonly inscribed on Buddha images show clear signs of being the products of an oral world timidly attempting to transfer some important cultural expressions into writing. Most people still actually met with texts orally, as is clear from the many public recitations, either from memory or supported by a manuscript, that are mentioned in the chronicles and inscriptions. This state of affairs provides yet another example demonstrating the pertinence of the idea, perhaps championed most eloquently by Finnegan (1977), that, with few exceptions, oral and written ways of communicating do not exist in separate, hermetically sealed worlds. There is no clearly demarcated line between them, and those living in premodern or developing nations were and are not necessarily confined to one or the other medium; but that is not to say that they did not privilege one over the other. As I have tried to show, they did.

Of the three northern Thai monastic orders, the newest one, composed of forest-dwelling *araññavāsīs* based at Wat Pa Dæng, was most interested in using writing both to communicate and to store Pali texts, and they therefore elevated writing to a somewhat privileged status. There were probably two copies of the Tipiṭaka and two libraries in which to keep them at their main monastery, and their sister *wat*, Chet Yøt (Mahābodhi), was the site of a council where the canon was redacted and written down. From the manuscripts that I examined, these monks appear to have sponsored far more than their numbers would have suggested, and in the area known as Tha Søi they also likely were at pains to take care of manuscripts once they were made by putting them into protective boxes from an early date.

Their main rivals, the older Sinhalese-derived order based at Wat Suan Døk and hence known as the "flower-garden order" or *pupphārāmavāsī*, certainly used written texts, but they did not incorporate them as much into their textual practices or their worldview. Their opus, the MS, rarely mentions writing, alludes to the use of libraries mostly in relation to the Mon, and strongly equates the health of the oral tradition with the well-being of the religion itself. It is not surprising, given these positions, that the new forest-dwellers were stricter in their interpretation of the disciplinary rules. It is reasonable to conjecture that along with the stricter ordination practices, and the more scholarly inclination of these monks, would have gone a greater reverence for books. In the particular context of the ordination practices of the monks in Lan Na as shown by details in the TPD, the debates were largely about matters of grammar, which are much easier to detect and thus root out through close examination of written texts. A heavier reliance upon the unchanging written word—a medium detached from contingencies—may have tended to make the monks less flexible. Just as the words on the leaves do not change, so their monastic practices may have been more resistant to modification. The close and more recent ties with Sri Lanka would also have likely instilled in the founding monks of this order a healthy respect for writing, for this island had historically had a strong literate culture.

Kings, moreover, were highly inclined to employ writing for the administration of the kingdom, for legal texts, and for interregnal communication. In many chronicles we hear of kings regularly sending and receiving letters, and there are myriad legal manuscripts still extant in library collections. This type of usage may have acclimatized them to writing, leading them to be more inclined to use it for religious purposes as well. Once they began to sponsor manuscripts, they probably began to realize that these projects and the texts that proceeded from them could be used to cultivate strong ties to the Dhamma and thus increase their prestige in the eyes of their subjects, who felt that the king gains much of his legitimacy from his role as upholder of the religion. Many of the monks, however, would have been somewhat resistant to this change because it afforded the king another source of cultural capital and thus lessened his dependence upon the Saṅgha. Furthermore, in an environment that restricted ostentatious displays of personal wealth, much of the prestige of being a monk grew out of his knowledge and wisdom. While these are rather nebulous concepts, the most effective way to demonstrate them is through the number of religious texts the monk has memorized. This provides a measurable indicator of these desirable attributes and was instituted by means of titles such as *vinayadhara, tipiṭakadhara,* and the like. If the memorization of texts were made obsolete, then this would deprive the monks of an important tool for achieving and displaying status.

Thus, like any new technology, writing was not a neutral process and occupied, for both explicit and opaque reasons, different positions in different sectors of society and in different monastic orders in Lan Na. It was likely a site of contention between kings and monks, among *araññavāsī*, *pupphārāmavāsī*, and *nagaravāsī* monastic orders, as well as between Thai and Burmese. My studies point to a technologically progressive, but doctrinally conservative group of scribal monks working with the support of certain kings steadfastly trying to expand the influence and uses of writing in the religious life of the region. They may have been passively, or perhaps even actively, opposed by some who were not eager to see the old ways of oral transmission become outmoded—but, of course, the irony is that the only way we can know about the latter is through the efforts of the former.

Some major changes took place after the two centuries of Burmese suzerainty. While only a few, poorly executed manuscripts from this period are now available, by the time of the reconstruction of King Kawila in the early nineteenth century, writing seems to have become much more accepted and used by all sectors of society. We see Ānisaṃsa texts praising the merits of making manuscripts; we see the word *pūjā* appear in colophons, entreating people to worship the manuscripts; and we see monks and kings working together to initiate very large manuscript-copying projects involving the production of hundreds of titles, many of which still survive. We also see title markers accompanying some of these texts, suggesting that they were made in order to constitute an active and accessible part of the texts in circulation. The Burmese invasion and the subsequent loss of the carefully nurtured literate world of Lan Na must at the time have been viewed by those involved as a great calamity. But the course of history is never predictable, and we can now say that this was merely a setback, for while great Pali texts were no longer composed in Lan Na, after the reconstruction the written word played a much more central role in the display and storage of Pali texts, and manuscripts finally reached the point of more general acceptance and even worship. One wonders whether the Golden Age scribes would be gladdened or dismayed to learn that today in the region old manuscripts are often burned and the ashes placed in amulets for good luck and protection.

NOTES

INTRODUCTION

1. This view has been held from T. W. Rhys Davids in his introduction to the Vinaya (Vin 1881), to G. P. Malalasekera (1958), through to Oscar von Hinüber (1989) and other modern scholars.

2. A number of different dating systems have been used in this book. I have endeavored to provide the common, western dates based on the Christian calendar wherever possible, and have marked these with (B)CE, for "(Before the) Common Era." The two Thai dating systems that I have used are the Cūlasakkarāja era, abbreviated CS and commonly used in manuscripts and inscriptions, that commenced in the year 638 CE, and the Buddhasakkarāja era, abbreviated BE, that commenced in the traditional year of the Buddha's death, 543 BCE. Any dates without a specific designation should be taken to be of the common era. For more information about the Thai calendar, see JKMI Appendix 2.

3. MV 1908, 33.100–101 and JKMp, 60–61.

4. For more information on the *paṇḍita* tradition, see Ingalls (1959) and Cenkner (1980).

5. The most successful electronic Dhamma project, used by many universities and Buddhist practitioners, has been the Vipassana Research Institute's CD-Rom and Web-based version of the *Chaṭṭhasaṅgāyana* edition of the Tipiṭaka, complete with all the commentarial and subcommentarial literature. This is available free from the group's website: http://www.vri.dhamma.org

6. The word "Tai" is generally used to distinguish the broad linguistic family that includes the Yuan, Thai, Lao, Shan, Khün, and other such languages that have a degree of mutual intelligibility and which are probably descended from the same proto-Tai group, distinct from either the Chinese to the north, the Vietnamese to the east, or the Burmese and Khmer to the west, south, and east. I have used the related word "Thai" to designate inhabitants of polities under Tai hegemony, such as the kingdom of Lan Na and the modern state of Thailand, as well as to refer to the official language of modern Thailand. Thus people who may in fact be descended from Mon, Chinese, or other originally non-Tai groups may be included under the term Thai, for it is impossible to know the genealogy of any one historical figure from the intermixed inhabitants of the region. For a brief overview of Tai history as it has been reconstructed by archaeology, anthropology, and historical linguistics, see Wyatt (1984, Chap. 1).

7. For a detailed study of this period, see Penth (1994, 13ff).

8. For an excellent study of the textual production of the period, see von Hinüber (2000).

9. McLuhan has presented his views concisely (1964, Chap. 1), as have Ong (1982, Chaps. 3–4) and Goody (1977, Chaps. 1–3).

10. I would like to present briefly some classic examples and arguments that have been used to support the idea that different forms of communication actually influence the very ways that cognition operates. McLuhan tells us that literate people tend to be better marksmen than nonliterates, because their brains are used to following a line visually and isolating targets in space like words on a page (1964, 296). Similarly, he claims that oral peoples do not have perspective in their art, not because of lack of ability, but because they simply do not perceive the world in such a manner (1962, 32). Goody says that "writing, and more specifically alphabetic literacy, made it possible to scrutinize discourse in a different kind of way by giving oral communication a semi-permanent form; this scrutiny favoured the increase in scope of critical activity, and hence of rationality, scepticism and logic" (1977, 37). Ong sums up the work of McLuhan, Goody, and others succinctly, saying that literate people are beings whose thought processes do not grow out of simply natural powers but out of these powers as structured, directly or indirectly, by the technology of writing. Without writing, the literate mind would not and could not think as it does (1982, 78).

11. Major studies of Pali literary history in Sri Lanka and Burma have been undertaken by G. P. Malalasekera (1958) and M. Bode (1909) respectively. These studies touch on some of the questions I wish to address, but are marked by an inadequate analysis of textual forms and communication technologies. Both are also quite dated and have not been supplemented by studies that critically examine all the newly available material. A study in a European language of the history of Pali in Thailand that is similar in scope to those of Burma and Lanka cited above has not been published yet, although a dissertation by Likhit Likhitanonta (1980) covers a lot of this ground. There is a thorough study in Thai by Suphaphan Na Bangchang (1986) whose title translates as *The Development of Pali Literature in Thailand: Inscriptions, Histories, Chronicles, Letters, Proclamations.*

12. An understanding of the oral world requires one to realize that it is very possible for people to memorize extremely large amounts of text. In fact, this is still done today not just in traditional cultures, but in modern western society. Stage actors are routinely required to learn scores of pages by heart for a show that may run only a few weeks, at which point they must learn another text by heart for the next performance. A veteran actor may have memorized hundreds or even thousands of printed pages over the years. Furthermore, actors that I interviewed did not talk of the raw memorization of lines as contributing in any major way to the challenges of acting.

13. Collins has provided a fairly detailed account of the methods of memorization (1992, 127).

14. Such a study of some oral aspects of the Tipiṭaka has been executed by Mark Allon in his Cambridge dissertation (1994).

15. This situation is seen elsewhere in the world, such as in classical Greece, as shown by R. Thomas (1992), and has been the case in South Asia itself with the Vedas.

16. For a detailed introduction to the themes and historical context of the CDV, see Part I of CDVe.

17. The version of this chronicle that I have used was edited by Bamphen Rawin and published as *Tamnan Mūlasāsanā Samnuan Lan Na.*

18. See Wyatt for a discussion of *tamnan* (1994b, 16). Pruess has conducted one such study of a chronicle centering on a relic (1976).

19. For a concise analysis of this problem, see Pollock (1989, 603–606).

20. Attempting to avoid what many felt were fanciful or legendary sections, George Coedès (1925), for example, translated only the portions of the JKM and CDV which he regarded as most likely to provide accurate names and dates with which to construct an event-history of the region. In doing so, he overlooked the religious and thematic concerns of the works and totally disregarded the frame stories, thereby stripping the texts of their poetic force.

21. In recent decades, questions about the limits and verisimilitude of historiography have been raised from many quarters. These issues, which range from whether it is possible to give an objective account of the past, to whether even the past itself can be said to possess a "true reality," are collected, discussed, and assessed by McCullagh (1998). In investing the term "reality" with some meaning here, I side with Joyce Appleby, Lynn Hunt, and Margaret Jacob, who argue that "truths about the past are possible, even if they are not absolute, and hence are worth struggling for" (quoted in McCullagh 1998, 3).

22. A detailed and thoughtful study of these *dhammacakka*s has been produced by Robert Brown (1996).

23. Harald Hundius has prepared a catalog of thirty Pali manuscripts and their colophons (1990) based on the SRI microfilms. I have cited these according to their number in Hundius's catalog in the form HH-00, and not according to their microfilm number. I have also examined some unpublished manuscripts from the microfilm rolls at the SRI. These have been cited according to their identification on these rolls commencing with the prefix MF. In all cases where published catalogs are available, I have cited them following the item number in that catalog. Thus citations from the catalog of manuscripts kept at the Siam Society (von Hinüber 1987) are in the form SS-00 and those from the SRI catalog edited by Buddharaksa (SRIcat) are SRIcat-00. In addition to these three catalogs, von Hinüber has written an article (1990) based on his reading of the colophons of manuscripts in the library at Wat Lai Hin in Lampang, and I have utilized a number of these colophons. Manuscripts from his article are cited according to the catalog number given to the actual manuscripts—not the microfilm—as part of the SRI project. I have also used these SRI numbers to cite unpublished manuscripts from Wat Duang Di and Wat Phra Singh, two monasteries in Chiang Mai with significant old manuscript collections. I examined these manuscripts myself from February 1999 through April 1999. In these cases, numbers starting with 04– are for manuscripts from Wat Lai Hin, Lampang; 07– are from Wat Phra Singh, Chiang Mai; and 19– are from Wat Duang Di, Chiang Mai.

24. The origins of the various scripts are obscure and cannot be presented in anything but the loosest of frameworks. Hans Penth (1992) presents the most detailed and critical account in English of the development of the various Thai scripts. See in particular pages 51–61. It is of note that the first appearance of the Dhamma script may be in the Pali portion, consisting of only a single dedicatory verse, of an inscription other-

wise in Sukhodaya script on a gold leaf that was discovered in a *cetiya* at Sukhodaya (EHS, 415–417). The inscription is dated CS 738 or 1376 CE. Unfortunately, the current location of this leaf is unknown, and the identification of the script at the end as northern was made by a monk who does not supply any evidence. Because the next known appearance of the script is not for over fifty years, I am tempted to believe that the script identified as northern Thai by this monk was perhaps not quite correct.

25. For more discussion of this question, see Collins (1990, 92).

26. For further discussion of these terms, their history, meaning, and deployment, see Collins (1990, 90–95).

27. Rahula sums up the situation succinctly: "Although there is evidence to prove the growth of the Pali Scriptures during the early centuries of Buddhism in India and Ceylon, there is no reason to doubt that their growth was arrested and the text was finally fixed in the 5th century A.C. when the Sinhalese Commentaries on the Tipiṭaka were translated into Pali by Buddhaghosa" (1956, xix).

CHAPTER 1: MONKS AND MEMORY

1. The coming of the Sinhalese dispensation will be discussed in detail in Chapter Three.

2. The origins of Buddhism in Thailand are obscure and largely a matter of conjecture. However, some basic components have emerged through careful study of the epigraphical, archaeological, and literary evidence which, though scarce, may serve to provide a provisional outline of the subject. The CDV itself commences with an account of the beginnings of Buddhism in the region, in which it is said that the Buddha himself flew through the air and visited the Mon, intent upon instructing them in the Dhamma (CDVe, 38–39). The early Buddhism of the region probably evolved independently of the Sinhalese forms and may have been in some way connected to missionaries that tradition holds were sent by Asoka (Skilling 1997a, 101). It is clear from Pali inscriptions on several *dhammacakka* wheels that beginning in the seventh century the Mon kingdom of Dvāravatī was already influenced by Theravāda teachings (Brown 1996, 96–120). Mon inscriptions found at Haripuñjaya from the early thirteenth century mention Pali canonical texts, further demonstrating that the Mon association with Theravāda continued at least until the advent of Tai kingdoms in the Menam region. We also know from Khmer inscriptions, Chinese accounts such as Yijing, and the remains of religious structures that Mahāyāna was flourishing at this time to the east and south (Finot 1926).

3. Some examples of popular Buddhist practices in the CDV are: Bodhiraṃsi claims protection from harm through worship of the Three Jewels (CDVe, 37); tree deities must vacate the area for the building of Haripuñjaya to commence (CDVe, 52); the king advocates transferring the merit from one's deeds to one's relatives (CDVe, 98); astrologers explain the meaning of the words of a crow that had been possessed by a *devatā* (CDVe, 128). While admitting that the nineteenth-century rationalist conception of "orthodox" Buddhism is a problematic one that conveniently overlooks the many widely accepted and ancient practices in Buddhism that do not conform to certain modern scientific notions, it is also important not to overlook the

fact that practices such as these are indeed condemned in important *sutta*s such as the *Brahmajāla Sutta* (DN, i, 8–11) and not just by modernists of a reformist bent.

4. The *Yājñavalkyasmṛti* (1.332) groups scribes with rogues and the *Aitareya Āraṇyaka* says that writing renders one impure and therefore unable to study the Vedas just as if one had come into contact with blood (cited in Nattier 2003, 59, n. 11).

5. There is an unusually acute anachronism here because Pagan did not exist until several centuries later.

6. Note the sequence of events occurring here: the teachings/words of the Buddha (which from the context must include the commentaries) are first recited in Sinhalese by Mahinda, then written down in Sinhalese, then translated into Pali by Buddhaghosa, and then written down in Pali.

7. By "mastery," I mean a deep knowledge of the different themes and styles of these three collections, which includes a copious amount of memorized passages, but not necessarily every word as may be found in printed editions. Recall that in the Introduction, I spoke about the fact that even written collections known in the chronicles and inscriptions as the Tipiṭaka were probably not complete.

8. *Kimatthaṃ āgatosīti āha. Buddhavacanaṃ uggaṇhatthāya, bhante ti. Thero uggaṇha dāni, sāmaṇerāti vatvā puna divasato pabhuti buddhavacanaṃ paṭṭhapesi. Tisso sāmaṇerova hutvā. ṭhapetvā vinayapiṭakaṃ sabbaṃ buddhavacanaṃ uggaṇhi saddhiṃ aṭṭhakathāya. Upasampannakāle pana avassikova samāno tipiṭakadharo ahosi. ācariyupajjhāyā moggaliputtatissattherassa hatthe sakalaṃ buddhavacanaṃ patiṭṭhāpetvā yāvatāyukaṃ ṭhatvā parinibbāyiṃsu. Moggaliputtatissattheropi aparena samayena kammaṭṭhānaṃ vaḍḍhetvā arahattapatto bahūnaṃ dhammavinayaṃ vācesi* (VRI-Dev, *Pārājikakaṇḍa Aṭṭhakathā*, 1: 41).

9. *Satthā "nāhaṃ, bhikkhave, yo bahumpi uggaṇhati vā bhāsati vā, taṃ dhammadharoti vadāmi. Yo pana ekampi gāthaṃ uggaṇhitvā saccāni paṭivijjhati, ayaṃ dhammadharo nāmā" ti vatvā dhammaṃ desento imaṃ gāthamāha*—

Natāvatā dhammadharo, yāvatā bahu bhāsati;
Yo ca appampi sutvāna, dhammaṃ kāyena passati
Sa ve dhammadharo hoti, yo dhammaṃ nappamajjatī ti

(VRI-Dev, *Dhammapada Aṭṭhakathā*, 2: 222)

10. The editors of the 1920 Thai printed edition of the CDV, published by the Wachirayan Library, insert this account into their edition of the CDV because the fascicle dealing with the actual arrival of Cāmadevī seems to be missing from the text that they used.

11. The event is also chronicled in inscriptions and Burmese chronicles that give a widely different version. According to them, the Tipiṭaka was taken from the Mon at Sudhammanagara in lower Burma (also known as Thaton) in 1057 CE (Sengupta 1994, 40). Ratanapañña makes an uncharacteristically large chronological error in placing the whole episode in BE 1200 (seventh century CE), instead of about BE 1600 (eleventh century CE), when the king probably reigned.

12. It is unclear here what is being considered the fourth basket. It is probably some form of commentarial texts.

13. For a detailed look at the wide variety of inscriptions to be found at Pagan,

and the definitive account of the history of early Pagan based largely upon epigraphic evidence, see Luce *Old Burma, Early Pagan* (1960–1970).

14. This process will be discussed in detail in Chapter Two.

15. Little is known about this civilization, including its exact dates and spatial extent. For a study that brings together the scant evidence that does exist, see Saraya (1999).

16. For examples of some Mon inscriptions, see Bauer (1991), Coedès (1924), Guillon (1974; 1977), and Halliday (1930).

17. This teacher is credited in the Epilogue of the TBK.

18. Changkachitt (1996) believes that the *cetiya*s of such monasteries as Wat Phra That Haripuñjaya and Wat Kukut, with their tiered facades with three Buddha images, display the influence of Mahāyāna schools that accepted the doctrine of the three bodies of the Buddha—Nirmāṇakāya, Sambhogakāya, and Dharmakāya.

CHAPTER 2: EARLY THAI ENCOUNTERS WITH ORALITY AND LITERACY

1. This episode is specifically said in the *Phongsawadan Yonok* to have taken place in Martaban (JKMI, 157; Epochs, 117, n. 5).

2. For a clear and detailed account based upon a number of chronicles and inscriptions of Sumana and the coming of the Sinhalese orders to this part of Southeast Asia, see Griswold (1975, 4–48).

3. There were monks living at what are referred to as forest monasteries before Kassapa founded the particular order that spread to Thailand, but this older order seems to have died out some time before Parakkamabāhu I.

4. More will be said about this mission in Chapter Three.

5. See, for example, VRI-Dev, *Uparipaṇṇāsa Aṭṭhakathā*, 4.182.

6. Another version of the TPD (Premchit and Swearer 1977) also says that Sumana brought the canon with him (82) and subsequently makes it clear that the transmission of these texts in manuscript form is indeed what is being talked about, for when the religion goes in 1373 to Chiang Tung, a library is built to house the scriptures (*maṇḍapadhamma*) (84). This version, whose provenance is unknown, focuses far more on written textual transmission than any of the other chronicles and even includes an episode in which the king dreams that an elephant eats the scriptures (86). While all versions of the TPD have problems with a host of dates, the dates in this version are the cleanest, which suggests to me that this version has had a heavier editorial hand over the years than some others. For this reason I have chosen to use Mangrai's edition as my main source for the TPD.

7. For a survey of Sukhodaya archaeology, see Gosling (1996). Gosling says that the library referred to in an inscription is not extant (1996, 32).

8. In 1975 considerable controversy erupted surrounding the authenticity of this inscription. Michael Vickery argued that the inscription was actually a hoax commissioned by Mongkut (for details, see EHS, 806–821).

9. See, for example, inscription 11 (EHS, 471) for a list of items donated, and PSC, 7: item 14, Face 1: ln. 22, for an inventory of buildings that seems to include everything save a library.

10. In the Pāṇinian tradition of grammatical scholarship, a reciter who relies upon a book instead of his memory is classified as one of the lowest types of reciters: "*Gītī śīghrī śiraḥkampī tathā likhitapāṭhakaḥ anarthajño 'lpakaṇṭhaśca ṣāḍete pāṭhakādhamāḥ*" (*Pāṇinīyaśikṣā* - *Ṛk* recension 32 [cited in Pant 1979, 50]). The terse arrangement of aphoristic grammatical texts such as the *Aṣṭādhyāyī* suggests that they were intended to be memorized, and this is indeed how they were learned. The seventh-century Chinese pilgrim Yijing tells us that in his day the study of grammar still began by memorizing the *Aṣṭādhyāyī*, which took under a year, after which the students underwent instruction in the commentaries in order to understand the root text (Pant 1979, 26). In fact, the memorization of key grammatical texts was still held as an ideal in the Benares *Pāṭhaśālā* of the nineteenth century (Pant 1979, 51).

11. The term *pūrī* found in the Wachirayan Library edition is here taken as *purī*. Long and short vowels are easily confused in Thai manuscripts. This reading, which takes the word to mean "city dweller," further suggests that Bodhiraṃsi did not associate himself with the forest-dwelling monks.

12. There are in practice many different forms that oral texts may take (Finnegan 1977, 16–24). I do not intend to simply plug the features of the CDV into any one theory about what marks a work as orally composed or transmitted. I appreciate that there are various features that may seem to be hallmarks of orality, but which may not in fact be such. However, as is discussed in this chapter, the CDV does display a number of characteristics that are generally associated with orality.

13. The Parry-Lord thesis involves not just meter, but also the use of formulaic passages that fit within these meters. This thesis understands formulae as groups of words that fit within metrical parameters to denote various ideas. Thus it is the very strictness of the meter which, instead of making the art even more difficult, actually facilitates its execution. The poet learns his vocabulary within the limits of this meter. With practice he intuitively composes in meter, and he does this by knowing formulae that are tailored to fit into the meter. They may range in size from a few words, to a line, to a whole verse. However, since these formulae in a technical sense do not appear to be employed in any of the chronicles I have been looking at, I will not explore the concept in detail.

14. For a detailed analysis of a South Asian example of an oral text, see Emeneau (1959, 114). Emeneau extends this understanding of textual production to the *Mahābhārata* itself, claiming that "the tradition of the transmittal of the *Mahābhārata* even illustrates the postulate that in a living oral tradition and barring special conditions, no two oral recitations of what purports to be the same work are identical, but each recitation is a fresh composition" (108).

15. As has been mentioned, the tradition, based largely on the MV (1908, 33.100–101), says that the Tipiṭaka was written down during the first-century BCE reign of King Vaṭṭagāmaṇi Abhaya. Bechert says that "there is not the least indication that the two stanzas are less likely to relate historical events than any other information of this section of the *Mahāvaṃsa*. On the contrary, the very fact that the verses are found in both sources [*Mahāvaṃsa* and *Dīpavaṃsa*] confirm that they were derived from the source book . . . and are thus to be considered reliable historical material" (1992, 50). Collins (1990, 98) suggests that the stated timing of the writing

down of the canon is indeed appropriate, for there was then a growing rivalry between the Mahāvihāra and Abhayagiri monasteries, and the fixing of the canon by the Mahāvihāra would have helped to establish their hegemony with respect to the religion. For more information on this subject, see Collins (1992).

16. For example, Pali *ācāriya* becomes *achan* and Ratanakosindra becomes Ratanakosin.

17. Justin McDaniel's 2003 Harvard PhD dissertation, "Invoking the Source: Nissaya Manuscripts, Pedagogy and Sermon-Making in Northern Thai and Lao Buddhism," is an important and painstakingly researched foray into the world of Thai Nissayas. For an excellent study of Burmese Nissayas and their influence upon the Burmese language itself, see Okell (1963).

18. Besides the fragmentary Jātaka from Wat Lai Hin (SRI 04 030–01; SRI 04 030–02; SRI 04 030–03; SRI 04 030–04) dated CS 833 (1471 CE) discussed by von Hinüber (1985, 1), there are at least two other manuscripts dated before 1500 CE that von Hinüber mentions: a copy of the *Milindapañha* from 1495 CE (von Hinüber 1986) and a *Yamakapakaraṇam* from 1497 CE (SRI 04–025). He adds that there are some manuscripts that are attributed to the late fifteenth century, although they are not precisely dated, and there is also supposedly a copy of the *Sāraṭṭhappakāsinī* in the National Library in Bangkok from 1440 CE, mentioned by Coedès, and a *Yamakavohāra* at the Siam Society from 1487 CE, neither of which von Hinüber has actually been able to trace (1990, 57).

19. This possibility will be examined in more detail in the next chapter.

20. The four stages of the path to enlightenment are *sotāpatti* (entering the stream), *sakadāgāmi* (returning to this world only one more time), *anāgāmi* (never returning to this world), and *arahant* (being enlightened and fully escaping the realm of rebirth). The four fruits are the benefits of being at each of these stages, and the ninth and ultimate attainment is reaching the state of *nibbāna*.

CHAPTER 3: GOLDEN AGE, GOLDEN IMAGES, AND GOLDEN LEAVES

1. Strictly speaking, the *araññavāsī* monasteries are not located "in" a town, but rather usually just outside it. For clarity, however, throughout this book I have identified these monasteries with the nearest large settlement.

2. To avoid confusion, it must be noted here that, as will be explained at the end of this section, Wat Pa Dæng in Chiang Mai was no longer tied to the lineage of its namesake after 1430 CE, at which point it became the center of a new lineage and gave rise to other monasteries named Wat Pa Dæng.

3. An interesting historical note is that this Sinhalese ordination actually died out in Sri Lanka itself in the seventeenth century due to persecution by the Portuguese, the Dutch, and the Shaivite king Rājasinghe. It was later reintroduced to its native land from Thailand during a series of missions starting in 1753. For details, see Blackburn (2003).

4. Although Sumana and his older Sinhalese forest-dwelling lineage was originally associated with the Wat Pa Dæng at Sri Sajjanālaya that provided the name for Wat Pa Dæng at Chiang Mai, after the newer ordination lineage came to

Chiang Mai, this monastery was no longer, strictly speaking, part of the lineage of its namesake.

5. All numbers refer to the paragraph number in Mangrai's English translation (1981).

6. There is an interesting historical note that speaks to the surprising reliability of the chronicles on matters of communications technologies. If, according to the JKM, the above prophecy was written 140 years prior to King Duṭṭhagāminī, it would have to have been written sometime in the mid-third century BCE, roughly contemporaneous with Asoka. It was thought until recently that writing was unknown in Sri Lanka at this time, but recent excavations have uncovered inscribed potsherds at Anurādhapura that have been dated through radiocarbon technology to the fourth century or even earlier (Salomon 1998, 12).

7. As will be discussed in Chapter Six, the belief that tattooing words on to the body can protect one from harm is common in northern Thailand, but this kind of power is not generally associated with writing in the chronicles. Also, the tattoos are not necessarily associated with Buddhism.

8. Most of the chapters in Schopen (1997) deal in some way with this topic, but see, in particular, chapter seven, "Burial *Ad Sanctos* and the Physical Presence of the Buddha in Early Indian Buddhism," and chapter eight, "On the Buddha and his Bones: The Conception of a Relic in the Inscriptions from Nāgārjunikoṇḍa."

9. In the version of the TPD translated by Premchit and Swearer (1977), the book-supported debate takes place a full century earlier, in CS 838 (1476 CE), which seems to me too early. I have therefore chosen to focus on the event as found in Mangrai's version of the TPD.

10. It is unclear exactly what the term *sarabhañña* means. Jayawickrama translates it as "vocal intonation" (Epochs, 130). As Collins concludes, it probably "involves something like a chant or recitative instead of ordinary speech" (1992, 125) but is something less than singing in a full voice, as this was forbidden by the Buddha.

11. This is the Buddha image from Wat Kesa Sri (Penth 1997b) that will be examined in detail in Chapter Four.

12. Bizot (1988) presents a detailed analysis of some of the variations found in Southeast Asian *pabbajjā* ceremonies. Just as in the TPD, these variations revolve largely around different pronunciation of the Three Refuges (*buddhaṃ saraṇaṃ gacchāmi, dhammaṃ saraṇaṃ gacchāmi, saṅghaṃ saraṇaṃ gacchāmi*), as well as minor grammatical alterations in this and related formulas.

13. Literally "houses for books" (*duve ca potthakālaye* MV 1925, 78.37) in this case.

14. A word must be said about the identity of Dhammagambhīra. The deeds of this monk mentioned in the JKM and some inscriptions seem to coincide with those of Ñāṇagambhīra as found in the TPD, leading one to believe that these two similar names refer to the same person.

15. That the scriptures were brought in written form is also suggested by the parallel account in Premchit and Swearer's edition (1977) where it is said that the scriptures were brought in a cart (97–98).

16. I agree with Mangrai's translation here of the term *mondok* as "library," although it is possible that it refers to some other sort of pavilion.

17. The *Tamnan Chiang Mai* will be studied in more detail in Chapter Five.

18. All citations refer to the fascicle and folio number of a manuscript compiled by Hans Penth and used by Wyatt in his edition of TCM.

19. Artifacts of this kind still exist, such as a set of golden plates from Sri Lanka inscribed with a Sanskrit text, probably dating to the tenth century as well. This set comprises seven gold plates in excellent condition that were found at the Jetavanārāma at Anurādhapura, and the text has been identified as the *Pañcaviṃśatisāhasrikā Prajñāpāramitā* (Jayasuriya 1988). It is surely not just a coincidence that both Kassapa's Abhidhamma and this text come from the same era. Rather, it is probably due to writing's acquiring a hieratic function that proceeded from ideas formulated in Sanskrit Buddhist works that had reached their apogee at this particular moment in Sri Lankan history (Paranavitane 1928).

20. The council to edit and copy the scriptures convened by Tilaka is the eighth council by Northern Thai reckoning and probably took place in 1477 CE.

21. Unfortunately, the eighth council itself does not appear in the JKM, and even the section about this council in the chronicle dedicated to the history of the very monastery where it was held, the *Tamnan Wat Chet Yøt*, is "a free translation, often amplified, of the passages in JKM which refer to Vat Ced-Yod" (Hutchinson 1951, 5). There is also no remaining evidence of the library today, although most of the other important edifices described in the chronicles have left some mark at the site (Hutchinson 1951, 8–18).

22. The garbled state of the lines renders them difficult to translate (Epochs, 168, n.1).

23. There is a slight problem with the chronology here, because the inscription is dated CS 854 (1492 CE) and says that at that time Bophit was ruling in Chiang Mai. If this is the same King Bophit mentioned in the Haripuñjaya inscription, which is likely based on the content, then the traditional date of the beginning of his reign derived from the JKM, which is 1495 CE, must be incorrect.

24. The Pali in the JKM is *Biṅgasenā Rattavanavihāre piṭakattayaṃ likhāpesi* (JKMp, 122). It is unclear from this sentence precisely who does the writing and who orders it to be done. From the grammar, it could be that a female person named Biṅgasena has it written, or it could be that the king had Biṅgasenā (taken as a feminine plural accusative) write it. In the latter case, Biṅga is the city of Chiang Mai (because the Biṅga River runs through it) and *senā*, usually used to mean "army," is probably a group of officials.

25. These are *Cakkavāḷadīpanī*, CS 900 (1538 CE), Wat Phra Singh: SRI 07–04–24–00; and another *Cakkavāḷadīpanī*, mid-sixteenth century, Wat Pubbārām: MF 78.009.01J.121–122; as well as two Jātaka manuscripts, CS 923 (1561 CE), Wat Lai Hin: SRI 04–28–01; and CS 922 (1560 CE), Wat Lai Hin: SRI 04–98.

26. *Anuṭīkāyamaka,* CS 873 (CE 1511), Wat Duang Di: SRI 19–04–034.

27. *Samantapāsādikā*, CS 950 (1588 CE), Wat Lai Hin: SRI 04–35.

28. *Mūlapaṇṇāsa-Aṭṭhakathā,* CS 904 (1542 CE), SRIcat-58; and *Mahosathajātaka*, sixteenth or seventeenth century, Wat Lai Hin: HH-03.

29. *Pārājika*, (1517 CE), Wat Latthivan (near Hot).

30. *Manorāthapūraṇī*, CS 894 (1532 CE), SS-55.

31. *Jātaka*, sixteenth century, Wat Lai Hin: SRI 04–16; *Dhammapada-Atthakathā*, early sixteenth century, Wat Lai Hin: SRI 04–69; *Jātakaṭṭhakathā-Aṭṭanipāta*, CS 911 (1549 CE), SRIcat-13; *Jātakaṭṭhakathā-Cattālīsanipāta*, CS 912 (1550 CE), SRIcat-20; *Jātakaṭṭhakathā-Paṇṇāsanipāta,* CS 912 (1550 CE), SRIcat-21; *Jātakaṭṭhakathā-Saṭṭhinipāta,* CS 912 (1550 CE), SRIcat-22.

32. *Itivuttaka*, CS 906 (1544 CE), Wat Lai Hin: SRI 04–08; *Ekanipāta Jātaka*, CS 909 (1547 CE), Wat Lai Hin: SRI 04–15; and *Suttasaṅgaha*, CS 903 (1541 CE), Wat Lai Hin: SRI 04–027.

33. *Mahāvagga*, CS 908 (1546 CE), Wat Lai Hin: SRI 04–36–06 was made by the monk Medhaṅkara and *Appadāna Aṭṭhakathā,* CS 898 (1536 CE), SRIcat-84 was made by Bhaddanta Ñāṇagambhīra.

34. One of these manuscripts is kept at Wat Phra Singh and is cataloged as SRI 07–04–24–00; the other is available on the SRI microfilm set as MF 78.009.01J.121–122.

35. Von Hinüber (2000, 129) cites the use of the term *pāṭhā* at *Samantapāsādikatthayojanā* 288, 13 for example.

36. This practice will be addressed in detail in Chapter Four.

37. This phrase is suggested and explored by Collins (1990).

38. Already in 1131 CE, an inscription records that Alaungsithu donated a copy of the Tipiṭaka to a temple in Pagan (Luce 1970, 131) and about one hundred years later, we find that the very first item donated to the Winido Monastery was a copy of the Tipiṭaka (Luce 1970, 146).

39. Frank Reynolds reminds us that kings were often aware of the potential problems represented by the Saṅgha. He points out that kings were happy to appear to promote the purity of the religion by seeing to it that the monks clung strictly to the Vinaya rules, not only to improve the royal image as a *dhammika* ruler, but also because these rules, of course, preclude the monks from participating in political affairs (1971, 200).

40. For studies of these texts, see Huxley (1996).

41. Their fears did not turn out to be entirely warranted, for even today, with the easy availability of printed texts, the oral mode of textual transmission still plays an important part in the life of Thai Buddhism. Most people encounter Buddhist texts through hearing them recited at the *wat* or on the radio or through tapes, and many monks have still memorized such large amounts of text that they seldom look at the manuscript in their laps when reciting.

CHAPTER 4: THE TEXT IN THE WORLD

1. This is not intended to be a catalog of the manuscripts surveyed and therefore does not necessarily include details such as how the manuscripts begin and end or how many lines of text there are on each leaf. This information is included in

catalogs published by von Hinüber (1987), Hundius (1990), Otani (1995), and Buddharaksa (2000).

2. This text is examined in detail by von Hinüber (1985).

3. For details on the scheme used in this book for citing manuscripts, see the Introduction, n.23.

4. Although I have not examined Pali manuscripts of Laotian provenance for this book, many of them are written in the Lan Na Dhamma script. Louis Finot comments that when he went to Luang Prabang, he was struck by the poor state of the manuscripts, their disorganization, and the dilapidation of the monastic libraries (1917, 2). Upon the suggestion of some French scholars, many of the manuscripts were collected and brought to the royal library for proper preservation. Finot's detailed analysis of some 1,200 Pali and vernacular manuscripts is reported in the *Bulletin De L'École Française D'Extrême Orient* (BEFEO) of 1917. He there concludes that the knowledge of Pali as evinced by the extant manuscripts was not great. He was not even able to collect a complete set of the Tipiṭaka because such important volumes as the *Majjhima Nikāya, Sutta Nipāta,* and *Theragāthā* were lacking (1917, 41).

5. Although the rules of Pali phonology can permit the elision of an initial *a* when following an *o*, it is standard practice to include it in this context. I have not seen it omitted in any other manuscripts.

6. In the absence of inscribed dates, dates may be estimated based upon the style of the design, as well as the style of clothing worn by any figures adorning the box. This is, admittedly, an imprecise science.

7. Unfortunately, the location of this important center of early manuscript production is unknown. It may lie beneath what is now water, as mentioned by Hundius (1990, 67), although as I show below, I believe it may have been in Phayao.

8. Penth argues that the term *abhinavabojarājarājā* should be translated in this way because King Tilaka considered Yudhiṣthira to be his younger brother (JKMI, 239).

9. Note that neither Pali morphology nor Pali phonetics are properly expressed in this text. Both retroflex and palatal sibilants are found in this passage, even though they are not found in Pali, being part of the Sanskrit phonetic system alone. This reflects a rather poor awareness of certain basic elements of Pali that may have been a result both of an underdeveloped Pali literate culture until this point, and of Sanskrit influence.

10. A feature of the Kammavācā texts of Burma, for comparison, are the ribbons, called *sarsekyo*, that are sometimes used to bind the manuscript. The earliest of these date from the late eighteenth century, although some undated examples may be slightly older. These ribbons often have some text woven into them, including such things as the title of the work, quotations from the Vinaya, prayers and wishes on behalf of the donor, and exhortations not to damage or steal the text.

11. Siamese examples can be seen in Pal's work (1988, 217) and the cover of Suphaphan (1986).

12. Not only are the titles, especially of older manuscripts, not clearly displayed, but in at least one case the copyist seems to have been unsure of what the

title actually was. The back page of what on the front is called the *Sadda-sāraṭṭhajālinī* (SRI 07-04-070) from CS 888 (1526 CE) has the title inscribed upon it as *Saddasārattani*, but this is marked with *x*'s and above it is written *Sadda-sāraṭṭhaṃ* in lacquer ink.

13. An example of such a manuscript can be seen in Pal (1988, 192).

14. Ginsburg's study of Thai manuscript painting (1989), as well as Pal's section on Thai illustrated Buddhist manuscripts (1988, 214–224), consist almost entirely of *samut khoi* manuscripts of vernacular texts such as Thai versions of *Phra Malai* and Jātaka tales.

15. A foundation script can be used to teach the basics of forming letters (Petrucci 1995, 61).

16. It is informative to compare the scribal praxis discussed here with that of Jewish scribes, who have approached their task with a famously reverential spirit. The sacred scripture of the Jews, known as the Pentateuch or Torah in Hebrew, is generally written with much more care and precision than the palm-leaf manuscripts that I have seen. Since the Torah is written on parchment with ink, minor corrections can be made by lightly scraping off the ink and rewriting the word. However, few such mistakes were permitted, and one does not see the number of mistakes, corrections, omitted letters, and the like in Torah scrolls that one sees in palm-leaf manuscripts from northern Thailand. In the early rabbinical era, a Torah scroll that contained too many mistakes or corrections was generally buried in an urn, often next to a prominent rabbi (Posner and Ta-Shema 1975, 29).

17. The best, and virtually only, work that explores the Nissaya genre is Justin McDaniel's 2003 Harvard dissertation.

18. A detailed analysis of these verses in Thai can be found at LNI, 169.

19. Griswold discussed the dating of this item with Hans Penth in a private communication, and the latter eventually published Griswold's opinion (Penth 1997b, 500).

20. The uniqueness of this inscription also seems to disprove the assertion in the JKM, as commonly interpreted, that a group of monks who had lived in Lanka and learned writing there came back to Lan Na in 1425 and spread this new knowledge or developed a native script based on it. The back of this pedestal also has an inscription, but it is written in the Grantha script from southern India and has thus far not been deciphered. Penth points out that some of the difficulty may lie in the possibility that this, too, is a heart-letter verse and therefore does not appear at first to be in any known language.

21. Griswold and Prasoert (EHS, 771) base this date on the visible portion, which shows the year of the hare of a CS year ending with a 1. Based on the orthography, they put it at CS 701.

22. In medieval Europe, access to the scriptorium was limited so as not to disturb the scribes, who were generally forbidden to speak. Furthermore, the illumination and rubrication was usually done by another team of craftsmen, contributing to the assembly-line feel of the larger scriptoria (McMurtrie 1943, 77–79).

23. It is, again, interesting to compare the position of the scribes in Lan Na to that of the contemporary Jewish scribe:

> The profession of scribe was indispensable to the Jewish community, and according to the Talmud a scholar should not dwell in a town where there is no scribe. In the talmudic period, scribes were poorly paid lest they become rich and desert their vocations, leaving the community without their services. The scribe writing a Torah scroll must devote attention and care to the writing; he is forbidden to rely on his memory and has to write from a model copy. His guide is the professional compendium for scribes, *Tikkun Soferim*, which contains the traditional text of the Torah, the specific rules concerning the decorative flourishes (*tagin* "crowns") on certain letters, the regulations as to the spacing of certain Torah sections. . . . When writing a Torah scroll a scribe must especially prepare himself so that he writes the names of the Lord with proper devotion and in ritual purity. It is, therefore, customary that he immerses himself in a ritual bath (*mikveh*) before beginning his work. (Posner and Ta-Shema 1975, 26)

24. For example, in a colophon from a set of Paritta texts (SS-11) written in BE 2447 (1904 CE), the scribe, Bhikkhu Candanasuvaṇṇa, and the makers (*phu sang*), Mr. Kæo and Mrs. Heiør, are clearly distinguished from each other in the statement that both the writer *and* the makers wish to get merit. Such a division is also suggested in many older manuscripts.

25. All currencies listed are those that were in wide use in Thailand except where otherwise noted.

26. Estimations of the length of palm-leaf manuscripts are based upon a comparison of other extant manuscripts with Pali Text Society printed versions of the texts, from which an average number of printed pages covered by each fascicle can be derived.

27. Although I have already pointed out that it seems that scribal duties were not carried out continuously, full-time work is postulated here for comparative purposes.

28. Penth has discussed the old system of weights (JKMI, 320). He actually weighed some bronze images and found the unit given in their inscriptions to be about one gram. He points out that a different unit may have been used to measure gold.

CHAPTER 5: TURNING OVER A NEW LEAF

1. The *yadu* poem has a melancholy tone and usually deals with separation, yearning, and the changing seasons; it possesses three stanzas, the last lines of which rhyme.

2. McDaniel is one of the few scholars of Thai culture and history who has begun to question the long-held position that the Burmese period was uniformly bad for the Thais. He alerts us to Sunait Chutintaranond, one of the very few Thai

scholars of Burma, who points out that a lot of the current negative feelings for Burma originated in early Ratanakosin historiography and that traditional Ayudhyā chronicles did not express overt antagonism towards the Burmese (McDaniel 2003, 29–35).

3. It is certainly not the case that the Theravāda Burmese were against the production of Pali manuscripts per se. In Burma itself around this time there was apparently a strong desire by the rulers to have copies of the Tipiṭaka made. According to a royal proclamation issued on the equivalent of April 4, 1638 CE, the Tipiṭaka was copied on a total of 1,008,000 palm leaves and was kept in the palace library (ROB, 1, 96). On April 22 of that same year, another order was given to use 10,008 ivory, 10,008 gold, and 10,008 silver plates to copy the canon (ROB, 1, 98).

4. For a detailed look at this monk and his work, see von Hinüber (1996a).

5. Von Hinüber (1996a) has examined these manuscripts and presents information on the circumstances of their production.

6. The severity of this final conquest of Chiang Mai is evident in the language of the Burmese royal chronicle quoted by Wyatt: "Then, having mopped up all the people in the towns of the 57 districts of Chiang Mai who insolently were unsubmissive, there was no trouble and everything was as smooth as the surface of water" (1984, 134).

7. In the traditional Thai *maṇḍala* system of political organization, in which borders are less important than intersecting fields of allegiance (see Thongchai 1994, 81–84), one would not be unjustified in defining the rather nebulous entity of "Lan Na" as the region in which the Lan Na scripts were used.

8. There is no evidence that the Burmese tried to foist the Burmese script upon the inhabitants of northern Thailand. I wish to be clear that I speak here of a resurgence of writing in Lan Na from a state of general decline and not from the writing having been done in Burmese.

9. It is not uncommon for orders or sects to merge during difficult times. In Burma, for example, after the animist Shans sacked Ava in 1527 and killed many of the monks, the forest-dwellers as a formally separate organization lost power and merged into the general community of monks (Lieberman 1984, 47).

10. For example, some Pali texts from Wat Duang Di dated CS 1170 (1808 CE) were sponsored by a forest-dwelling monk named Paññāvajira, along with his students. A *Visuddhimagga* from this *wat* dated CS 1171 (1809 CE) was made by the Mahārājaguru, who would have been an *araññavāsī* as well. Another text, the *Suttasaṅgaha* CS 1174 (1812 CE) from Wat Duang Di (SRI 19-04-008), was made, once again, at the behest of the Rājāguru, who is said in the colophon to be an *araññavāsī*.

11. The Nan chronicle was written in 1894 CE by a royal official named Sænluang Ratchasomphan, in the aftermath of the Paknam Crisis and the French assumption of control of the eastern portion of Nan, which strangely enough it does not mention. Like the other chronicles of more recent provenance, it is based on unnamed older chronicles as well as oral testimony and the experience of the author. I have used Wyatt's translation (Nan).

12. A *salüng* was at this time equivalent to 0.25 *bat.* Prices paid for manuscripts are discussed in more detail in Chapter Four.

13. Wednesday, November 3, 1886.

14. For example, an *Apadāna* commentary (SRI 04–09) consisting of thirty-three fascicles, cost 72,000 cowries in 1537 CE, which comes to about 2,200 cowries per fascicle.

15. If each fascicle contained the usual number of leaves, twenty-four, the total number of leaves used would be 100,800. Compare this with the number of leaves—1,008,800—given earlier for a Burmese copy of the Tipiṭaka in ROB, 1, 96.

16. Tambiah says, "It is difficult to say who at any particular period owned the region in which today lies the village of Phraan Muan; it is less difficult to guess what were the cultural and religious elements deposited in it by the parade of historical events" (1970, 31).

CHAPTER 6: OVERLOOKED OR LOOKED OVER?

1. Pal cites a number of colophons from India and Nepal that give voice to the hope that a variety of felicities will accrue to the writer and other people (1988, 37–38). The colophons also contain admonitions to take good care of the manuscript and to overlook mistakes on the part of the humble scribe (1988, 39).

2. Schopen has presented many inscriptions on *stūpa*s and images indicating that they were funded by the donor in order for him or herself or other beings to gain merit and reach *nirvāṇa* (1997, 34–39).

3. For an analysis of some of the wording of these sentiments, see Hundius (1990, 38–41).

4. As will be discussed later, it is unclear to me whether the term *prasong* actually does mean "worship" in these cases.

5. The merit in these colophons is always directed to someone specific and not to "all beings." This conforms exactly to the pattern pointed out by Schopen (1997, 38–41) in early Indian donative inscriptions, where only Mahāyāna inscriptions mention a desire to help all beings in general.

6. Tepiṭako is a secondary formation based on the word Tipiṭaka. It is roughly synonymous with the term *tipiṭakadhara* and means "one who is familiar with the canonical texts" (PTSD, 80).

7. It is possible that the elision of one "ñ" in the word *puña* as found in the colophon is a result of the influence upon the scribe of Thai vernacular orthography, in which the letter is not doubled as it is in standard Pali.

8. One often sees some form of the phrase *khø hü suk 3 prakan mi nibbana pen yøt* (may it lead to the three kinds of happiness, with *nibbāna* at the pinnacle) in the colophons. See, for example, Otani (696, 702, and 725).

9. These sentiments are commonly found in donative inscriptions on Buddha images as well as in colophons. See, for example, CLNI 5, 165; 176; and 187.

10. The *Mahāparinibbāna Sutta* is one of the main sources of inspiration for Buddhist cultic practice. After the Buddha dies, his disciples honor the body with flowers, perfume, and music, and Ānanda says that the Buddha's remains are to be

treated as those of a wheel-turning monarch (*cakkavatti*), which is to say interred in *stūpa*s and venerated (DN, ii, 161).

11. For a discussion of the commentarial background to the classification of relics, see Trainor (1997, 89).

12. The role of cultic objects in devotion and ritual in Theravāda Buddhism has been addressed at some length by Schopen (1997) and Trainor (1997), and I draw on many of their insights in what follows.

13. Dependence upon rules and rituals is generally seen as one of the fetters (*saṃyojana*) that prevent one from reaching enlightenment. For examples, see Trainor (1997, 139, n. 8).

14. An example of the irrelevance of good karma to the attainment of enlightenment is illustrated in the *Aṅguttara Nikāya*. The Buddha is asked whether there will be a difference in the future lives of two laypeople only one of whom regularly gives food to the monks. The Buddha replies that if they are both reborn in the realm of the gods (*deva*s), for instance, the one who gave will be happier, more beautiful, and will live longer. However, should they both choose to renounce and eventually attain enlightenment, there would be no difference between them (AN, v, 31).

15. Many of Schopen's works deal with the topic of monastic involvement in relic worship. See, for example, "Monks and the Relic Cult in the *Mahāparinibbāna Sutta*," "Burial *Ad Sanctos* and the Physical Presence of the Buddha in Early Indian Buddhism," and "On the Buddha and his Bones," published as chapters six, seven, and eight in *Bones, Stones and Buddhist Monks* (1997).

16. Some examples of this kind of genealogical chronicle, to name only a few, are the *Dāṭhavaṃsa*, which traces the history of the tooth relic, the *Chakesadhātuvaṃsa*, which traces the history of six hair relics, and, of course, the CDV itself, which focuses on the authenticity of the relic kept at Wat Phra Dhātu in Haripuñjaya.

17. Slightly differing accounts of the origins and career of the Phra Buddha Singh image can be found in the JKM (Epochs, 120) and Bodhiraṃsi's *Sihiṅganidāna.*

18. The issue of oral authority and the Vedas has been widely studied. See, for example Cenkner (1980); Ingalls (1959); Rocher (1994); and Staal (1986).

19. For a discussion of the authorial colophon and its implications for the provenance of this text, see Penth (1977). The author is not identified specifically as Thai or Siamese, but it is said that he settled in a monastery called Laṅkārāma in Yodaya, which is most likely the Siamese capital of Ayudhyā, in which there is a monastery of that name.

20. See, for example, the catalog of Burmese manuscripts compiled by Bechert, Khin Su, and Myint (1979, item numbers 9; 10; 39; 53; 60; 64; 68; 73; 91; 92; 93; 97; 100; 115; 131; 133; 134; and 136).

21. Daniel Stevenson (1995) provides a brief overview of the text, from which the quotes and paraphrases are taken.

22. The Three Jewels, or *tiratana*, are the Buddha (often represented by an image), the Dhamma, and the Saṅgha.

23. This sentiment is listed at the beginning of this chapter as sentiment #3 found in the colophons.

24. For a detailed study of the sources and provenance of the Māleyya story and its Pali versions, see chapter three in Brereton (1995). She notes that many manuscripts of this work from Lan Na as well as an old Nissaya from 1516 CE are still extant. Saddhatissa says that the text as we now have it was probably written in Lan Na around 1500, but was based upon earlier, less detailed tellings from Sri Lankā (1974a, 215).

25. There is a very slight possibility that the phrase "give the gift of the Truth" (*Dhammadānaṃ denti*) could be an oblique reference to donations of manuscripts, inasmuch as the Dhamma is written upon them. However, this possibility is strongly discouraged by the fact that any such connotations are left out of the vernacular versions and by the lack of any reference in the commentarial literature connecting this term with the donation of written texts. The worship of the Three Jewels also does not specifically point to worship of manuscripts because the Dhamma could just as easily be represented by a Buddha image or the Saṅgha.

26. There are actually more than fifty stories in total if one considers all of the Thai, Burmese, Laotian, and Cambodian recensions of this work, but each version generally has only fifty tales. There are, in fact, only twenty-one stories that occur in all four recensions (Fickle 1978, 14–19).

27. A number of the tales can be found in a Laotian manuscript dated to 1589 CE, and therefore the bulk of the text must have been composed before that period.

28. For a discussion of the date and authorship of these tales, see Fickle (1978, 7–10) and Jaini (1983, xl–xli). Some of these Jātakas are elaborations of episodes found in the canonical Jātakas, and others are based on stories found in the Avadāna literature. Still others are based on local oral traditions or on nothing at all other than the imagination of the author. Jaini (1983, xii–xl) provides a brief assessment of the possible sources in his introduction, and Fickle provides a detailed analysis on two of the tales in chapter three of her dissertation.

29. One other example can be found in the *Saddhammasaṅgaha* (Law 1963).

30. When I commenced this project in 1999, I asked monks, scholars, curators, and other learned Thai Buddhists if they knew of texts of Thai provenance that spoke of the importance of writing the Tipiṭaka. A few people mentioned that some Ānisaṃsa texts deal with this topic, but no one directed me to the *Paññāsa Jātaka*, suggesting that this particular tale is not well known among the Thai Buddhist community.

31. Some of these *Anisong Sang Tham* texts are cataloged in Coedès (1966) as Laos 63 (1805 CE), Laos 64 (1812 CE), Laos 65 (1816 CE), Laos 66 (1819 CE), and Laos 67 (1828 CE).

32. Charles Keyes describes the work of King Mindon:

> Although King Mindon, like other Theravadin rulers, ensured that the city was protected by spirits and that it was oriented cosmologically, his primary efforts to draw upon sacred power in ensuring the prosperity of his kingdom followed orthodox Buddhist patterns. King Mindon is still remembered for his great acts of merit, the greatest of which was unquestionably the convening

of what the Burmese hold to have been the Fifth Buddhist Council [in 1871]. . . . The text of the *tripiṭaka*, after having been agreed on by the most learned of Burmese monks in sessions that lasted over a five-year period, was engraved upon stones. The 729 engraved "pages" of the scriptures, each of which had their own shrine located at the Kutho-daw ("royal merit") temple monastery remain to this day as graphic reminders of the great merit that King Mindon acquired. (1977, 267)

33. Approximately half of the inscribed images that Penth (1976) collected from the fifteenth and sixteenth centuries were sponsored by monks.

34. Frank Reynolds, in a very interesting study (1978a), has examined an example of how these two forms of the body of the Buddha operate in tandem in the form of the Emerald Jewel image and the scriptures, which have been kept in close proximity for centuries, to legitimate the rule of Thai kings. Swearer's text and the cases examined here are examples that seem to dissolve that distinction somewhat.

35. In Burma, for example, a 1658 CE Buddha image in the Ngahtatgyi Pagoda at Sagaing contains Tipiṭaka passages written on gold and silver (Singer 1991, 133). The Japanese from at least the twelfth century also commonly placed scriptures, sometimes brought from China, inside Buddha images and statues of other important personalities such as Prince Shotoku (Pal 1988, 270) and Kṣitigarbha (Pal 1988, 272–273). To give but one of many examples, the Royal Ontario Museum possesses a monumental thirteenth-century Kuan Yin from Daning, China, that was carved from a hollowed tree trunk (Accession no. 921.1.14). There are three openings in the back intended to allow for the insertion of scriptures.

36. For examples of these *yantra*s and how the words are hidden within them, see Swearer (2004, 64–68).

37. This Pali passage means: "Those things that originate due to a cause, the Buddha has spoken about their cause, and their cessation. The great ascetic speaks thus."

38. For a detailed study of these inscriptions, see Suphaphan (1986, 16–34). Prince Damrong had noticed this absence already in 1926 (Damrong1962, 17).

39. Swearer (2004, 205–210) presents an account of the origins of this highly venerated stone Buddha image.

40. The term *lao* means "recite," rather than "read," as von Hinüber translates it.

41. See von Hinüber (2000) for a discussion of the works of these two scholars.

42. The oldest copies of this text were made in the 1850s (Bizot and Lagirarde 1996, 80).

43. In early modern Europe a person learned to read Latin in school before moving on to the vernacular languages, which led to a situation where many who did not stay in school into the advanced stages had never read a book that they could understand (Darnton 2001, 171). Because of the high rate of students who left the Thai monasteries before being able to comprehend Pali, this must have been the case in Thailand as well.

44. *Badloüang* is a monastic title that is one rank higher than an ordinary *bhikkhu* and can be conferred only upon those who are twenty-one years of age or older.

45. Note that Gervaise made this casual observation a century before William Jones presented his famous thesis that the Indo-Aryan languages are related to Latin and Greek.

BIBLIOGRAPHY

Adikaram, E. W. 1946. *Early History of Buddhism in Ceylon*. Migoda: D. S. Puswella.

Aeusrivongse, Nidhi. 1994. "The Early Bangkok Period: Literary Change and Its Social Causes." *Asian Studies Review* 18:69–76.

Allon, Mark. 1994. "Style and Function: A Study of the Dominant Stylistic Features of the Prose Portions of Pali Canonical Sutta Texts and their Mnemonic Function." PhD dissertation. Cambridge University.

Altekar, Anant S. 1934. *Education in Ancient India*. Benares: The Indian Book Shop.

AN. 1900. Hardy, Edmund, ed. *Aṅguttara Nikāya* V. London: Pali Text Society.

Anderson, Benedict. 1991. *Imagined Communities*. London: Verso.

Aronson, Harvey. 1979. "The Relationship of the Karmic to the Nirvanic in Theravāda Buddhism." *Journal of Religious Ethics* 7:28–36.

Atiyeh, George, ed. 1995. *The Book in the Islamic World*. Albany: SUNY Press.

Bauer, Christian. 1991. "Notes on Mon Epigraphy." JSS 79:31–73.

Becchetti, Catherine. 1994. "Une ancienne tradition de manuscrits au Cambodge." In *Recherches nouvelles sur le Cambodge*, edited by François Bizot, pp. 47–62. Paris: L'École Française d'Extrême Orient.

Bechert, Heinz, ed. 1980. *The Language of the Earliest Buddhist Tradition*. Göttingen: Vandenhoeck and Ruprecht.

———. 1992. "The Writing Down of the Tripitaka in Pali." *Wiener Zeitschrift fur de Kunde Sudasiens* 36:45–53.

Bechert, Heinz. 1979. With Daw Khin Khin Su and Daw Tin Tin Myint. *Burmese Manuscripts*. Wiesbaden: Franz Steiner Verlag.

BEFEO. *Bulletin de l'École Française d'Extrême Orient.*

Bernot, Denise. 1975. "Influence of Burmese Language on Some Other Languages of Burma." JSS 63:96–109.

Bierman, Irene. 1988. *Writing Signs: The Fatimid Public Text.* Berkeley: University of California Press.

Bizot, François. 1976. *Le figuier a cinq branches.* Paris: L' École Française d'Extrême Orient.

———. 1988. *Les traditions de la Pabbajjā en Asie du Sud-Est*. Göttingen: Vanderhoeck & Ruprecht.

———. 1993. *Le Bouddhisme des Thais*. Bangkok: Cahiers de France.

———. 1994. "La consecration des statues et le culte des mortes." In *Recherches nouvelles sur le Cambodge*, edited by François Bizot, pp. 101–135. Paris: L'École Française d'Extrême Orient.

Bizot, François, and François Lagirarde. 1996. *La pureté par les mots*. Paris: L'École Française d'Extrême Orient.

Blackburn, Anne. 1996. "The Play of the Teaching in the Life of the Sasana:

Sārārthadīpanī in Eighteenth-Century Sri Lanka." PhD dissertation. University of Chicago.

———. 2001. *Buddhist Learning and Textual Practice in Eighteenth-Century Lankan Monastic Culture.* Princeton: Princeton University Press.

———. 2003. "Localizing Lineage: Importing Higher Ordination in Theravādin South and Southeast Asia." In *Constituting Communities*, edited by J. C. Holt, J. N. Kinnard, and J. S. Walters, pp. 131–150. Albany: SUNY Press.

Bode, Mabel. 1909. *The Pali Literature of Burma.* London: The Royal Asiatic Society of Great Britain and Ireland.

Boucher, Daniel. 1991. "The *Pratītyasamutpādagāthā* and Its Role in the Medieval Cult of the Relics." JIABS 14, no.1: 1–27.

Brereton, Bonnie. 1993. "Some Comments on a Northern Phra Malai Text Dated C.S. 878 (A.D. 1516)." JSS 81:141–144.

———. 1995. *Thai Tellings of Phra Malai.* Tempe: University of Arizona Press.

Brown, Robert L. 1996. *The Dvāravatī Wheels of the Law and the Indianization of Southeast Asia.* Leiden: E. J. Brill.

Buddharaksa, Balee. 1996. "The History of Pali Chronicles Composed in Chiang Mai during the 14th-16th Centuries." In *Proceedings of the 6th International Conference on Thai Studies: Theme VI Chiang Mai,* pp.185–202.

Bunnag, Jane. 1973. *Buddhist Monk, Buddhist Layman.* Cambridge: Cambridge University Press.

Camille, Michael. 1992. *Image on the Edge: The Margins of Medieval Art.* Cambridge, MA: Harvard University Press.

Carruthers, Mary. 1990. *The Book of Memory: A Study of Memory in Medieval Culture.* Cambridge: Cambridge University Press.

Carter, T. F. 1925. *The Invention of Printing in China and Its Spread Westward.* New York: Columbia University Press.

CDV. 1920. *Cāmadevīvaṃsa* (in Thai and Pāli). Bangkok: Wachirayan National Library.

CDVe. 1998. Premchit, Sommai, and Donald Swearer, trans. *The Legend of Queen Cāma.* Albany: SUNY Press.

Cenkner, William. 1980. "The Pandit: The Embodiment of Oral Tradition" *Journal of Dharma* 5, no.3: 237–251.

Chandrangaam, Saeng. 1980. "Lanna Thai Kingdom and its Religion." In *Buddhism in Northern Thailand*, pp. 87–99. Chiang Mai.

Changkachitt, Sadubhon. 1996. "Phra Phuttha Satsana Mahayana Nai Lan Na." In *Proceedings of the 6th International Conference on Thai Studies: Theme VI Chiang Mai*, pp. 359–384.

Chartier, Roger. 1995. *Forms and Meanings: Texts, Performances and Audiences from Codex to Computer.* Philadelphia: University of Pennsylvania Press.

Cherniack, Susan. 1994. "Book Culture and Textual Transmission in Sung China." *Harvard Journal of Asian Studies* 54:5–126.

Chutima, Tham, ed. 1970. *Tamnan Mūlasāsanā.* Chiang Mai.

CLNI. *Corpus of Lān Nā Inscriptions.* Chiang Mai: Social Research Institute.

CNPT. *Charük Nai Prathet Thai.* Bangkok: National Library.

Codrington, H. W. 1924. *Ceylon Coins and Currency.* Colombo: Government Printer.

Coedès, George. 1915. "Note sur les ouvrages Palis composes en pays Thai." BEFEO 15:39–45.

———. 1924. *Recueil des inscriptions du Siam.* 2 Vols. Bangkok: Wachirayan National Library.

———. 1925. "Documents sur l'histoire politique et religieuse du Laos occidental." BEFEO 25:1–206.

———. 1966. *Catalogue des manuscrits en Pali, Laotien et Siamois provenant de la Thailande.* Copenhagen: The Royal Library.

———. 1968. *The Indianized States of Southeast Asia.* Translated by Susan B. Cowing. Honolulu: East-West Center.

Collins, Steven. 1990. "On the Very Idea of the Pali Canon." JPTS 15:89–126.

———. 1992. "Notes on Some Oral Aspects of Pali Literature." *Indo-Iranian Journal* 35:121–135.

———. 1993. *Brah Māleyyadevatheravatthuṃ.* JPTS 18:1–96.

———. 1998. *Nirvana and Other Buddhist Felicities.* Cambridge: Cambridge University Press.

Conze, Edward, trans. 1975. The Large Sutra on Perfect Wisdom. Berkeley: University of California Press.

Cousins, Lance. 1983. "Pali Oral Literature." In *Buddhist Studies Ancient and Modern,* edited by P. Denwood and A. Piatagorsky, pp. 1–11. London: Curzon Press.

Crook, Nigel, ed. 1996. *The Transmission of Knowledge in South Asia: Essays on Education, Religion, History and Politics.* Delhi: Oxford University Press.

Current Biography. 1967. New York: H. W. Wilson.

Dagenais, John. 1994. *The Ethics of Reading in Manuscript Culture.* Princeton: Princeton University Press.

Damrong, Rachanuphap. 1962. *A History of Buddhist Monuments in Siam.* Bangkok: Siam Society.

Darnton, Robert. 2001. "History of Reading." In *New Perspectives on Historical Writing,* edited by P. Burke, pp. 157–186. Pennsylvania: Pennsylvania State University Press.

Davis, Richard. 1984. *Muang Metaphysics: A Study of Northern Thai Myth.* Bangkok: Pandora.

De Hamel, Christopher. 1992. *Scribes and Illuminators.* Toronto: University of Toronto Press.

De la Loubère, Simon. 1693. *A New Historical Relation of the Kingdom of Siam.* London: T. Horne.

De Silva, Lilly A. 1974. *Buddhism: Beliefs and Practices in Sri Lanka.* Colombo.

Deegalle, Mahinda. 1997. "Reconsidering Buddhist Preaching: *Baṇa* Tradition in Sri Lanka." In *Recent Researches in Buddhist Studies: Essays in Honour of Professor Y. Karunadasa,* edited by K. L. Dhammajoti, A. Tilakaratne and K. Abhayawansa, pp. 427–447. Colombo.

Deibert, Ronald. 1997. *Parchment, Printing and Hypermedia: Communication in World Order Transformation*. New York: Columbia University Press.

DN. 1890. Rhys Davids, T. W., and J. Estin Carpenter, eds. *Dīgha Nikāya* I. London: Pali Text Society.

———. 1903. Rhys Davids, T. W., and J. Estin Carpenter, eds. *Dīgha Nikāya* II. London: Pali Text Society.

Donadoni, Sergio. 1997. *The Egyptians*. Chicago: University of Chicago Press.

Doré, Pierre, and Sommai Premchit. 1991. *The Lan Na Twelve-Month Traditions: An Ethno-historic and Comparative Approach.* Chiang Mai: Chiang Mai University.

Dubey, P. K, ed. 2001. *Cakkavāladīpanī.* Delhi: Bharatiya Vidya Prakashan.

Eade, John. 1996. *The Thai Historical Record: A Computer Analysis.* Tokyo: Centre for East Asian Cultural Studies.

EHS. 1992. Griswold, Alexander, and Prasoert na Nagara. *Epigraphic and Historical Studies.* Bangkok: Historical Society.

Eisenstein, Elizabeth. 1983. *The Printing Revolution in Early Modern Europe.* Cambridge: Cambridge University Press.

Emeneau, Murray. 1959. "Oral Poets of South India: The Todas." In *Traditional India: Structure and Change*, edited by Milton Singer, pp. 106–118. Philadelphia: American Folklore Society.

Epigraphia Birmanica. Rangoon: Superintendent, Government Printing.

Epochs. 1968. Jayawickrama, N. A., trans. *Jinakālamālī: The Sheaf of Garlands of the Epochs of the Conqueror*. London: Pali Text Society.

EZ. *Epigraphia Zeylanica.* Colombo: Department of Government Printing.

Fa-Hsien. 1965. *A Record of Buddhistic Kingdoms.* Translated by James Legge. New York: Paragon Books.

Falk, Harry. 1993. *Schrift im Alten Indien.* Tubingen: Gunter Narr.

Fickle, Dorothy. 1978. "An Historical and Structural Study of the *Paññāsa Jātaka*." PhD dissertation. University of Pennsylvania.

Finnegan, Ruth. 1977. *Oral Poetry*. Cambridge: Cambridge University Press.

Finot, Louis. 1917. "Recherches sur la littérature Laotienne." BEFEO 17:1–219.

———. 1926. "Outlines of the History of Buddhism in Indo-China." *The Indian Historical Quarterly* 2, no.4: 673–689.

Fraser-Lu, Sylvia. 1984. "Sadaik: Burmese Manuscript Chests." *Arts of Asia* (May-June): 68–74.

Freeman, Michael. 2001. *A Guide to Northern Thailand and the Ancient Kingdom of Lanna*. Trumbull: Weatherhill.

Galbraith, John Kenneth. 1983. *The Anatomy of Power.* Boston: Houghton Mifflin.

Geertz, Clifford. 1973. *The Interpretation of Cultures*. New York: Basic Books.

Gervaise, Nicolas. 1989. *Natural and Political History of the Kingdom of Siam.* Translated by John Villiers. Bangkok: White Lotus Press.

Gesick, Lorraine. 1995. *In the Land of Lady White Blood: Southern Thailand and the Meaning of History*. Ithaca: Cornell Southeast Asia Program.

Gethin, Rupert. 1992. "The *Mātikā*s: Memorization, Mindfulness and the List." In *In the Mirror of Memory*, edited by J. Gyatso, pp. 149–172. Albany: SUNY Press.

Ghosh, Manmohan, ed. 1986. *Pāṇinīyaśikṣā*. Madras: Asian Humanities Press.

Ginsburg, Henry. 1989. *Thai Manuscript Painting*. Honolulu: University of Hawai'i Press.

Gombrich, Richard. 1988. *Theravada Buddhism: A Social History from Ancient Benares to Modern Colombo*. London: Routledge.

———. 1990. "How the Mahāyāna Began." In *The Buddhist Forum*, edited by T. Skorupski, pp. 21–31. London: University of London.

Goody, Jack. 1977. *The Domestication of the Savage Mind.* Cambridge: Cambridge University Press.

———. 1980. "Oral Composition and Oral Transmission: The Case of the Vedas." In *Oralita*, edited by Bruno Gentili and Giuseppe Paioni, pp. 7–18. Rome: Edizioni dell'Ateneo.

Gosling, Betty. 1996. *A Chronology of Religious Architecture at Sukhothai.* Ann Arbor: Association for Asian Studies.

Graham, William. 1987. *Beyond the Written Word: Oral Aspects of Scripture.* Cambridge: Cambridge University Press.

Gray, James, ed. 1892. *Buddhaghosuppatti*. London: Luzac & Co.

Griffiths, Paul. 1999. *Religious Reading: The Place of Reading in the Practice of Religion.* Oxford: Oxford University Press.

Griswold, Alexander. 1959. "Two Dated Images from the Shan States." *Artibus Asiae* 22:59–60.

———. 1975. *Wat Pra Yün Reconsidered.* Bangkok: Siam Society.

Griswold, Alexander, and Prasoert na Nagara. 1977. "The Inscription of Vat Jyaṅ Hman." JSS 65:111–144.

Guillon, Emmanuel. 1974. "Recherches sur quelques inscriptions Môn." BEFEO 61:339–348.

———. 1977. "Recherches sur quelques inscriptions Mônes." BEFEO 64:83–113.

———. 1999. *The Mons: A Civilization of Southeast Asia*. Translated by James Di Crocco. Bangkok: Siam Society.

Gutman, Paula. 1978. "The Ancient Coinage of Southeast Asia." JSS 66:8–20.

Hackforth, Reginald. 1953. *Plato's Phaedrus*. Cambridge: Cambridge University Press.

Hall, David. 1996. *Cultures of Print: Essays in the History of the Book.* Amherst: University of Massachusetts Press.

Halliday, Robert. 1930. "Les inscriptions Mon du Siam." BEFEO 30:81–105.

Hallisey, Charles. 1988. "Devotion in the Buddhist Literature of Medieval Sri Lanka." PhD dissertation. University of Chicago.

Havelock, Eric. 1986. *The Muse Learns to Write: Reflections on Orality and Literacy from Antiquity to the Present.* New Haven: Yale University Press.

Hinüber, Oskar von. 1983a. "Notes on the Pāli Tradition in Burma." *Nachrichten der Akademie der Wissenschaften in Göttingen* 3:67–79.

———. 1983b. "Pali Texts of Canonical Manuscripts from Northern Thailand." JSS 71:75–88.

———. 1985. "Two Jataka Manuscripts from the National Library in Bangkok." JPTS 10: 1–22.

———. 1986. "The Oldest Dated Manuscript of the Milindapañha." JPTS 11:111–119.

———. 1987. "The Pali Manuscripts kept at the Siam Society, Bangkok. A Short Catalogue." JSS 75:9–74.

———. 1988. "Die sprachgeschichte des Pali im spiegel der sudostasiatischen handschriftenuberlieferung." In *Abhandlungen der Akademie der Wissenschaften und der Literatur*. Mainz.

———. 1989. *Der beginn der schrift und fruhe schriftlichkeit in Indien.* Mainz: Akademie der Wissenschaften und der Literatur.

———. 1990. "On Some Colophons of Old Lanna Pali Manuscipts." In *Proceedings of the Fourth International Conference of Thai Studies.* 4:56–79.

———. 1991. "The Oldest Pali Manuscript." *Abhandlungen der Akademie der Wissenschaften und der Literatur.* Mainz.

———. 1993. "Pali und Lanna in den kolophonen atler palmblatthandschriften aus nord-Thailand." In *Indogermanica et Italica*, edited by G. Meiser, pp. 223–236. Innsbruck: Universität Innsbruck.

———. 1996a. "Chips from Buddhist Workshops: Scribes and Manuscripts from Northern Thailand." JPTS 22:35–57.

———. 1996b. *A Handbook of Pali Literature*. Berlin: Walter de Gruyter.

———. 2000. "Lān Nā as a Centre of Pāli Literature During the Late 15th Century." JPTS 26:119–137.

Hoffman, Frank J. 1991. "Evam Me Sutam: Oral Tradition in Nikāya Buddhism." In *Texts in Context*, edited by Jeffrey Timm, pp. 195–220. Albany: SUNY Press.

Holt, John C. 1996. *The Religious World of Kīrti Śrī.* New York: Oxford University Press.

Hundius, Harald. 1990. "The Colophons of Thirty Pali Manuscripts from Northern Thailand." JPTS 14:1–174.

Hutchinson, E. W. 1951. "The Seven Spires: A Sanctuary of the Sacred Fig Tree at Chiengmai." JSS 39:1–50.

Huxley, Andrew. 1996. *Thai Law, Buddhist Law*. Bangkok: White Orchid Press.

IHP. 1995. *Inscriptional History of Phayao.* Bangkok: Matichon Publications.

Ilangasinha, H. B. M. 1992. *Buddhism in Medieval Sri Lanka*. Delhi: Sri Satguru Publications.

Indian Antiquary. Bombay: Popular Prakashan.

Indorf, Pinna. 1984. "Study of the Ordination Hall (Bot) in the Context of the Thai Monastery (Wat)." In *Buddhism and Society in Thailand*, edited by B. J. Terwiel, pp. 43–62. Gaya: South East Asia Review Office.

Indrawooth, Phasook. 1996. "The Ancient Civilization in Lamphun Province Prior to the Mid-13th Century." In *Proceedings of the 6th International Conference on Thai Studies: Theme VI Chiang Mai*, pp. 1–8.

Ingalls, Daniel. 1959. "The Brahmin Tradition." *Traditional India: Structure and Change*, edited by Milton Singer, pp. 3–9. Philadelphia: American Folklore Society.

Innis, Harold. 1951. *The Bias of Communication.* Toronto: University of Toronto Press.

Ishii, Yoneo. 1986. *Sangha, State, and Society: Thai Buddhism in History.* Honolulu: University of Hawai'i Press.

Jaini, Padmanabh S, ed. 1983. *Paññāsa Jātaka.* Vol. 2. London: Pali Text Society.

———, trans. 1986. *Apocryphal Birth-Stories.* London: Pali Text Society.

Jayasuriya, M. H. F. 1988. *The Jetavanarama Gold Plates.* Kelaniya: University of Kelaniya.

JKMI. 1994. Penth, Hans. *Jinakālamālī Index.* Chiang Mai: Silkworm Books.

JKMp. 1962. Buddhadatta, ed. *Jinakālamālīpakaraṇaṃ.* London: Pali Text Society.

Jones, Robert B. 1971. *Thai Titles and Ranks.* Data Paper No. 81. Ithaca: Cornell University Southeast Asia Program.

Jory, Patrick. 2000. "Books and the Nation: The Making of Thailand's National Library." *Journal of Southeast Asian Studies* 31:351–373.

Kæmpfer, Engelbert. 1998. *A Description of the Kingdom of Siam.* Bangkok: Orchid Press.

Kapstein, Matthew. 1998. *The Tibetan Assimilation of Buddhism.* Oxford: Oxford University Press.

Kasetsiri, Charnvit. 1979. "Thai Historiography from Ancient Times to the Modern Period." In *Perceptions of the Past in Southeast Asia*, edited by A. Reid and D. Marr, pp. 156–170. Singapore: Heinemann Educational Books.

Keyes, Charles. 1970. "New Evidence on Northern Thai Frontier History." In *In Memoriam Phya Anuman Rajadhon*, edited by T. Bunnag and M. Smithies, pp. 221–250. Bangkok: Siam Society.

———. 1977. *The Golden Peninsula.* Honolulu: University of Hawai'i Press.

———. 1988. "Three Worlds According to King Ruang (review)." JSS 76:315–322.

Kingshill, Konrad. 1991. *Ku Dæng: Thirty Years Later.* DeKalb: Northern Illinois University.

Klein, Anne. 1994. *Path to the Middle: Oral Mādhyamika Philosophy in Tibet.* Albany: SUNY Press.

Klimburg-Salter, Deborah. 1988. "The Gilgit Manuscript Covers and the 'Cult of the Book.'" In *South Asian Archaeology, 1987: Proceedings of the Ninth International Conference of the Association of South Asian Archaeologists*, pp. 815–830.

Knox, Robert. 1966. *An Historical Relation of Ceylon.* Dehiwala: Tisara Prakasakayo.

Kumar, Bimalendra, ed. 1992. *Gandhavaṃso.* Delhi: Istarna Buka Linkarsa.

Lagirarde, François. 1996. "Les manuscrits en Thaï du nord de la Siam society." JSS 84: 91–115.

Law, Bimala Churn. 1933. *A History of Pali Literature.* London: Trubner.

———, trans. 1963. *Saddhammasaṅgaha: A Manual of Buddhist Historical Traditions.* Calcutta: University of Calcutta.

Levitt, Stephan H. 1984. "The Indian Attitude Toward Writing." *Indologica Taurinensia* 13:229–250.

Lieberman, Victor. 1976. "A New Look at the *Sāsanavaṃsa*." *Bulletin of the School of Oriental and African Studies* 39:137–149.

———. 1984. *Burmese Administrative Cycles: Anarchy and Conquest, c. 1580–1760.* Princeton: Princeton University Press.

Likhitanonta, Likhit. 1987. "Pali Literature of Thailand." PhD dissertation. Chiang Mai University.

LNI. 1991. Prasoert Na Nagara, ed. *Lan Na Inscriptions* Part I. Bangkok: James Thompson Foundation.

Lord, Albert B. 1960. *The Singer of Tales.* Cambridge: Harvard University Press.

Losty, Jeremiah. 1982. *The Art of the Book in India.* London: The British Library.

Luce, Gordon H. 1960–1970. *Old Burma, Early Pagan.* 3 Vols. New York: J. J. Augustin.

———. 1970. "Aspects of Pagan History: Later Period." In *In Memoriam Phya Anuman Rajadhon*, edited by Tej Bunnag and Michael Smithies, pp. 129–146. Bangkok: Siam Society.

———, trans. 1976. *The Glass Palace Chronicle.* New York: AMS Press

———. 1985. *Phases of Pre-Pagan Burma: Languages and History.* Oxford University Press.

Luce, Gordon H., and Tin Htway. 1976. "A 15th Century Inscription and Library at Pagan, Burma." In *Malalasekera Commemoration Volume*, edited by O. Wijesekera, pp. 203–256. Colombo.

Malalasekera, G. P. 1958. *The Pali Literature of Ceylon.* Colombo: M. Gunasena.

Mangael, Alberto. 1996. *A History of Reading.* New York: Penguin.

Martin, Henri-Jean. 1994. *The History and Power of Writing.* Chicago: University of Chicago Press.

McCullagh, C. Behan. 1998. *The Truth of History.* London: Routledge.

McDaniel, Justin. 2003. "Invoking the Source: Nissaya Manuscripts, Pedagogy and Sermon-Making in Northern Thai and Lao Buddhism." PhD dissertation. Harvard University.

McKitterick, Rosamund. 1988. *The Carolingians and the Written Word.* Cambridge: Cambridge University Press.

McLuhan, Marshall. 1962. *The Gutenberg Galaxy: The Making of Typographic Man.* Toronto: University of Toronto Press.

———. 1964. *Understanding Media: The Extensions of Man.* New York: McGraw Hill.

McMurtrie, Douglas C. 1943. *The Book: The Story of Printing and Bookmaking.* London: Oxford University Press.

McWhirter, Norris, ed. 1986. *The Guinness Book of World Records.* New York: Sterling Publishing.

Mirando, A. H. 1985. *Buddhism in Sri Lanka in the 17th and 18th Centuries.* Dehiwala: Tisara Prakasakayo.

Mitchiner, Michael. 1991. "Early Trade Between India and Mainland Southeast Asia as Reflected by Coinage." In *Coinage, Trade and Economy*, edited by A. K. Jha, pp. 62–83. Maharashtra: Indian Institute of Research in Numismatic Studies.

MS. 1995. Rawin, Bamphen, ed. *Mūlasāsanā Samnuan Lan Na.* Chiang Mai: Social Research Institute.

Mudiyanse, Nandasena. 1967. *Mahayana Monuments in Ceylon*. Colombo: M. D. Gunasena.

MV. 1908. Geiger, Wilhelm, ed. *Mahāvaṃsa*. London: Pali Text Society.

———. 1912. Geiger, Wilhelm, trans. *The Mahāvaṃsa*. London: Pali Text Society.

———. 1925. Geiger, Wilhelm, ed. *Cūlavaṃsa* I. London: Pali Text Society.

———. 1927. Geiger, Wilhelm, ed. *Cūlavaṃsa* II. London: Pali Text Society.

———. 1929. Geiger, Wilhelm, trans. *The Cūlavaṃsa* I. London: Pali Text Society.

———. 1930. Geiger, Wilhelm, trans. *The Cūlavaṃsa* II. London: Pali Text Society.

Myint, Ni Ni. 1996. "Victory Land of Golden Yun: A Queen and Her Poem." In *Proceedings of the 6th International Conference on Thai Studies: Theme VI Chiang Mai*, pp. 9–17.

Nan. 1994. Wyatt, David K, trans. *The Nan Chronicle*. Ithaca: Studies on Southeast Asia.

Nattier, Jan. 2003. *A Few Good Men: The Bodhisattva Path according to* The Inquiry of Ugra. Honolulu: University of Hawai'i Press.

Neusner, Jacob. 1987. *Oral Tradition in Judaism: The Case of the Mishnah.* New York: Garland Publications.

Nguanphiyanphak, Usa. 1990. "Vivathanagan læ Salagan Phriyay læ Kwam phen ma khøng Hø Trai." In *The Development of Thai Buddhist Temple Architecture*, pp. 191–217. Bangkok: National Museum.

Niditch, Susan. 1996. *Oral World and Written Word: Ancient Israelite Literature*. Louisville: Westminster John Knox Press.

Norman, Kenneth Roy. 1983. *Pali Literature*. Wiesbaden: Otto Harrassowitz.

———. 1989. "The Pali Language and Scriptures." In *The Buddhist Heritage*, edited by T. Skorupski, pp. 29–53. London: Tring.

———. 1990. "Pali Philology and the Study of Buddhism." In *The Buddhist Forum*, edited by T. Skorupski, pp. 31–40. New Delhi: Heritage Publisher.

Notton, Camille.1926–1933. *Annales du Siam*. 3 Vols. Paris: Charles Lavauzelle.

Okell, John. 1963. "Nissaya Burmese: A Case of Systematic Adaptation to a Foreign Grammar and Syntax." *Lingua* 15:186–227.

Olson, David. 1994. *The World on Paper*. Cambridge: Cambridge University Press.

Ong, Walter. 1971. *Rhetoric, Romance and Technology: Studies in the Interaction of Expression and Culture.* Ithaca: Cornell University Press.

———. 1982. *Orality and Literacy: The Technologizing of the Word.* London: Routledge.

Otani. 1995. *Catalogue of Palm Leaf Manuscripts kept in the Otani University Library*. Kyoto: Otani University.

Pal, Pratapaditya. 1988. *Buddhist Book Illuminations.* New York: Ravi Kumar Publishers.

Pant, Mahes Raj. 1979. *On Sanskrit Education*. Kathmandu: Lusha Press.

Paranavitane, Senarat. 1928. "Mahāyānism in Ceylon." *Ceylon Journal of Science* 2:35–71.

Parry, Milman. 1971. *The Making of Homeric Verse.* Oxford: Clarendon Press.

Patton, Laurie, ed. 1994. *Authority, Anxiety, and Canon: Essays in Vedic Interpretation.* Albany: SUNY Press.

Pavie, August. 1898. *Recherches sur la littérature du Cambodge, du Laos et du Siam*. Vol. 2. Paris: E. Leroux.

Penth, Hans. 1974. "A Note on the History of Wat Umong Thera Jan (Chiang Mai)." JSS 62:269–272.

———. 1976. *Kham Charük thi Than Phra Phuttha Rup nai Nakhøn Chiang Mai* (*Inscriptions on the Base of Buddha Images in Chiang Mai*). Bangkok: Samnak Nayok Ratthamontri.

———. 1977. "Reflections on the *Saddhammasaṅgaha*." JSS 65:259–279.

———. 1992. *Thai Literacy*. Chiang Mai: Social Research Institute.

———. 1994. *A Brief History of Lan Na*. Chiang Mai: Silkworm Books.

———. 1997a. "Buddhist Literature of Lan Na on the History of Lan Na's Buddhism." JPTS 23:43–82.

———. 1997b. "An Inscribed Buddha Image in Wat Ket Sri." *Indica et Tibetica* 30:495–507.

Petrucci, Armando. 1995. *Writers and Readers in Medieval Italy*. New Haven: Yale University Press.

Pollock, Sheldon. 1989. "Mīmāṃsā and the Problem of History in Traditional India." JAOS 109, no.4: 603–610.

Posner, Raphael, and Israel Ta-Shema. 1975. *The Hebrew Book: An Historical Survey*. Jerusalem: Keter Publishing House.

Premchit, Sommai. 1976. *Tamnan Mūlasāsanā*. Transliteration Series IX. Chiang Mai: Social Research Institute.

———. 1980. "Palm Leaf Manuscripts and Traditional Sermon." In *Buddhism in Northern Thailand*, edited by S. Chandrangam, pp. 81–86. Chiang Mai.

———. 1986. *Lan Na Literature: Catalogue of Palm-leaf Texts on Microfilm at the SRI*. Chiang Mai: Social Research Institute.

———. 1996. "Phra Phuttha Satsana Chiang Mai 700 Pi: Atit læ næo nom nai anakat." In *Proceedings of the 6th International Conference on Thai Studies: Theme VI Chiang Mai*, pp. 437–456.

Premchit Sommai, and Donald Swearer, trans. 1977. "A Translation of Tamnān Mūlasāsanā Wat Pā Dæng." JSS 65:73–110.

———. 1978. "The Relation Between the Religious and Political Orders in Northern Thailand (14th-16th Centuries)." In *Religion and Legitimation of Power in Thailand, Laos and Burma*, edited by Bardwell Smith, pp. 20–33. Chambersburg: Anima Books.

Premchit, Sommai. With Puangkam Tuikeo. 1975. "A Catalogue of Palm Leaf Texts in Wat Libraries in Chiang Mai." Unpublished mimeograph from University of Chiang Mai.

Pruess, J. B. 1976. *The That Phanom Chronicle: A Shrine History and Its Interpretation*. Ithaca: Cornell University Press.

PSC. *Prachum Sila Charük*. Bangkok: Khana Kammakan Phicharana.

PTSD. 1966. Rhys Davids, T. W., and William Stede, eds. *Pali–English Dictionary*. London: Pali Text Society.

Rahula, Walpola. 1956. *History of Buddhism in Ceylon: The Anuradhapura Period.* Colombo: M. D. Gunasena

Rajadhon, Anumon. 1952. "Phra Cedi." JSS 40:66–72.

Rajani, M. C. C. 1976. *Guide Through the Inscriptions of Sukhothai.* Honolulu: University of Hawai'i Southeast Asian Studies Program.

Rawin, Bamphen, ed. 1995. *Tamnan Wat Pa Dæng.* Chiang Mai: Social Research Institute.

Ray, Niharranjan. 1936. *Sanskrit Buddhism in Burma.* Amsterdam: H. J. Paris.

———. 1946. *Theravāda Buddhism in Burma.* Calcutta: University of Calcutta.

Reid, Anthony. 1988. *Southeast Asia in the Age of Commerce 1450–1680.* Vol. 1. Chiang Mai: Silkworm Books.

Reynolds, Craig J. 1979. "Religious Historical Writing and the Legitimation of the First Bangkok Reign." In *Perceptions of the Past in Southeast Asia*, edited by A. Reid and D. Marr, pp. 90–107. Singapore: Heinemann Educational Books.

Reynolds, Frank E. 1971. "Buddhism and Sacral Kingship: A Study in the History of Thai Religion." PhD dissertation. University of Chicago.

———. 1978a. "The Holy Emerald Jewel: Some Aspects of Buddhist Symbolism and Political Legitimation in Thailand and Laos." In *Religion and Legitimation of Power in Thailand, Laos and Burma*, edited by Bardwell Smith, pp. 175–193. Chambersburg: Anima Books.

———. 1978b. "Ritual and Social Hierarchy: An Aspect of Traditional Religion in Buddhist Laos." In *Religion and Legitimation of Power in Thailand, Laos and Burma*, edited by Bardwell Smith, pp. 166–174. Chambersburg: Anima Books.

———. 1978c. "Sacral Kingship and National Development: The Case of Thailand." In *Religion and Legitimation of Power in Thailand, Laos and Burma*, edited by Bardwell Smith, pp. 100–110. Chambersburg: Anima Books.

Reynolds, Frank E., and Mani Reynolds, trans. 1982. *The Three Worlds According to King Ruang: A Thai Buddhist Cosmology.* Berkeley: University of California Press.

Reynolds, L. D., and N. G. Wilson. 1990. *Scribes and Scholars: A Guide to the Transmission of Greek and Latin Literature.* Oxford: Clarendon Press.

Rhum, Michael. 1994. *The Ancestral Lords: Gender, Descent and Spirits in a Northern Thai Village.* DeKalb: Northern Illinois University Center for Southeast Asian Studies.

Rhys Davids, T. W, trans. 1890. *The Questions of King Milinda* I. Oxford: Clarendon Press.

ROB. 1983–1990. Tun, Than, ed. *The Royal Orders of Burma 1598–1885.* 10 Vols. Kyoto: Center for Southeast Asian Studies.

Rocher, Ludo. 1993. "Law Books in an Oral Culture: The Indian *Dharmasastras*." *Proceedings of the American Philosophical Society* 137, no. 2: 254–267.

———. 1994. *Orality and Textuality in the Indian Context.* Philadelphia: University of Pennsylvania.

Rungrüangsi, Udom. 1990. *Phachanukhrom Lanna-Thai* (Lanna-Thai dictionary). Bangkok: Amarind Printing.

Saddhatissa, H. 1974a. "Pali Literature of Thailand." In *Buddhist Studies in Honour of I. B. Horner*, edited by Lance Cousins et al., pp. 211–225. Dordrecht: D. Reidel Publishing.

———. 1974b. "The Dawn of Pali Literature in Thailand." In *Malalasekera Commemoration Volume*, edited by O. Wijesekera, pp. 315–324. Colombo.

———. 1979. "Pali Literature from Laos." In *Studies in Pali and Buddhism: A Memorial Volume in Honor of Bhikkhu Jagdish Kashyap*, pp. 327–340. Delhi.

———. 1980. "Pali Studies in Cambodia." In *Buddhist Studies in Honour of Walpola Rahula*, pp. 242–250. Sri Lanka: Vimamsa.

———. 1989. "A Survey of the Pali Literature of Thailand." In *Amala Prajña: Aspects of Buddhist Studies*, pp. 41–46. Delhi.

Salomon, Richard. 1998. *Indian Epigraphy*. New York: Oxford University Press.

———. 1999. *Ancient Buddhist Scrolls from Gandhara: The British Library Kharosthi Fragments.* Seattle: University of Washington Press.

Sāratthadīpanīṭīkā. 1961. Yangon: Chaṭṭha Saṅgāyana Editions.

Saraya, Dhida. 1999. *Dvāravatī: The Initial Phase of Siam's History*. Bangkok: Muang Boran.

Sasaki, G. H, ed. 1992. *Sārasaṅgaha*. London: Pali Text Society.

Schopen, Gregory. 1975. "The Phrase '*sa pṛthivīpradeśaś caityabhūto bhavet*' in the *Vajracchedikā*: Notes on the Cult of the Book in Mahāyāna." *Indo-Iranian Journal* 17:147–181.

———. 1997. *Bones, Stones, and Buddhist Monks*. Honolulu: University of Hawai'i Press.

Seidenfaden, Erik. 1958. *The Thai Peoples*. Bangkok: Siam Society.

Sengupta, Sukumar. 1994. *Buddhism in South-East Asia: Mainly Based on Epigraphic Sources.* Calcutta: Atisha Memorial Publication Society.

Shorto, Henry.1971. *A Dictionary of the Mon Inscriptions from the Sixth to the Sixteenth Centuries*. London: Oxford University Press.

Singer, Noel. 1991. "Palm Leaf Manuscripts of Myanmar (Burma)." *Arts of Asia* (Hong Kong) 21, no.1: 133–140.

———. 1993. "Kammavaca Texts: Their Covers and Binding Ribbons." *Arts of Asia* (May-June): 97–106.

Skilling, Peter. 1994. "Kanjur Titles and Colophons." In *Tibetan Studies*, edited by Per Kvaerne, pp. 768–780. Oslo: Institute for Comparative Research in Human Culture.

———. 1997a. "The Advent of Theravāda Buddhism to Mainland South-east Asia." JIABS 20, no.1: 93–107.

———. 1997b. "New Pāli Inscriptions from South-east Asia." JPTS 23:123–157.

Smith, Bardwell, ed. 1978. *Religion and Legitimation of Power in Thailand, Laos, and Burma.* Chambersburg: Anima Books.

SN. 1884. Feer, L, ed. *Saṃyutta Nikāya* I. London: Pali Text Society.

———. 1888. Feer, L, ed. *Saṃyutta Nikāya* II. London: Pali Text Society.

———. 1890. Feer, L, ed. *Saṃyutta Nikāya* III. London: Pali Text Society.
Spiro, Melford. 1982. *Buddhism and Society,* 2nd ed. Berkeley: University of California Press.
SRIcat. 2000. Buddharaksa, Balee. *Warnakon Pali Nai Lan Na (Catalogue of Pali texts in Lan Na)*. Chiang Mai: Social Research Institute.
Staal, Frits. 1986. *The Fidelity of Oral Tradition and the Origins of Science.* Amsterdam: North Holland Publishing.
Stargardt, Janice. 1990. *The Ancient Pyu of Burma*. Cambridge: PACSEA.
———. 1995. "The Oldest Known Pali Texts, 5th-6th Century." JPTS 21:199–213.
Stevenson, Daniel. 1995. "Tales of the Lotus Sūtra." In *Buddhism in Practice*, edited by Donald Lopez, pp. 427–451. Princeton: Princeton University Press.
Stock, Brian. 1983. *The Implications of Literacy*. Princeton: Princeton University Press.
Suphaphan Na Bangchang. 1986. *Wiwathanakan Ngan Khian Phasa Bali Nai Prathet Thai.* Bangkok: Mahamakut Rachawithalay.
SV. 1897. Bode, Mabel. *Sāsanavaṃsa*. London: Pali Text Society.
Swanson, Herbert. 1996. "Using Missionary Records for the Study of Northern Thai History." In *Proceedings of the 6th International Conference on Thai Studies: Theme VI Chiang Mai*, pp. 31–49.
Swearer, Donald. 1974. "Myth, Legend and History in the Northern Thai Chronicles." JSS 62:67–88.
———. 1976. *Wat Haripuñjaya*. Missoula: Scholars Press.
———. 1995. "Consecrating the Buddha." In *Buddhism in Practice*, edited by D. Lopez, pp. 50–58. Princeton: Princeton University Press.
———. 2004. *Becoming the Buddha: The Ritual of Image Consecration in Thailand.* Princeton: Princeton University Press.
Tambiah, Stanley J. 1968. "Literacy in North-East Thailand." In *Literacy in Traditional Societies*, edited by Jack Goody, pp. 86–131. Cambridge: Cambridge University Press.
———. 1970. *Buddhism and the Spirit Cults in Northeast Thailand.* Cambridge: Cambridge University Press.
———. 1984. *The Buddhist Saints of the Forest and the Cult of Amulets.* Cambridge: Cambridge University Press.
Tarling, Nicholas, ed. 1990. *The Cambridge History of Southeast Asia*. Vol. 1. Cambridge: Cambridge University Press.
TCM. 1998. Wyatt, David K., and Aroonrut Wichienkeeo, trans. *The Chiang Mai Chronicle*. Chiang Mai: Silkworm Books.
Terwiel, B. J. 1975. *Monks and Magic.* Lund: Studentlitteratur.
Thiphakorawong. 1978. *The Dynastic Chronicles Bangkok Era: The First Reign.* Vol. 1. Translated by Chadin Flood and Thadeus Flood. Tokyo: East Asian Cultural Studies.
Thomas, Rosalind. 1992. *Literacy and Orality in Ancient Greece*. Cambridge: Cambridge University Press.

Thongchai Winichakul. 1994. *Siam Mapped: A History of the Geo-body of a Nation.* Honolulu: University of Hawai'i Press.

TPD. 1981. Mangrai, Sao Sāimöng, trans. *The Pa Dæng Chronicle and the Jengtung State Chronicle Translated.* Ann Arbor: Michigan Papers on South and Southeast Asia.

Trainor, Kevin. 1997. *Relics, Ritual and Representation in Buddhism: Re-materialising the Sri Lankan Theravada Tradition.* Cambridge: Cambridge University Press.

Trakulhun, Sven. 1997. "The View from the Outside." JSS 85:75–84.

Troll, Denise. 1990. "The Illiterate Mode of Written Communication: The Work of the Medieval Scribe." In *Oral and Written Communication: Historical Approaches*, edited by R. Enos, pp. 96–125. Newbury Park: Sage Publications.

Varadarajan, Lotika. 1995. "Glimpses of Seventeenth Century Currency and Mensuration in Siam." JSS 83:199–204.

Vickery, Michael. 1974. "A Note on the Date of the Traibhūmikathā." JSS 62:275–284.

———. 1979a. "The Composition and Transmission of the Ayudhya and Cambodian Chronicles." In *Perceptions of the Past in Southeast Asia*, edited by Anthony Reid and David Marr, pp. 130–154. Singapore: Heinemann Educational Books.

———. 1979b. "A New Tamnan about Ayudhya." JSS 67:123–186.

———. 1991. "On Traibhūmikathā." JSS 79:24–33.

Vilanilam, John. 1987. *Religious Communication in India.* Trivandrum: Kairali Books.

Vin. 1881. Oldenberg, Herman, and T .W. Rhys Davids, eds. *Vinaya Texts.* Oxford: Clarendon Press.

Virawong, Mahasila. 1964. *History of Laos.* New York: Paragon Books.

VRI-Dev. 1998. Chaṭṭha Saṅgāyana Edition of Pali Tipiṭaka and Commentaries (Devanāgarī Script Edition). Igatpuri: Vipassana Research Institute.

Wales, H. G. Q. 1969. *Dvāravatī: The Earliest Kingdom of Siam.* London: Quaritch.

Weeraprajak, Kongkaew. 1989. "Conservation of Palm-leaf Manuscripts." *Sinlapakøn* 33:23–33.

White, Hayden. 1978. *Tropics of Discourse.* Baltimore: Johns Hopkins University Press.

Wichienkeeo, Aroonrut. 1996. "Lanna Customary Law." In *Thai Law: Buddhist Law*, edited by A. Huxley, pp. 31–40. Bangkok: White Orchid Press.

Wyatt, David K. 1969. *The Politics of Reform in Thailand: Education in the Reign of King Chulalongkorn.* New Haven: Yale University Press.

———, trans. 1975. *The Crystal Sands: The Chronicles of Nagara Sri Dharrmaraja.* Ithaca: Cornell University Press.

———. 1984. *Thailand: A Short History.* New Haven: Yale University Press.

———. 1994a. *Temple Murals as an Historical Source: The Case of Wat Phumin, Nan.* Bangkok: Chulalongkorn University Press.

———. 1994b. *Studies in Thai History.* Chiang Mai: Silkworm Books.

———. 1994c. "Five Voices from Southeast Asia's Past." JAS 53:1076–1091.

———. 1997. "History and Directionality in the Early Nineteenth-Century Tai

World." In *The Last Stand of Asian Autonomies*, edited by A. Reid, pp. 425–443. Basingstoke: MacMillan.

———, trans. 1999. *Chronicle of the Kingdom of Ayutthaya*. Tokyo: Centre for East Asian Cultural Studies.

Yājñavalkya. 1909. *Yājñavalkyasmṛti*. Allahabad: Sacred Books of the Hindus.

Yijing. 2000. *Buddhist Monastic Traditions of Southern Asia*. Translated by Li Rongxi. Berkeley: Numata Center for Buddhist Translation Research.

Zürcher, Eric. 1959. *The Buddhist Conquest of China: The Spread and Adaptation of Buddhism in Early Medieval China*. Leiden: E. J. Brill.